Ten Generations of Bondage

Eleven Generations of Faith

The Lewis and Green Family History

Johari Ade

Ten Generations of Bondage

Edited by Zuton Green Lucero
Foreword by Olisa Yaa Ajinaku

Copyright © 2017 by Johari Ade

3rd Edition

ISBN 978-1-9441390-4-9

This book was printed in the United States of America.

To order additional copies of this book, contact:
Sakhu Shule Publications 303-320-1525

Or order online at:
www.tengenerationsofbondage.com
orders@tengenerationsofbondage

Contents

Introduction

In looking at the history of African American people, next to the Black church, the Black family has been the strongest resource for overcoming various forms of adversity. Ten Generations of Bondage: Eleven Generations of Faith draws on biography and family studies, on history and culture, sociology, religion, politics, and psychology toward outlining the essential elements of adaptation which shaped the families over the span of the generations.

Driven by the desire to capture historical relevance of the family background for her grandchildren and other family members, Johari Ade projects onto the reader a dazzling array of life value lessons which each generation taught the next. The complexity of the family life is skillfully revealed with the pouring forth of insights gathered through everyday conversations and family stories, placing a wide variety of emotions before the reader to digest. In a time period of which mobility patterns and other social forces have tremendously changed the structure of the overall American family, this book is truly refreshing in the regard that the notion of "biography" is illuminated in perfect measure, placing the connecting points of historical moments, culture, and personality, at center stage. A ten-generation African American family study is something to be celebrated, a rare treasure not encountered on a day-to-day basis.

Although a book to be read by laypersons and academia alike, the material within the pages will especially thrill historians and genealogists, serving as a uniquely useful contribution to scholarship as it renders invaluable resource points for those engaged in serious undertakings to tell the complete story of the American landscape.

Dennis L Green
Professor of African American Studies
University of Colorado, Denver

Dedication

THIS BOOK IS DEDICATED TO

My Parents:
Tommie Tim Lewis, Sr. and Bessie Mae (McGhee) Lewis,
and "Mama" ...my beloved Aunt

This book would not have been possible without their
willingness to openly and honestly share their past, their pain,
and their joy. "Madear" and Daddy, and Mama, I love you!

Special Dedication

To
Zumante

You will forever be in my heart and soul. Thank you for
nine years, eleven months, and six days of pure joy.
May your legacy be one of life, peace, and hope.
With eternal love,
Nana

Acknowledgments

I owe a debt of gratitude to all of those who have contributed to this book.

To the creator through which all things are possible, thank you for walking with me through this journey.

To the ancestors, I recognize your struggle, your pain and your progress. Thank you for paving the way for your children, and your children's children. I honor you with this book, for it would not exist, but for your love and your guiding light.

To my father Tommie Tim Lewis Sr. (T.T.), who insured that I walked with pride, no matter what the path. To my mother Bessie Mae (McGhee) Lewis, who taught me the power of "the Word" and who unselfishly, relived some very painful memories to help me on my quest for the family history. To Mama (Aunt Hattie), who did not sugar coat some of the horrors and the difficulties of the past, but taught me "we always get up."

To my husband Professor Dennis Green, the true historian in the family, who patiently guided me on my mission for the truth, and always gave me encouragement. Thanks for always listening to my ranting and ravings when I found out about some wrong that had been done to a family member and thanks for sharing in my joy, when I managed to add to the family tree. I thank you for your patience during all of those hours that you were "reading" at the library while I poured over census reports, old wills, manuscripts, records, and book after book, trying to find tidbits about our family.

To my daughters: Olisa, the Psychotherapist, who helped me to understand the impact that the past had on our present psyche. Thanks for the perspective on slavery and other civil wrongs. Thanks to Niecy, the Business Strategist and the real "brains" in the family who gave me practical advice about the business of business. And to Zuton, the poet, journalist, and editor of this book, Thanks for helping me get the words in the proper order, and turning my thoughts into a book. All of you encouraged me to continue the search, even while teasing me relentlessly about my spyglass, and my "Mr. Magoo" glasses.

To my grandchildren, Raisha, Kiante, Brianne, Zumante, Ashantay, D.J., Monye, Elijah, Yekpewa, and Maxwell, Aina, Ojo, and NiaMani the tenth generation documented as of this writing. Thanks for the laughs, the love, and the joy you brought into my life. Although you never had the opportunity to know many of your ancestors mentioned in this book, it is my wish that you will enjoy reading about the journey of their past. Learn from it, and continue to share it.

To my brothers, Calvin and Tommie Jr. and my sister, Stella, who never let me forget that I was supposed to write, and then share, the family history.

To the myriad of other relatives, cousins, and friends including Aunt Arlie, Aunt Essie, Charley Lewis, Jr., Charles Willis, Archie Aubrey, Mary White, John and Ernestine Stovall, Earline Hayes, Mrs. Minnie Walker, Mozilla Walker, Cousin Girtha, Cousin Aggie, James Walker, The Courtney's, The Willis', Lee Jur, John Richards, Irma West, Rodell, Dorothy Ingram, Sinclair Ingram, Edith Lowery, Parnese Lowery, Aunt Bert, Aunt Clara, Barbara Walker, and all of those who often, without ever having met me, would invite me into their homes, and share the memories just because I was "family."

Foreword

By Olisa Yaa Ajinaku (formerly Lisa K Green)

Shortly before my grandfather, T.T. Lewis passed, I was sitting with him at his shop. I remember how he looked at me as if something important was on his mind. He got up from his seat and pointed to the pictures of his parents and grandparents on the wall. He said, "Me and you and them are the same." I nodded in agreement, but Grandpa apparently was not convinced that I understood what he was trying to say. He gave me that look again and said slowly and deliberately, *"we are them."* After he was satisfied that I understood, he sat peacefully in his chair next to me.

The work that my mother has done in this book is invaluable. It is because she has insisted on finding out who our ancestors were that we know who we are. The Yoruba people of West Africa have a saying; "A person does not truly die as long as someone remembers her name." Thanks to my mother, those old souls in our family remain alive. They are alive in their own right, and they are alive through us. My mother's work makes it possible for us to be whole, to be complete as a family, and internally as African people.

It is because of my mother's work that we were able to grieve for those who were taken from us and never buried properly, albeit scores after they were killed. It is because of my mother's work that we are able to truly understand what our people lived through and know the true meaning of the words strength and power. And it is because of my mother's work that we are able to know our way, their way, and reclaim it.

The Ghanaian people have a concept called Sankofa. It suggests that you have to know where you are coming from to know where you are going. This book represents the notion of Sankofa in its truest form.

We are truly grateful for the patience, diligence, and discipline that it took Nana to write this book. The countless hours, days, months and years that it has taken to do this work have paid off. All of the trips to distant and sometimes hostile places; all of the painful searches through property records and wills, all of the arguments with Europeans who tried to hide the truth in order to protect their own interests. Through all of that, you have persevered. I salute your Ase. We adore you Nana, and hope that you know that your name will never be forgotten. Nana Coumba Johari Ade Mary Jane Green, Medasi Pa (we lay ourselves at your feet).

Ase, Ase, Ase.

A Note About The "N" Word

Because of the peculiar history of slavery, and Black people in America, there has been a variety of terms that attempt to identify our race. We have been referred to as "nigger, Negra, Negro, Negress, Colored, Afro-American, African American, American African, Afrikan, Africana, Black, Black American," and many others.

The word *nigger* is a powerful word in today's culture. Depending on who uses the word and how it is used, it may have both positive and negative connotations. Typically the word has been described as negative and categorized as being "derogatory," "offensive," "hurtful," "insensitive," " insulting," a "racial slur," "abusive" and/or "cruel." Others describe or use it in a positive way and believe it to be an acceptable form of "affection" a "term of endearment," "friendly," "constructive," or "sociable." Use of the word is often debated in both Black and white circles with never-ending opinions on whether or not we should allow its use, and if so, who is allowed to use it. Historical novels are increasingly banned from schools because of use of the "n-word." Despite the danger of this book ending up on the "banned" list, the author has decided that the word must be used if we are to be true to its historical context.

The reader will find that in this book, the terms change over time. Moreover, depending on the time period and the context, you will find the word capitalized at times, and lower cased in others.

In *Ten Generations of Bondage,* many manifestations of the term "nigger" are used at different times throughout. The author of this book believes that it is of utmost importance to allow the reader to see and feel the true "face" of race and racism. The reader will gain a better understanding of the varying degrees of the power of the word and the prejudices surrounding it.

The
Homeland

The First Generation

First, We Were Free

Dakar, Senegal, West Africa

"First, We Were Free"

The year was 1764. Violet was out in the Virginia fields cutting tobacco. She was a bundle of nerves one minute, and on cloud nine the next. Nevertheless, Violet tried to think only positive thoughts. She was a spiritual woman, and she prayed very hard every day. Surely, her prayers would be answered. She thought about how wonderful it would be to be a free woman again. She had been bound to Peter Rhem for 8 years. Violet's contract as an indentured servant was over. She had brought a lawsuit against Rhem for holding her against her will.

"What is there to decide?" Violet thought to herself. "I had a contract for seven years. This is year number eight. The judge will surely make Rhem let me go." Tomorrow she would have her day in court and become a free woman again.

"The indenture of the Negro Violet has been completed," the judge would say. "Violet must be freed at once!" Then Violet would be given her head right of 50 acres, some tools to work the land, and a workhorse. She would walk on her own land, and till her own soil. Perhaps she would sell enough vegetables to buy out her child's indenture. She would finally have the means to care for her daughter Bett.

Her daydream was rudely interrupted by Nan, who was running towards her and wildly waiving her arms. Nan had been bound to Rhem for about 5 years, and was older than Violet. Nan usually did all of the cooking for the field hands. She was out of breath when she finally reached the fields. There were tears in her eyes. She stopped just in front of Violet to catch her breath. "He gonna do it!" she gasped.

"Who's gonna do what?" Violet asked

"Rhem!" Nan stated. "I hear'd him and Judge Crane talking. Crane tol' Rhem not to worry 'bout nothin' tomorrow. He tol' im he goin keep you wit Rhem!" she cried. "You's still bound," she continued. "Dat judge goin keep you heah! He say dat you's gonna belong to Rhem fuh two mo' yeah's! Two mo yeah's!!" Nan went on to talk about the conversation she had overheard between Judge Crane and Rhem. She repeated what she had heard. Rhem and Judge Crane had been discussing some new law in the county that allowed the judge to extend the time for indentured servants two years for every child they had during their time of indenture. Nan's voice seemed far away as Violet thought about Bett. Little Bett was eight years old, now. When Violet carried Bett, she worked right up until the time of labor. She had Bett at around sundown and the next day Violet was back in the fields. While Violet toiled, Bett was either cared for by a wet nurse, and slept most of the day or Violet would carry Bett on her back while she worked.

Violet scarcely remembered Nan leaving. She absentmindedly went about her work. At sundown, she headed back to her cabin and passed Rhem along the way. He had a smirk on his face, and remarked, "Well, tomorrow's a big day! That judge'll surely make up for you cheatin' me out of my time. He should extend you for 5 years! Nigger wenches ain't no good 'til the child is bout 5 years old." Then he turned and abruptly walked off. Violet had heard of others who had their time extended. She heard that not a single Negro servant had won in court against the planter when the planter wanted to keep them. Some said that at least sixteen Negroes had petitioned the court because their masters were illegally holding them. Sixteen times the judge ruled against them. Word was that the judge thought it was ridiculous for these "uncivilized creatures" to think that they should be free. Already, in some parts of Virginia, Negroes were not allowed to roam around free. Rhem said that the court was guided by the Bible. He insisted that the Bible said that Black people should be slaves to white people.

There were many stories about other servants who were now slaves for life. Nan said that enslavement of Africans had been increasing since about 1640 and had actually been legalized in some places in 1641. According to Nan, an African man who went by the name of John Punch came to the colonies as an indentured servant. Punch and two white servants tried to run away from their masters, but they were caught. As punishment, the two white servants were required to serve an additional four years. John Punch was required to serve his owner for "the rest of his natural life." Nan said that since Punch, more and more African's and even some Indians were required to serve for a lifetime whenever they were sentenced for committing a crime.

The soil in the colonies was rich and fertile, and planters tried to find ways to keep servants for a longer time. Nan learned a lot from working closely with the slavers and she kept the servants informed. In her heart, Violet knew that that the stories were true. She had heard it repeatedly. She heard about slavers going to court and always getting their indentures extended. Laws were frequently being changed. There was always some new law that made a Negro servant stay enslaved. Even free Negroes were being captured and sold into slavery. But Violet hoped that she would be different. She prayed that Rhem would treat her fairly. She had signed a contract. Rhem was usually a fair man. Violet worked hard, and certainly had kept her part of the bargain. She hoped that Rhem would reconsider and keep his.

However, Rhem didn't have to keep his word. The court case was quick. Violet scarcely remembered it. She remembered that the Judge asked her to stand and that her legs felt like rubber. She remembered hearing "Two more years," as the Judge extended her indenture. She remembered trying to keep the hot tears from running down her face, but failing miserably. She didn't remember leaving the courtroom but she clearly remembered the look on Rhem's face when she saw him after court. He looked like a cat that had just trapped a canary. He was smiling and talking to several of the other planters. He was in an especially gay mood that day. He was talking about something called the Virginia Act XII, where non-Christian negroes could be slaves for life. He said it had been decided by the court under almighty God that a Negro could not be a Christian. Even after all of her hopes and all of her prayers, at the end of the day Violet was no different from the rest. In court, she was "Violet," a freeborn negro." Not even a last name, just Violet.

"You're one lucky nigger," Rhem snarled. "You only have two more years!" But it was over. Violet knew that although the Judge had not called her a slave, she was in fact, being held in slavery. Her 7-year contract didn't matter. She knew that like the others, her indenture would not end until she was too old and too sick to work. Violet was born a free woman. Rhem had promised her land and more. Now she was sure Rhem would not stop until he had enslaved her daughter Bett, too. With a heavy heart, Violet went back to the plantation with Rhem. When they got off the wagon, Rhem turned and walked towards the big house. Violet was glad to see him go. After her evening chores were done, she fell into an exhausted, fitful sleep. She would need all of her strength for tomorrow because Rhem would certainly drive home his point by making her work twice as hard. She would break the news to the other servants. She would tell them that everything that Nan said was true. They were no longer servants. Now they were slaves.

The Middle
Passage

The Second Generation

Enslaved

2

"Enslaved"

The next morning Violet arose at sun-up and headed to the fields. She dreaded this day. Her situation now seemed a lot more hopeless than it had just one day earlier. She would tell the others about her conversation with Rhem the night before. They would say positive things like, "The Lord will see us through. God doesn't give us more than we can bear."

While Violet was walking out to the fields, she thought about another court case four years ago. That time the fight was about her daughter, Bett. The year was 1760, and Violet was 20 years old. She was in the courtroom that day, and was sitting on a hard bench wondering what would become of her first-born child. Her four-year-old daughter Bett, sat by her side, kicking the seat in front of her. Violet grabbed Bett's feet, and Bett began to squirm, trying to get out of her mother's clutches. Bett was tired. She was a very active child, and had been sitting for what seemed like hours. Violet was grim. She was anxiously awaiting the Judge's decision. Violet had bound herself to Rhem when she was fourteen years old. Two years later, she had Bett. However, Foy, a neighboring planter, had taken her precious Bett because of some business dispute he had with Rhem. Rhem, to Violet's delight had retrieved Bett from Foy's plantation and petitioned the court to have Bett returned to her mother, Violet. Even though technically Bett would belong to Rhem, it meant that Violet could be with her daughter.

Violet remembered looking at Foy who sat at a desk directly in front of the Judge. He was so angry that his face was as red as a beet. Foy told the judge that Bett was *his* slave under the new law in the county. Rhem disagreed, and told the judge that that under the law, Bett was free because her mother was free. Violet could not understand all of the legal talk, but she did know that if Rhem won, she would get to hold her precious Bett again. Violet was a proud woman. She had worked hard so that she could make a good home for Bett. Now the judge had Bett's life in his hands. Would the judge say that Bett was a slave? Or would she be free? She knew that if the judge said that Bett was a slave, Foy would take her daughter and she would never see her again. But Violet had a deep spiritual belief that God would take care of her and her daughter. She would accept God's will.

Most people thought that Violet was just asking for trouble when she said that she would help Rhem fight for Bett. "You gonna fight in the white man's court?" they asked. "What chance you got against a white man?" Nevertheless, here she was, in the white man's courtroom, and the judge was looking right at her. Actually, he was glaring at her. The look in his eyes was a mixture of disgust, and boredom. Finally he spoke. "Will the Negra Violet please stand?" Violet stood up. "The Negra Bett shall be returned to the care of her mother Violet." Violet breathed a sigh of relief. She got her daughter back!

Violet returned to the present with a start. She had reached the fields. The other field hands sadly looked at her. They had already heard that Violet was still bound to Rhem. Nan briefly looked up and said, "The Lord will see us through." Violet nodded, picked up her tools, and set to work. She began to wonder if they would ever be free.

As the years passed, she began to lose hope. Three more times she and Bett found themselves in court. Three more times their service was extended. Finally in 1775, when Violet was almost 40 she was freed. Two years later, Bett was given her freedom. By this time, Violet had eight children who were conceived while she was in bondage. Two of her daughters, Hanna and Abigail remained enslaved to Rhem. Two of her sons, Steven and Isaac were sold to other plantation owners. Violet's other son Thomas had been given to John Foy to settle a debt and was still enslaved to Foy. Foy was not willing to let Thomas go. Nanny, Violet's youngest daughter who was born crippled, was the only child to remain free.

Violet and her children were encouraged after the American Revolution and America's Declaration of Independence. They had heard that the Declaration proclaimed, "All men were equal." They rejoiced at hearing that Thomas Jefferson had berated King George for condoning slavery. In 1776, America declared her independence from Great Britain, and they all felt that they would soon be free. When Foy heard what was being said among the servants, he quickly quashed the speculation. He told the servants that the Declaration of Independence had no effect on slavery in the Colonies, and that servants must serve out their terms. Any attempts to use the Declaration of Independence to try to gain freedom would not be tolerated! Violet and her children watched as the "freedom celebrations" went on. They watched the Colonies proclaim themselves free, while her children were still in bondage.

Finally, in 1777 a planter petitioned the court claiming that Thomas was being unjustly withheld from his liberty. The court ordered Foy to set Thomas free.

The 1700's were a time of contradiction. In some states, slavery had not yet been written into law. Slavery existed, but it was sometimes a temporary condition that was a test of wills between the dominator's and the dominated.

Ten Generations of Bondage

Crossing The
Ocean

The Third Generation
"Snatched"

Tom and Jane

THE DOOR OF NO RETURN
Dakar, Senegal, West Africa

3

"Kidnapped"

It was a proud day for Thomas when his son and name-sake, Timothy Thomas married Nancy. It was near the turn of the century (1800), and things were rapidly changing for Blacks. In just eight more years, according to the United States Constitution, importing slaves from Africa would not be allowed. Many looked upon 1808 as the end of slavery. However, the new law was rarely enforced. Because of the need for free labor, and overwhelming greed, enslaved Africans were still illegally imported into America until at least 1857. In addition, a very troublesome and disheartening practice was taking place in the New America. Many called it "home grown slavery." Others put it bluntly. "Breeding slaves."

There was double-edged sword cutting into this new land. The U.S. had begun to grow rich with cotton and tobacco. The desire for wealth and the need for workers to harvest these crops led to an increase in the price of slaves. Once enslaved, Blacks were "encouraged" to have more children, often being "bred" by their owner who would then use his own offspring in the same manner that he did all of the other slaves. "Breeding farms" expanded as planters forced "strong bucks" to mate with "good wenches."

Thomas became concerned that he and his children would someday be re-enslaved. He had good reason to worry. Soon after Timothy and Nancy got married, Foy petitioned the court to obtain Timothy. Foy claimed in court that when Timothy was born, his mother was still a slave. Because she was a slave, that meant that Timothy was a slave. Foy's slave.

They saw no way out. Black slavery happened gradually, and now more were enslaved than free. They were surrounded by the overseer, who had guns, whips, and the law.

A few years later, Foy moved his lot from Virginia to North Carolina. He sold some of his slaves to a man named Martin Lewis. North Carolina was a fertile planting ground. The work was hard. Many enslaved blacks tried to run away or revolt. Some headed for the hills and joined the Native American societies. Timothy considered both. But because slave insurrections had killed or maimed some of the white enslavers, the slave laws were becoming tougher. By this time, North Carolina had revised their laws. The new laws said (in part) that;

Slaves are not allowed to be armed with any weapon (including items that may be perceived as a weapon)

No slave shall go as a free person...or have discretion of his/her own time.

It shall not be lawful for any slave to be insolent to a free white person...play dice or cards. preach or exhort in public...rebel. testify in court...own property...be set free...spend time in idleness...(etc).

It shall not be lawful for any slave to hire out his or her time, nor teach or attempt to teach any other slave to read or write.

Many of these infractions were punishable by the whip. Many others were punishable by death. For the next 10 years or so, Timothy and Nancy, and the seven children they had, remained enslaved to Foy. Foy's wealth began to grow as the tobacco proved to be profitable. But he wanted more. More money. More things. More slaves.

Timothy and Nancy were in the fields one day when they heard a terrible commotion. The other slaves gathered to see what the noise was all about. Off in the distance, they saw an African woman, sobbing, and trying to break her shackles to chase after a horse-drawn wagon that was moving down the road. But the horses picked up their pace and the woman fell to her knees screaming and sobbing. Though her accent was thick, and her English poor, they knew what she was saying. They had witnessed similar scenes over the years, and it never failed produce a heart-wrenching sob that stuck in their own throats.

"No! No! Not my child," the woman sobbed. "Please don't take my child!" But the wagon rolled on. The woman had been put out of the wagon and was left sobbing on her knees. She stayed there for what seemed like hours. Finally, she arose, head down and walked towards the Big House.

The next day, Nancy saw the woman in the fields. "Yo baby?" The question needed no explanation.

"Sold." the woman said. Her heartbreak was evident in the one-word response. Much later, after sunset, they talked as they headed back to their cabins. The woman's African name was Abena, but now they called her Jane. Nancy had heard similar stories, from other enslaved Africans, but each time she heard it, her heart grew heavier.

Jane spoke of her home in Africa. "My people is the 'Ga'. My Paw was the head of my village. I got me a husband, and three chillun. I got five sisters and three brothers. I got lotsa family in da village." Then her eyes turned cold as she remembered her last night in the village. "One night dey comes. Dey seemed lak a hundred. Dey has guns, and chains. Dey raid our village. I waked up when I hear'd my husband shout. I tried to get to him and den somebidy grabbed me from ba'hind. I kick. I scream. But I cudn't break free." Jane's eyes had a far-away look as she remembered the horrible scene that took place that dreadful day. She had tears in her eyes as she thought about the family that had been literally torn from her arms. She continued to speak. "I neva seed dem no mo', 'cept for my last born.

Nancy could feel the woman's pain. She had seen children ripped from their parent's arms. She could feel her own tears begin to fall as she listened to Jane. Jane continued to speak of her horrific ordeal.

"We was took to a dungeon and kep dere fo' months. No light. Little food. Den one day they taken us in chains to a jail by the wata."

ENTRANCE TO SLAVE MANSION
Goree Island
West Africa

Jane took a deep breath and tried to gather her strength as she thought about what happened next. After she composed herself, she continued the story. "Den, I seed my baby, but dey dint let me get close to her. Dey makes us get on da ground with our head on the dirt. Dey had three fire irons and dey put em in da fire. Den while we fight and cry, dey taken us one by one and burn our backs with the irons."

Jane put her hand on her shoulder as she remembered the scar that was still seared into her skin. "My baby got da same mark I got. Dey say that if we try to run away dey know who we be 'cause of the marks. Den da boat come. Dey taken us to the bottom of the boat and chain us together, side by side, so tight that we cain't move. Dey put they smallest babies between the legs of somebidy so that they could get mo' slaves on the boat. We sail many days. Some got sick. Dey got sick and died right dere."

Jane looked as though she was going to be physically ill as she remembered the ship. Her face became contorted as she remembered her journey across the water.

"The smell was horrible from the urine and the waste we lay in. One day dey unchain some of us so dat they could throw off da dead. The light hurt my eyes after being in dat dark hole fo' so long. I looked over and seed dead African bodies laying on the flo' of da boat. One by one they picked 'em up an' throwed 'em in da wata. I saw a necklace that was just lak mine on the neck of one of the slaves they throwed overboard. It was my sista. I were glad dat she free and would not have to go through what we did. I try with all my might to jump in da wata to be wit my sista but I could not loosen dat chain. When we gits to America, I's tol' we'd been on dat boat fo' bout 90 and some days. Den dey put us on the block. They say I's young and kin have mo babies. I's sold for $200. I thought my baby was sol' wit me, but they jes leave me here, and take her away."

By now, they had reached the chicken coop that was near the cabins. Jane held her head down, clearly exhausted from the sheer memory of her ordeal.

Nancy told Jane about the ways of the plantation as they walked along. They finally reached "slave row," a straight little row of five run-down, log cabins. "Dis where the slaves be. It usta not be locked at night, but the white folks is scared after that insurrection up at Stono. Now we's locked in at night, and cain't leave the plantation 'lessen we got a note from Massa."

They continued on their journey. "This Clara's house. Clara looks after all the chillun when we out in the fields."

They came upon a long trough, about 6 feet long and about a foot wide. It looked exactly like the one in the pigpen that they used to feed the pigs, but it was taller. "Dis where we eat." Jane continued. "Harriett, the house slave fills it up wit grits when it time to eat. Mens stand on dat side, and the womens stands on dis un." She saw the look of disgust on Jane's face. "But Foy better 'n some. He don't whup da women wit da big whip, jes the smalla one. An after yo' whuppun he don't rub no salt in it like some does."

They continued to walk down a path behind the big house. There were several graves, some with flat stones, and some with large elaborate tombstones. "Dis where we be buried when da time come. Culled on dat side. White over yonder." When one of us crosses ova', Massa only let 6 at a time come and pray, cuz they don't want nobidy to run off."

Jane soon got the hang of things and settled down into a kind of a rhythm. It was a hard, cruel life. It was very hard for Timothy to try to be protector and head of his family, when he was under control of the slaveholder. Every whip of the lash would eat away at his dignity, especially when the other slaves were made to watch. Harder still, was when he would see the women whipped or abused and could do nothing to come to their aid. Frequently, women were bred with selected slaves, or even with the slaver or overseer, in attempts to produce more slaves. No consideration was given to whether they were "married" or not. Timothy often thought of ways in which he could strike out against the overseers and get his family out of slavery. "How can I be a man and be the head of this house" he grieved, "when Foy owns all of us?"

Over the years, fewer Blacks would obtain their freedom. As profits grew for the slaveholders, and the year 1808 became closer slaveholders became more desperate. Slaves were bought, sold, bred, loaned, traded, and mortgaged with zeal as their value increased. As 1808 came and went, the underground slave trade flourished as the illegal importation of slaves continued. More "Jane's" were brought to the colony and separated from their families. They were stripped of their names and given new ones at the whim of the slaveholder. Legally, the enslaved Blacks had no last names. Naturally, first names became very important. Both the women and the men often named their children after themselves. They felt that this would continue the family link, and help to find their children if they ever became free.

One night, sometime between midnight and dawn, the sound of horses, woke everyone up. Nancy tried the door and was surprised to find it unlocked. She stepped outside and saw several Indians on horses. Some had abandoned the horses and were heading for slave row. Timothy and Nancy had heard about the band of Choctaw and Creek Indians who lived in Maroon colonies not far from the plantation. Some said that these Indians had many Negroes living among them. They said that the Indians would sometimes raid the plantations and steal slaves for themselves. Others said that the Negroes and Indians planted crops and peacefully coexisted in the maroon colonies. The commotion outside certainly seemed like a raid. There was an Indian running out of the cabin that Jane lived in. He was carrying Jane, and she was kicking and trying to get away. He was saying something in a hushed tone that sounded like "Quiet! No hurt! No hurt!" Suddenly shots rang out. Most of the Indians rode off on their horses. But the one who was carrying Jane suddenly dropped her and clutched his side. He was immediately surrounded by Foy and several of the overseers. "We got you now you slave-stealing Indian!" Foy shouted. The Indian was led away with the dogs nipping at his heels, and his hands bound behind his back with a piece of rope. They were heading for the Big house. One of the overseers hustled the slaves back into the cabins and locked the doors.

About a week later, Nancy and Jane were heading back to the cabins after leaving the fields. Jane leaned over to Nancy and pointed to a man, limping badly and coming in their direction. He took short steps to accommodate the chains that bound his feet together.

"Ain't dat the Injun?" whispered Jane as she nodded her head towards the man.

"Sho nuf is!" When the man reached them he slowed down, and then looked around, as if he was making sure no one was watching. He looked as if he was going to say something. He apparently thought better of it, however. With a nod and a sly little grin at Jane, he headed in the direction of the men's cabins.

"I bet he don't talk no English." Nancy proclaimed.

"You's probly right." Jane answered. "But he sho like to flirt!"

They were doing the evening chores about thirty minutes later, when Jemmy, one of Foy's overseer's rode up on his horse. When he reached them, he pulled back on the reins. "Hey, Yah!" The horse stopped and Jemmy looked down at Nancy. "You tell yo' Timmy that he gotta break in that Injun tomorrow. I don't want no problems. I want him pulling his load by tomorrow!"

"Ya Suh." Jemmy road off, and left Nancy and Jane to speculate about what had happened to the Indian.

"He done got himself caught and now he slave for Massa!" Nancy exclaimed.

"I reckon so," Jane said. She thought of her family back in Africa. She wondered who else had been caught and brought to America? Who was slave? Who was free? Now she wondered if the Indian had family that was looking for him. Who was taking care of his wife and children? She felt an incredible sadness and anger as she looked over at the Big House.

"These people thank they's God!" she said under her breath. "Tearin' apart families! Whipping babies! And dey makes us call 'dem "Massa." She turned her palms upward towards the sky. "I have only one Massa," she emphatically stated. "And he goin' rescue me out of this white man's slavery!"

The Indian was with them in the fields the next day. Timothy arose extra early so that he would be sure to have his quota of tobacco by sunset. If any of the slaves came up short on their tobacco, they were in for a whipping. It usually came out okay though, because those who were faster, did an extra pound or two for the slower workers. They set themselves up so that a faster one worked next to a slower one. That way, nobody was whipped. When Timothy and the Indian reached the fields, Timothy gave the Indian a bag of seeds and began to show him how the plant the tobacco trays. The Indian looked at Timothy and said, "Too many seeds." He went over to a tree and looked at it carefully. He broke off one of the branches that made a nice even, three-prong fork. He then showed Timothy how to plant three rows at a time with the same amount of seed Timothy was using to plant one row. "Won't they come up too weak?" Timothy asked.

"No. You see, the tree branch makes the wells that give the seeds the extra room that they need. They don't choke each other and they grow bigger and stronger. White man plant all wrong. They think if you put twenty seeds in a hole that you get strong plant. Not true. Plant will die." By the time the sun was up, they had been in the fields for about two hours and the overseer rode up to make sure they were working hard. He looked at the nice even rows and was pleased that the work was moving along nicely. He knew he could go back and tell Foy that he had whipped the Indian into shape. However, the overseer didn't want them to see his approval. He had been taught by the other overseers that if you told a nigger that they were doing a good job, then they thought it meant they could slack off for the rest of the day. "Y'all need to work faster if you think you gonna git this plot done by sundown." Then he rode off to report to Foy. Tom non-chalantly went back to his planting.

Timothy looked curiously at Tom.

"What you so happy about?" he asked. "You done got caught,

and now you slavin' jes like the rest of us. And here you is plantin' pretty little rows for Massa. Ain't you rankled a'tall?"

"Me? Nope! I'm fine! You see, I know these parts betterin' most. I kin leave whenever I get ready to leave! Especially if massa ain't spectin it. An' maybe I take my pretty little tobacco plants with me." he said with a wink as he went back to his planting.

By the end of the day, the Indian had taught them many short-cuts about planting and working the fields. Jane was familiar with many of his methods from her days in Africa and they worked nicely together. They learned more about the Indian. His name was Tom. He lived in a maroon colony not far from the plantation. The colony had good, fertile planting ground and they raised corn and many other crops. Mostly Choctaw and Cherokee Indians inhabited their colony. Tom said that quite of few Africans who had run away from their slaveholders had joined the colonies.

"We hear tell that Indians catches Africans and slaves em jes like white folks." Nancy said sarcastically. Tom seemed amused.

"Some does. But not our tribe. We catches em and marries em," he said. Then he turned serious. "There no slavery like the white man's slavery. Yes, sometimes we raid a plantation and take slaves back with us. But we work together side by side. After three or four moons, we tell them they can go or stay. No one go back to the white man's slavery. Many stay and marry and raise their children as Indian."

He looked at Jane. "I see the many time, the overseers leave the cabins unlocked. Many Saturday night they drink whiskey and sleep drunk. I see Miss Jane when wagon bring her here. I want to take her away. I come for Miss Jane. I'm not leavin' here without Miss Jane. "

However, the right time never came. For the next five years or so things remained pretty much the same. Timothy and Nancy had three more children. Tom and Jane stood out under the oak tree one day. They said vows to each other, promising to care for each other in sickness and in health, for as long as they lived, or were separated by slavery's ways. They knew that under the law their union was not legal. Slaves could not legally marry. Nevertheless, they felt that the Gods would bless their union. If it was God's will, they would stay together and have children together. Foy did not oppose the union. He knew from experience if a slave took a "wife" he was easier to control. Sometimes the male slaves would run off, beating or no beating. But they usually stayed "in their place" if the overseer threatened to beat the wife or child. So he usually let the slaves "marry" as long as their work was done.

One day, Clara, a house slave came running out into the fields. Timothy, Jane and the others looked up, wondering what was wrong. It was not unusual for Clara to bring them water, or grits for lunch, but now she was waving her arms wildly, and motioning for them to come. She was not carrying the meal on her head like she usually did, and she had nothing in her hands. They ran towards her, knowing that something was wrong. She was out of breath when she reached them. "Massa Foy dead," she screamed.

"What?" Nancy had heard her, but she wanted to make sure that she had not misunderstood.

"Massa Foy!" Clara said again. "Dr. Scully come to the house. Massa Foy been coughing up blood all night long. He was burnin' up. I fixes him elderberry tea, and cold cloths. This mornin' Dr. Scully say that Massa Foy done died of the Dysentery. Oh Lawd! Oh Lawd! What we goin' do?"

Some of the slaves headed out further to the fields to give the news to the other field hands. Timothy and Nancy stopped working and just sat down right where they were in the fields. No overseers were in sight. They were all at the Big house, no doubt huddled in a meeting. The field hands finished their work a little while later and slowly went back to the cabins.

The next day the overseer rode out to the fields and told them to gather at the Big House. When they arrived, they were alarmed to see the county Judge there. They knew that seeing the judge after the slaveholder died could mean that their lives were about to change in a very big way. When the slaveholder died, his will was read, if he had one. Most slaveholders who had many slaves, had wills. When the will was read, they learned their fate. Timothy hoped that Foy would do right by him and set him free.

"This is the reading of the last Will and Testament of the late John Foy, the judge started. "To my loving wife ____ I leave my affection and all of the lands that I possess except for the north 1/2 of sec 10 twp 19. That portion of my land shall be evenly divided between my son's _____. To my daughter ___ I leave $20. To my daughter-in-law ___, I leave $15 with my love and affection."

The slaves anxiously waited. Where would they go? Would they stay together? What kind of master would they be enslaved to? They hoped that somehow each of their families would get to stay together. But they knew that their loved ones could be taken from them at any moment. The judge continued to speak.

"To my Son-in-Law Samuel, I leave my two black horses. To my son Josiah, my negroes Ben, and Delia. To Joshua Abston of Mississippi, to settle my debt I leave my Negroes Timothy, Nancy, and their daughters Margaret, Lucretia, Sally, and Mary. Also to Joshua Abston, I leave my negroes Tom, Jane and their child, Penny. The balance of my negroes, Nancy's sons Richard, Joshua, and Willis, I leave to Joseph Tucker, as settlement in full of my debt.

The judge continued to speak about the cows, tools, and other property. But Nancy did not hear another word that the judge said. Her screams drowned out the bequest of the 300 acres of land that rightfully belonged to Timothy when he was unjustly enslaved, but was left to Foy's estate. All she heard was that three of her sons were given to a slaveholder that she had never heard of. She would never see her son's Richard, Joshua and Willis again! "Oh God no!" screamed Nancy. "Not my sons! Not my sons! Please don't take my sons!" She sank to the ground sobbing. Timothy put his arms around her and tried to comfort her through his own tears. The yard had become chaotic in the last few minutes, as the enslaved families learned of their fate. Some stayed together. Most did not. Foy had led a lavish lifestyle and left a lot of debt. That meant that the boys who were about thirteen to eighteen were willed to some of the planters to whom Foy owed a debt. Nancy cried uncontrollably until no more tears would come. Jane made Nancy a special tea to comfort her. Although Jane was grateful that she, Tom and their child Penny would stay together, she could feel Nancy's pain. She had known the same kind of pain when she was taken from Africa. And she was like a mother to Nancy's children. She had helped deliver two of them herself, and she had nursed Willis who was born about the same time as her daughter Penny. The judge said Abston and Tucker would come for them tomorrow. They would make the most of tonight.

That night they prayed together and talked about finding each other again. They promised to find a way to keep track of each other. Nancy tried to memorize every detail of her son's faces and every birthmark on their bodies.

The next day, Abston and Tucker arrived at dawn with three horse-drawn wagons. Everyone loaded up their meager belongs and climbed onto the wagons. They rode to the Mississippi River and then took a riverboat down the river. They were met on the other side, and two days later, they were on their new plantation in Marshall County, Mississippi. The year was 1825.

They found the new plantation to be just about the same as the old one, in many ways. It was a smaller plantation. There were fewer slaves, but there was a smaller field to plow. The only difference on this plantation was that each family pretty much cooked for their own family after the day's work was done. This was preferable to Jane and Nancy. They usually quit work in the fields about an hour before sundown so that they could get their evening chores done before the light was gone. Meals typically consisted of the vegetables they grew in their own gardens. When they cleaned and cured the meat for the Abston's they were allowed to keep the parts, such as the pig's feet and ears which would otherwise be thrown away as waste. They managed to spice up the vegetables and the meals with these parts. Their cabins were left unlocked at the end of the day, which gave them some degree of autonomy. Because of family ties, there were few who attempted to run away. Even Tom, who had a much better life in the maroon colony, would not go because he was now far away from home, and he and Jane had made a life together. Running away meant leaving family members behind, and they felt that the family had been split up too much already.

Jane still thought about her family in Africa. But she knew that the chance of ever seeing any of them again was very slim. It was well after 1808, and the Constitution now prohibited importing slaves from Africa. Now, most people were born into slavery in America. Although slaveholders still managed to illegally obtain people from Africa and enslave them, this practice was not nearly as frequent as it had been 20 years before. But the slaves still dreamed of the day that they would be free. The system was set up on fear. The tools of slavery told the story. Whips. Thumb screws. Slave collars. All were used to keep enslavement in place. New laws were made frequently, and slaves knew them well because they were always reminded of them. It was against the law to be insolent to a white person. "Negroes" were not allowed to drink alcoholic beverages. Dancing was against the law. Preaching in public was against the law. Many of these laws made the slaves very unhappy. However, it was against the law for a slave to admit the he was unhappy. As Jane put it, "Dey make a law that we like slavery and den dey believes it." Fugitive slave laws meant that any person who saw an unattended Black person was obligated to turn him in, preferably alive, but dead was fine too. There were books, pamphlets, and instructions on how to get the most profit out of a slave. Slaveholders were told to pit dark skin against light skin. Slaves who had never seen Africa were told that others were "rescued" out of Africa. American born Blacks were taught to view African born Blacks with suspicion. Slavers told tales about "African savages who eat people." African religion was ridiculed as a "heathen" religion or simply "superstition," and Africans were not allowed to practice it. Then they were taught the slaveholders version of Christianity. This version always included "the Lord said that you should be kind to your masters and obey them." When the slave families attempted to worship on Sunday, they were always scrutinized to ensure that they were not plotting a revolt, or something similar. A white person had to be present at their service. They had to seek permission to worship and after this permission was granted, Jane, like other Africans was prohibited from "blasphemes" dances or using any drums. She was not allowed to pray or talk in her native language. There was a fear among slaveholders that drums would be used to signal other Africans of a revolt or rebellion. Jane felt discouraged at this foreign method of worship. When she was alone, she would call out to the ancestors, and pray in the manner she had been taught as a child. Some of these rituals were incorporated into their worship when their enslavers were not looking.

The years came and went. They had been on the Abston plantation for twenty-five years. Timothy and Nancy had two more children. Tom and Jane had five more, which included a set of twins. Nancy's daughter, who was named after her mother but nicknamed "Nini," had "taken up" with Jane's son Harmon. Nini and Harmon had two children by 1852. Then, in about 1853, they noticed that the Doctor frequently visited the Abston House. They began to worry. Soon, they were again called for the reading of a will. Heart in throat they went to the yard in front of the house to be told of their fate. Once more hearts were broken as some of the children were taken away. Tom was 58 years old, and could do little field work now, because slavery had taken its toll on his body. Jane was only a few years younger. Ben Lewis, who purchased their lot, paid only a small fee for Tom and Jane. He needed field hands and paid top dollar for Harmon, and Harmon's son Huey. He felt that Huey was an investment that would pay off in a few years. However, he didn't need Harmon's wife Nini. Nini was sold with Timothy and her mother's lot. This time it was Nini in tears, begging Lewis not to take her husband and son from her. Her tears were in vain. She never saw her husband Harmon, or her son Huey again.

A few days later, the country again celebrated "America's birthday" By this time Blacks had watched their white enslavers celebrate "Independence day" for about 75 years. Each year they grew angry as their enslavers talked about "how great a country this America is, and how great freedom was. And about how rich the country was growing with cotton, sugar, and tobacco. "Our backs!" Tom said. "Dey gits rich off our backs," an' den say how hard dey work to make dis country rich an' free."

About this time, they had heard about an ex-slave by the name of Frederick Douglas. He was said to be an abolitionist. A slave named Ned who could read worked on their plantation. He had several handbills and a bible buried in a box in the fields, which he sometimes dug up and read to the other slaves. That 4th of July, when the overseer was too drunk to oversee, Ned brought out a yellowed crumbled piece of paper. It was a 1-page copy of the North Star, which was a newspaper published by Douglass during the late 1840's. Although he knew he could be whipped for just having the paper, he took it out and read Douglas' words to the other slaves.

"I am not included within your glorious July 4th anniversary! Your independence only reveals the immeasurable distance between us. The rich inheritance of justice, liberty, prosperity and independence obtained by your forefathers, is shared by you, not by me. The sunlight that brought life and healing to you, has brought stripes and death to me. This 4th of July is yours, not mine. You may rejoice. I must mourn."

The day after America's "celebration of freedom," Tom, Timothy, and their fragmented families left the Abston plantation, and went to their new ones.

Sun Up to Sun Down

The Fourth Generation

"Entrenched in Slavery"

Nancy, Harmon, Kitty, Syntha

GOREE ISLAND FROM A DISTANCE

"Sold Down the River"

Harmon and his sons Huey and William arrived at the Lewis plantation in Marion County, Mississippi on a hot summer day. A wealthy man, he had at least seven children who each owned homes in the area. Lewis owned over 1000 acres. He was a wealthy man. His brothers and a sister lived in the area. Benjamin Lewis envisioned a fine home for his family. Harmon, and some of the other slaves were very good carpenters. They cut the wood, and built Benjamin's home from the ground up. And what a fine home it was! It was a 5-bedroom Victorian that was grand in style. A neat white porch, just right for drinking iced tea while enjoying the warm weather, surrounded the entire home. Then they built their own one-room cabins. The slave cabins were small and dark, and were a stark contrast to the grand home they built for Ben Lewis. The tiny log cabins had dirt floors where the enslaved slept on wooden slats that were covered with burlap. Tom once said that Massa had a finer home for his chickens than he did for his slaves. At times, Benjamin loaned some of his slaves to his brothers who lived on

51

nearby plantations.

Benjamin's main crop was cotton. Picking cotton required a good back and a strong will. With the methods that Tom had taught them on the Foy plantation, they had few problems making their quotas. Harmon missed his wife Nancy and thought about her often. When they were sold, Nancy had been sick off and on. Now, Harmon wondered if she was dead or alive.

After Benjamin had been in Marion County, for a few years, he became a sheriff in the county. The whites in the neighborhood respected him. The Blacks thought he was better than most. They knew he would not treat them too badly because of his standing in the community. Benjamin needed more slaves to work his vast holdings of land. Soon the word was out that more slaves would arrive. One day, Benjamin pulled up to the Big House, and two wagons followed closely behind him. Several slaves got off the wagons and stood in front of it, eyes to the ground. One of the overseers came down from the fields and led them down to the slave cabins. One by one, they were told which cabin they would be in. Harmon knew that his cabin could hold another slave or two. He was also aware that Benjamin considered him prime age to produce more children. Talk around the plantation was that Benjamin was looking for a "good wench" to put with Harmon. So he was very interested in seeing who was on the wagon. There were two women. One of the women looked like she was about 30 or 35. She was pleasant looking and Harmon could tell that she was a field hand. She had strong, muscular arms, the way women's arms looked when they did field work. She had a kindly looking face. Her eyes were wide, like most of the others as she looked around. She looked up at the trees, as if she expected to see someone hanging from them. Her skin was dark, almost black. Harmon wondered if she was brought from Africa. The other woman was medium brown and she looked like she was about 18 or 20 years old. She didn't look afraid like the others. She looked angry. She kicked the ground as she walked along. When she got out of the wagon, she looked the overseer right in the eye. That kind of look would have gotten her whipped on the Foy plantation, but the overseer acted as if he didn't see it. Harmon guessed that the woman had missed the law that said that negroes were not allowed to be sullen or show any displeasure. She didn't hold her head down like the others as they walked. She looked about the plantation, taking in her surroundings, no doubt wondering what kind of place she was being brought to. She didn't seem to see anything she liked. When they were being shown to their cabins, she kind of hung back, preferring to let the others go first. Finally, they stopped at the cabin next to Harmon's.

"Syntha," the overseer growled at the woman, clearly showing his displeasure at her. "This is your cabin. Go on now! Get in there!" She walked through the broken door of the cabin, saying nothing. Harmon muttered under his breath, "Oh shoot! I sho hope Massa ain't totin' her heah fuh me! That kind uh woman is goin' to get herself whipped and me whipped too." He was not looking forward to their union.

The overseer came, got Harmon, and told him that the new slave was his to train.

"Sho hope he jes talkin 'bout field trainin'," Harmon thought. He joined Syntha in her cabin. He planned to explain the field routine to her, and let her know how she would start her mornings. She barely looked up. She just sat on the floor making circles in the dirt floor.

Not really knowing what to say, but wanting to break the ice, Harmon said, "You want some wata or somethin? Jane cooked and they's still peas lef."

"I don't want nothin but free from here!" she said. Harmon glanced at the door, hoping that the overseer didn't hear her. He had seen both men and women whipped for suggesting such a thing. He was trying to figure out something else to say. Then Jane came to the door of the cabin with Harmon's son Huey. Huey was about 3 years old, and not yet old enough to understand what slavery was all about. All he knew was that there was someone different in the house. Huey was a friendly child. He was used to people coming and going. Different slaves cared for him all the time. They all considered him an "easy child." He went straight to the woman. "What's yo' name, Lady?" he asked her. She turned and looked at him. For the first time since she got off the wagon, her eyes softened, and she looked like she was going to cry.

"My name Syntha. What yo' name baby?" she asked.

"Huey," he said. "Do you have any kids?" Syntha's eyes filled with tears and she didn't answer for a few moments.

Finally, she said. "I got a son, not much older than you."

"Can I play wit him?" Huey asked.

Syntha took a deep breath, as if to muster up all of her strength. "He don't live here," she answered.

"Oh!" said Huey. "Okay." He went to the corner and started building circles with his rocks.

It was nightfall. Harmon made Syntha a pallet on the dirt floor. Then he told her about the schedule for the next day. Finally, he rounded up Huey and went back to his cabin.

At sunrise the next day, Harmon showed Syntha what she was expected to do. She already knew about picking cotton. She filled her bags and said very little the whole day. Harmon was glad he didn't have to try to think of something to say to her. The work didn't allow much time for talking. It was nearing dusk when they got back to slave row that evening. Nancy had made enough dinner for all of them. Syntha seemed friendly enough when the overseer wasn't around. They made small talk and cleaned up after dinner. Harmon and Syntha finished their chores and sat in front of her cabin. Huey was playing a game of tag with the other children. As he ran and laughed, he seemed to alternately lighten Syntha's mood and make her sad. The evening grew dark and Harmon and Syntha went into Syntha's cabin to light the candles. Harmon silently watched the flickering candle, not sure whether or not to acknowledge Syntha's efforts to hold back the tears when she watched the children play. The only sounds were the crickets outside. Finally, Harmon broke the silence.

"Do you know where he is?" Harmon finally asked.

"Who?"

"Yo' son."

"Naw. I don't know where he at." Silence again fell over the cabin. Finally, Harmon got up and headed for one of the candles to check the flame. As Harmon bent over the candle, Syntha spoke.

"Dey took 'im! Took 'im right out of my arms. Last thang I saw was his little arms, stretched out, cryin' fo' me! Reaching for me!" Harmon stood up, leaving the candle lit. He turned around and looked at Syntha. She was looking straight ahead. She was in another time, another place. She shook her head in disbelief. "I got about fo' yeah's wit my baby and then they takes im! They say he be a full hand in a few mo' yeah's."

Now Harmon spoke. "They don't see chillun as chillun, Syntha. They see's lil' boys as bucks an' field hands and they sees little gals as wenches."

"I reckon dey does," Syntha said. "Dat how dey sees me when I's a youngun. I don't know how ol' I is but one slave say I was about tha'teen when I had im. When I was bout 10 yeahs old, slava name Joe Tucka put me on the block. He say, "This slave's prime fo' breedin' yo' younguns." He say "She be about prime child bearin age to put wit some strong black buck.' He say I's fo'teen but I weren't no mo den ten or eleben. I's big though. Them slavers took me and 'fo long dey had dey way wit me. I had me my baby when I twelve, or maybe tha'teen yeahs ol."

Harmon grew angry. "Dem no good slavers," he said. "If we'd of done that to they women, they calls it rape and talk about puttin us to death. When they does it to our women, it sposed to be "the way things is! Lawdy. When this goin end? When this goin end?"

Syntha had no answer. Harmon knew that there wasn't one. He knew Syntha needed to talk. She had to purge her soul before the pain ate her at her insides. She talked about another enslaved child, who she thought of as her son because his Momma was dead. The boy was just coming into his working days when he was sold. He'd started picking cotton, but he didn't have a quota yet, so he didn't get the lash. Syntha knew that he would soon get the lash.

Then Harmon asked about her parents.

"My Momma was sol' when I's about 3 yeah's old. Don't know nothing bout my Ma. Don't know if she dead. Don't know if she alive. She could be right here on this plantation and I wouldn't know she my Ma. But I know about my Paw. Dey say Paw was a good field hand. Say he was born in Mississippi. I reckon he still in Mississippi somewhere." She continued to talk, her voice becoming stronger as she went on. "Ol' Joe Tucka was one ob dem mean slavers. If slave don't do right he whup you, den rub salt in it. Man, woman, child; it don't matta. It jes' don't matta. I seed him whup a slave raw for bein' one hand down on his quota. One time he whupped a field hand who was in the family way so bad, she pert near dead. Baby were born dead. When ol' Joe died I's glad cuz I know'd they weren't no slaver bad as Joe. But den he done gone an' take muh baby. Even dead he bad! Even dead he take mah baby!" It became quiet. The candle was almost out. As the room grew dimmer, Harmon said "goodbye" to Syntha and headed back to his cabin. He knew she would sleep a restless sleep. He knew that it would be a long time before she could sleep without crying for her lost child. As he lay on his pallet that night, he fell into a restless sleep.

Harmon and Syntha got along well after that. They came to truly care for one another. Syntha had lost track of time and she didn't know her true age. However, she thought she must be about 17 now. Harmon and Syntha soon started a family. In addition to Harmon's sons William, and Huey, they soon welcomed twins named Emily Ann and Emily Jane, and a son named Johnnie. However, the vestiges of slavery still proved brutal to the make-up of the family. Slavery was a peculiar institution. Even when those enslaved belonged to a slaveholder who vowed to keep them together, things frequently happened to make that vow impossible.

Even though Ben Lewis did prove to be kinder than Tucker was, the overseer still needed to get maximum work out of the slaves. In addition, the law specified how many lashes you would give a slave who misbehaved. The only way to keep the slave institution intact was to mete out punishment to keep the other slaves in line.

A slaveholder's death was one of the things guaranteed to upset the rhythm and balance of the family. Benjamin Lewis died in about 1859. Once again, the enslaved Blacks anxiously awaited their fate. Once again, there was a reading of a will. And sadly, once again Syntha was separated from her children by the slaveholder's will. Benjamin's children still lived in Marion County, Mississippi in the Waterhole area. His will made a gift of Harmon's son's William and Huey to each of his sons Lemuel and Martin. But it was good that the brother's lived near each other because they sometimes loaned their slaves to one another. William and Huey still worked on the old Ben Lewis Plantation from time to time. But the twins Emily Ann and Emily Jane were just infants. Benjamin bequeathed one of the twins to his daughter ___ as a token gift. Slaves were looked at much the same as real estate, or a colt. Their value would increase over time. Even though an infant was a token gift, the infant would some day be a full-fledged slave. A slave wet nurse would nurse the small infants. As the children became older, other slaves would care for them. The enslaver never tended to the slaves needs. Other slaves on the plantation did that. The enslaver bided their time until the child grew older and became either a field hand or a breeder. Very young children, some as young as 4 years old, would begin doing errands and cleaning tasks around the plantation.

However, to Syntha, that gift that Benjamin made of her child was the life to which *she* had given birth. It was her baby. Her blood. And she didn't know if she would ever see her baby again. Even though Syntha had been separated from her children before, she found that one could never be prepared for that kind of heartache.

"Dey's a hole in muh heart. They's a special place in a mother's heart for alla her children. When one taken, a new hole is made in yo' heart. Dat space stays empty. They's nothing that can heal that empty hole. It hurt fuh the rest uh yo' life."

57

Because Benjamin's children owned land in the area, most of the slaves who were willed away were no more than 10 miles from their old plantation. Emily Jane was taken only seven miles from Syntha, but neither ever knew of that fact. It could have been one mile or a thousand. The end result was the same for the slaves who were separated. It was the sign of the times. Few considered the wishes of the slaves when it came to business and slaves were a business. According to the law, they were property. Property had no feelings. Property had no voice.

Most of the slaves remained hopeful that they might someday escape to the north and obtain freedom. Slaves in the north had been free for over 30 years. Surely there was a chance that slavery would be abolished in the south as well, and all of the slaves would be let go. There was a slave named Dred Scott who had traveled with his owner to the North. Then Scott sued for his freedom. He told the court that he was in free territory and he should be freed. Nevertheless, when the judge handed down his opinion, he said that the Missouri Compromise, which had previously allowed a slave state admitted for every Free State admitted, was invalid. He said that slavery was legal in both the north *and* the south. According to Judge Taney, Congress didn't have the right to outlaw slavery in *any* territory! But the Judge didn't stop there. He declared that Scott was property, and had no rights under the Constitution. Furthermore, he declared that since blacks were property, they could never be citizens. Then he attacked the very soul of Black men when he said that blacks were "…beings of an inferior order, and altogether unfit to associate with the white race, either in social or political relations; and so far inferior that they have no rights which the white man is bound to respect."

Then just to insure that there was no question about the status of Blacks, he wrote that Blacks were not human, just animals. He said that they were made only for slavery. His blistering decision was a blow to the physical and mental health of the enslaved, in the North as well as the South.

After word of the decision got around, it seemed to Harmon,

Syntha and the others that the overseer's treated the slaves much harsher. The Judge had said that Blacks were not human. Blacks were then treated less humanely.

For many whites the Dred Scott decision was empowering. The white race was granted the status of superiority both legally and morally. It gave them license to condone harsh treatment of the entire black race. The decision clearly eradicated any notion that Blacks had any humanity whatsoever that needed to be respected. Therefore, there was no need to treat Blacks any better than work horses or cows.

As morally degrading as the Dred Scott decision was for Black people, it fundamentally set one basic foundation that was paramount above others; The Supreme Law of the land had said that Blacks could never be free!

Then in 1860, Lincoln was elected President. Things became even more contentious between the north and the south. The southern whites were always talking about how the north should mind their own business and leave the south to run things as they saw fit. They complained about "agitators" and "abolitionists." They worried that "negroes were going to start to get ideas about being free." They were right. Many enslaved Blacks became encouraged by Lincoln's presidency. When the slaveholder was out of earshot, they talked about freedom. The songs in the field changed from *"Some-times I-ah fee-l like a mo-ther-less chi-ld,"* to *"Oh-oh free-dom. Oh-oh freedom. Oh free-dom over me-e. And before I be a slave - - I be buried in my grave. Goin home to my Lo-rd and be free!"* Often the songs had a hidden meaning as some of the slaves enlisted the help of the abolitionists and the Underground Railroad. Songs like *"Wade in the Water"* signaled a meeting place and reminded the slaves to cross the water to throw their scents from the dogs. Or hearing the song *"Swing low Sweet Chariot,"* signaled a time to gather.

Jane ran excitedly out to the fields one day. She was out of breath when she reached the field hands. "Ol' Massa and Mr. Lemme be talkin las' night. They say South done quit the North," she said. "Ol' Jefferson Davis is President of the South. An' Abe Lincoln is President of the North!" The slaves awaited their fate, some thinking that freedom might come soon, others certain that a lifetime of enslavement was their destiny.

Changes came to the south very rapidly after that. The slaves kept an ear to the ground at all times. They knew that their future was uncertain. They heard many different versions of the truth. They heard that they were free and "Massa is keeping it from us." Then they heard that nothing had changed. Finally late in January 1863, one of the slaves came running up to the field hands. He was laughing and yelling. He was jumping over tree limbs like he was playing hopscotch. Finally, he reached the others. "Put down those hoes! We don't have to slave no mo'. Lincoln done freed the slaves! Mancipaton Placamaton say we's free." The others started whooping & hollering, and jumping. They went into a happy dance and started singing "Thank God we Free!" Their celebration was cut short by a gunshot. Startled, they looked up and saw the overseer riding his horse towards them. "What's wrong with you niggers, he growled? Ain't nobody free, and ain't nobody gonna be free. De South ain't no part of da Union no mo'. We gots us a new President. Jefferson Davis is President of the South. And Jefferson Davis ain't freed nobody, and ain't gonna free nobody. Now Jefferson Davis and this here gun say you a slave and you gonna stay a slave." He fired another shot. They went back to work, but that evening there was an excited buzz in the air.

The overseer was right about one thing. They were still slaving. The civil war was in full swing. They heard that both the Union and the Confederacy would give a slave his freedom if he fought on their side. The slaves on the Lewis plantation never received such an offer though. On the contrary, Jefferson Davis ordered the soldiers to pick up any Negro who was running around loose and put them on the auction block. Many of the plantations were in chaos as the men went off to war and fewer people were able to keep control of the slaves and the plantations. Some of the Lewis brothers were among those who went off to war.

The slaves continued to labor under the overseer, but the farm rapidly declined. The overseer's became tougher on all of the slaves to keep them from running off. Whippings became more frequent. Quotas for the cotton increased to unreasonable quantities. By this time, Huey had become a teenager. The overseer frequently chastised Huey for not making his quota. One day, in answer to the request to pick more cotton, Huey said to the overseer.

"I doin de bes' I can, suh!" Apparently, it was the wrong thing to say. The next thing Huey knew, the overseer snatched him up and hauled him to the big oak tree in front of the barn. It was about two o'clock in the afternoon and it was a hot day. The sun was high. With some of the others gathered around, Huey was strapped to the tree and the overseer got his whip. One of the children ran to find Harmon and Syntha to tell them that Huey was about to be whipped, and they came running over to the tree. Syntha pleaded with the overseer, but her cries fell on deaf ears.

"He jes a baby, suh!" she cried. "Oh Lord please don't whup my baby!"

Harmon was concerned that because of Huey's small physique, the beating would be too much for him to bear. Additionally, the overseer was angrier than anyone had seen him in a very long time. This likely meant that the beating would be longer and harder, with other slaves required take turns whipping Huey. Harmon tried reasoning with the overseer. He promised longer hours, and better training to help Huey to work faster. He tried to get the overseer to let him make up Huey's slack, but the overseer refused. Nothing that they said had any effect.

The whip came down hard on Huey's back. One... Two... Three... Eighteen... Nineteen... Twenty. After the first twenty, the overseer was tired and the whip was passed off to another slave to continue the beating. Twenty more lashes! Finally the whipping stopped. Harmon and Syntha ran towards the tree, but the overseer stopped them. "I ain't through with this nigger yet." With that, he tied Huey's arms to the saddle on his horse. He gave the horse a tap and the horse dragged a limp and bleeding Huey toward the barn. The overseer untied Huey and hammered four stakes in the ground. Then he bound Huey's arms and legs spread eagle style, to the stakes. There he left him in the burning sun and warned the other slaves not to untie him until the sun came up. There, bound to the stakes, Huey lay in the hot sun all day long. Mercifully, the sun went down about 5 hours later. When the sun came up again, Huey was burned red and parched from being withheld water. The blood and puss oozed from his body and formed bright red streaks and blisters down his back. His back was cut raw from the whip, and it looked like bone was sticking out of parts of his flesh. Harmon and Syntha had been awake all night and worried that Huey was going to die out there. They were not allowed to stay with him. At sunrise the next morning, the overseer told one of the slaves to untie Huey. He sent Harmon to the fields, and told Syntha and Nancy to take Huey back to the cabin to "lick his wounds, and learn him his lesson." Huey had a high fever and a slow pulse. Syntha and Nancy got him some cool water and treated his wounds with juice from an aloe vera plant. They bathed his forehead with cold rags to reduce his fever. Two days later, Huey was back in the fields. However, he was making a plan.

He told Harmon of his plan. "Cain't stay heah no mo Pa! Dey says the wah done turn and we goin be free sho nuf. I knows somebody who can hep me git away from heah."

Harmon pleaded with him not to go. "Huey, Ah don't know if Syntha's heart kin take it. She the only Momma you ever knowed, and you's huh son just as sho as she giv you life." But Huey was determined. He didn't want to hurt Harmon and Syntha, but it also pained him to see the anguish on his parent's faces, when he was healing from the whipping. He couldn't bear it to see them hurt that way again.

"I'm gonna fine somewheah fuh us. We be free any day now. Den I come back and get ya'll."

Huey stayed on the plantation until he saw a good chance to run. That chance came one Sunday, when Massa Lemme's wife got sick and the overseer was distracted all day by attending to her needs. The timing was perfect because all day long the field hands sang about the "Chariot" coming. Huey knew that there would be help to escape that night. When nightfall came Huey ran. And he didn't stop running until he got to Louisiana. He planned to stay there until the next freedom train came.

The war was fought long and hard. More of the Lewis brothers went off to war. Not all of them returned. The slave-owners donated all the money they had to the confederate cause. The plantation was in ruins. The writing was on the wall. The South was losing badly. Enslaved Blacks all over the south were hopeful that they would soon be freed. Then finally, one hot day in 1865, the slaves looked up from the fields and saw the Union soldiers marching up to the Big House. Their hearts pounded as they wondered what the soldiers were doing on the plantation. By that time, Mass Ben was dead, and the slaves belonged to his children Lemuel, Giles, and Joshua. At sundown, they got their answer. The overseer went to slave row and instructed the slaves to go to the big house. An excited buzz was in the air as they gathered there. Some of them had a sense of foreboding because it was generally not good news when they were gathered together in that way. Others had heard rumblings that the war was over.

Lemuel came out of the big house. He looked very sad. Two of his brothers were with him. His wife stood beside him, tears in her eyes. Lemuel had a scroll in his hand.

"I want ya"ll to listen up." I know you have heard rumors about the war. And I'm gonna read this just as it's written."

He began to read from the scroll;

"The people of Mississippi are informed that in accordance with a Proclamation from the Executive of the United States, all slaves are free. This involves an absolute equality of rights and rights of property between former masters and slaves, and the connection heretofore existing between them becomes that between employer and free laborer."

Lemuel looked up from his paper. "War's over." he said, sadly. "So I guess you're all free."

It was pure pandemonium on the grounds. There was shock. There were tears of joy. There was confusion. And there were praises to God. After they had calmed down a bit, Lemuel continued to speak. "You are all free now, but you've never had to take care of yourself. You never had to want for nothin' because we gave you everything you needed. You wouldn't know how to live on your own." He took a deep breath and continued speaking.

"You can't support yourself if you leave, and I can't support my family and tend to this plantation without somebody to work the land. It would be best for everybody if you stay on the plantation. And anyhow, the government says that you are not allowed to leave until this planting season is over. Now the law says that I have to pay you. I can't pay you much but you can take a share of the crop that you raise. Most of you have been here a long time, and you know that I am a fair man. You can stay in the cabins rent-free. But we must work together if any of us will survive these dreadful times."

The former slaves looked around the plantation and off in the distance, taking in the vast world that was soon to be theirs. They looked at the Big House that was built with their own labor. It was a fine house, nice and white. The garden, once blooming with beautiful red and yellow roses, was now overgrown with weeds. They looked at their cabins. The cabins were poorly built. Some looked like they might fall down any minute. The cabins were built with left over material, and had to be made in a hurry so they could get back and tend to the Massa's work. Massa Ben saw no need for floors and separate rooms in the cabins. Most of the cabins had make shift walls to keep separate areas. At times, only a rope holding several pieces of cloth separated the parents from the children. In the early days, they didn't even have beds. They just had slats nailed together, and a mattress made of scraps of old rags that they could put together. Then Syntha thought of all of her children. She wished that she could find them. She didn't know where they were or what they looked like. She knew that the notes that the slaveholders sometimes made in their Bible records rarely listed much information about the slave's parents. And she knew that the new master often gave the slaves he acquired new names, especially when they were children. A new name reduced the chance of some runaway slave looking for their kin. She doubted that Emily was still Emily. Harmon thought of his first wife, Nancy. If she was alive, he now had two wives. He felt a duty to both of them, but it was a Herculean task to find her. They both thought of their sons, Huey and William. They had not seen William for months and they didn't know what happened to him. They heard that Emily was still in the area somewhere. If that were true, they might be able to find her. And of course, they had to stay and wait for Huey. Huey had said that he would be back after freedom came. They wanted to be there for Huey. In the end, they agreed to stay on at the Lewis Plantation. They needed the work. They reasoned that it would be better, because their time would be their own, and they could find their children.

At their first opportunity, they walked for miles in each direction trying to locate their children. They were not alone. They ran into other newly freed slaves who were trying to do the same. Some families were reunited. While enslaved, many had taken steps to ensure that they found their children after slavery. Often the men and women would give their children their own name. They hoped that this would help reunite the family after freedom. Mothers often took care to make a mental note of anything that would help them identify their children.

Harmon and Syntha walked for days. They finally found William. He had been willed to one of Lemuel's brothers. But the plantation was in ruins. There was very little left of the plantation that William was on. He happily joined his parents in sharecropping for Lemuel. They took William back to Lemuel's place. They walked in vain in their search for Emily. No one could help them put the pieces together to find her. Syntha did not know how big Emily was. She could not describe her. She wasn't sure if Emily had kept her honey brown color, or had darkened over the years. She couldn't find Emily, so she went back to the plantation. She watched. She waited. And she hoped.

Syntha was out in the fields picking cotton one day when she looked up to see William walking towards her with an older woman. William supported the woman's elbow as they slowly made their way towards the fields. He excitedly motioned for Syntha to join them. Syntha took a few steps toward them and cupped one hand above her eyes to shield the sun and get a better look. Still, she did not recognize the woman. As Syntha got closer she saw that William and the woman had huge grins on their faces. Suddenly, the woman broke free of Williams grip.

"Syntha!? Syntha!? Is you Syntha?"

"Yessum." answered Syntha.

"Let me see the back of yo' neck!" the woman demanded.

"Ma'am?" Syntha questioned, startled by the request.

"Yo' neck! I wants to see the spider on the back of yo neck!" the woman repeated. Syntha quickly slapped the back of her neck and looked at her hand. If there had been a spider there, it seemed to be gone now. Undeterred, the woman stepped behind Syntha, and removed the head wrap that covered Syntha's head and neck. The old woman immediately let out a loud, high-pitched squeal and began to jump up and down, although her feet barely left the ground in their crippled condition.

"My baby! Yes you is! You my long-lost baby! Thank you Lord! Thank ya! Thank ya!"

The old woman's words slowly began to sink into Syntha. Her mother? Could this woman be her mother?

"My Mama?" Syntha asked, the words barely escaping her lips.

"Yes, child, I's Matilda. I's yo Mama! And you still got that spider birthmark on the back of yo' neck. When you was took away from me I know'd dat mark would help me find you. I done heard that Ol Massa Tucka sold you heah! Thank the Lord you's still heah! But I couldn't believe that you was *my* Syntha till I saw dat mark on yo' neck! I'd ponder on that mark goin to sleep and wakin up ever' day of my life!"

The women gazed at one another. Tears streamed down both

of their faces. Syntha had long given up on ever finding her mother. She actually believed that her mother was dead after so many years passed without a word. All the bravado that Syntha had shown over the years slowly crumbled as she and Matilda held each other. William watched the scene unfold before him as he wiped a tear from his eyes. Matilda had reclaimed her child. Syntha had regained a mother, and he had gained a grandmother.

Finally Free

The Fifth Generation

"Freedom"
Huey, Arthina, Frank, Mary, Green and Harriett

This is a photo of the last Slave House in the Family
Florence, South Carolina
The Green Family

5

"Free At Last"

Tom, Jane, Harmon, and Syntha, and the others finally tasted freedom. They were grateful to God, the Union army, and to President Lincoln for their freedom. Even working from sun-up to sun down didn't seem as hard because they looked forward to getting their share at the end of the season. They dreamed of someday getting their own land.

There was talk about a government agency that helped the freedmen get their lives set up. Jane heard some of the white Lewis' talking and she told the former slaves what she'd heard. "The law done created a Freed Men's Agency," she said. After the wah' Gen'l Howard say he gonna give each ex-slave 40 acres, a mule, and $10. He say dat da lands dat was 'bandoned in de war gonna go to da ex-slaves."

However, that dream died quickly when the confederate soldiers returned from the war. After hearing the latest news, Jane gave them an update.

"Them Confederate soldiers done come back an' da President say dat the cullud has to give that lan' back to dem soldiers. Boy, I'm tellin you. When I went down by the Mississippi riva I sees dat dey runnin nigga's off that land left and right! Even dem soldiers dat didn't hab no land befo' the wah' got some ob dat land after it. Dey jest had to sign up and go git it. Dem soldiers were mad as a hornet at da niggas though. Dem niggas could fugget bout gitten some land. Jes settin' on that land uh git ya a bullet in da head. They's got all they can do jes to stay alive, and stay free! You could set dere if you don't mind dodgin' bullets."

Harmon became agitated, and spoke sarcastically. "How ya'll thank dey gonna give us some property, when dey still thank of *us* as dey property? Jes 8 yeahs ago dey done said we wuz property. Dey done said we ain't even human, and dey all believes it. Jes' cuz you ain't slave no mo don't mean you can run around like a white man, actin' like you free. Now dey's stayin' up nights trying to figure out a way to slave us again. "Freedom ain't much differn't den slabry. Difference is – now yo' life ain't worth a nickel."

Harmon was right. After emancipation when the legislature convened, they debated about slavery. Many southern whites still thought that they could use the Constitution to get their slaves back.

On the senate floor, Senator Davis who was speaking about the emancipated slaves quoted the constitution.

".. no person shall be deprived of life, liberty, *or property* without due process of law." Many of the Senators were upset, because they didn't get "due process" before their "property in slaves" was taken away. They demanded reparations for the loss of their property!

The Senators also debated about granting reparations to the former slaves. There was a resolution on the house of the senate floor given by Senator Sumner on July 3, 1867. Sumner resolved that:

> "...(so) that the reconstruction of the rebel states would be hastened and the best interest of the country promoted if the President of the United States, in the exercise of his pardoning power, would require that every landed proprietor who has been engaged in the rebellion, before receiving pardon ... would convey to the freedmen, his former slaves, a certain portion of the land on which they have worked, so that they may have a homestead in which their own labor has mingled, in that the disloyal master may not continue to appropriate to himself the fruits of their toil...I move that the resolution be printed and laid on the table!"

President Johnson would have none of that. He moved quickly to veto the action.

Nevertheless, changes came quickly now. Every Saturday the freedmen looked forward to the telegram that would tell them they local and national news.

One Saturday evening in 1868, William ran into Syntha's cabin, out of breath, apparently excited about something. "Dey's finally makin laws *fuh* the culled Pa!" he said excitedly.

Shortly after the war, they knew that the 13th Amendment had abolished slavery. They weren't slaves any more. Now William was explaining the new laws.

"This one is different, Pa." William was the one that they always looked to to explain about the laws. In slavery, he had been able to sneak and learn to read and write a little bit, and he could decipher pretty well. "Dey's done passed anotha amendment fuh us. The 'mendment say that we's all citizens of the United States now! Da 'mendment say we hafta be treated jes de same as whites. Mendment say that cain't no State in America make us slaves no mo', or treat us like slaves no mo'. Dey say whatever white folks can do, colored folks kin do. And they's mo Pa. A bunch of Colored folks done got the Court to take they side. The Court say that the States have to do what the Fedral Gub'ment say do."

William smiled a wide smile. He felt a great sense of pride. He was thinking about striking out on his own and buying some land. When things got going good enough, he would come and get his parents and others in the community. The Lewis plantation would have to do for now. But in two, maybe three years, they could own their own land.

William's smile disappeared as he looked up at his parents. He had expected to see great big smiles of excitement and joy. Instead, what he saw on his parent's faces was more of a frown. They looked at each other and then looked back at him again. Their expressions looked just like they had when he was a little boy, and found a nickel. He thought that it was a lot of money and he was going to buy them their freedom. Harmon and Syntha marveled at his hopefulness, but they knew they had to tell him some hard truths about slavery. They had the same look now.

"What wrong?" He couldn't figure out why they weren't more excited.

Syntha spoke first. "William. You's young. And Lawd knows that I want you to always have hope. But son, ain't no law on no piece uh paper gonna let Colored folk do what white folk do. Now Lawd knows I hopes I's wrong. But when I sees it, den I believes it."

William looked at his father. "What you thank Paw?"

"Son, yo' Momma's right." I done seen it befo'. Dey's gonna try ever thang in dey power to keep us from gitten so much as a cotton seed."

William realized that Harmon and Syntha were right. Their former masters outright refused to obey the new laws. They said that they didn't have to obey the law because each state had their own laws. The Federal government and the Supreme Court couldn't protect them. Harmon paused and shook his head. "Welcome to freedom, son!"

However, William still believed that things would slowly get better. The law was the law. Even white men had to abide by the law didn't they?

William's hopefulness arose again when two years later, in February 1870; the Government gave colored men the right to vote! Now *that* Amendment surprised even Harmon and Syntha.

Moreover, things indeed seemed to improve. The Federal government had sent in the army to make sure that the whites did right by the colored. Colored folks were learning how to read and many even held political offices in the south. Southern white men were mad as a hornet about it. However, it didn't last too long. In 1876, there was a U.S. Presidential election Between Samuel J Tildon and Rutherford B Hayes that was too close to call. The Tildon side made a deal with the Hayes side that if Hayes pulled the army out of the South, and gave more control back to the States, Tildon would let Hayes have the office. So the army pulled out and whites went back to business as usual. Lynching and murder increased. Blacks holding political office became non-existent. Once again, Blacks were completely disinfranchished in every southern state, even though they were a majority in several of them There was no more reconstruction for the Blacks. Reconstruction had failed.

***

After years of searching and hoping, Harmon and Syntha still had not heard from Huey or found Emily. Although they had wanted to have their family back together for the occasion, Harmon and Syntha made plans to remarry. They had jumped over the broom during slavery to celebrate their nuptials, but this time their marriage was legal and they felt that God had sanctioned their union. They remarried under the old oak tree one sunny July afternoon. An old friend, who was a minister, officiated at their wedding, with most of their family and friends looking on. What a grand party it was that night! There were many other parties that summer, as other former slaves re-married to legalize their unions.

Harmon and Syntha lived out their lives on the Lewis Plantation. In addition to the six children they had before emancipation, they had eleven more children born free: Johnny, Willis, Franklin, Elizar, Ibbia, Alax, Pennie, Nancy, Polly Ann, and Robert. However, they never saw Huey or Emily Ann again.

Harmon died in about 1887 leaving Syntha a widow. She never remarried. Tom outlived his son Harmon. He never forgot his Cherokee teachings, and attributed his long life to respecting the rhythm of nature. He arose and retired with the sun every day. Even in slavery, he took care of his spirit the way that they had in the maroon society. Jane died before Tom. Syntha lived near her son William and his family for the rest of her life. She died in 1918 after her house burned to the ground with her in it. No one knew how the fire started. She was about 80 years old.

Although she never knew her mother, Emily Ann had died four years earlier in much the same way. She died in a fire at about age 60. She was badly burned on her back, shoulder, and her breast. Her birth certificate listed her father and mother as unknown. It listed her birthplace as "don't know". She was buried about eight miles from her mother. She never knew that her mother lived less than seven miles from her!

6

"Twenty Minutes of Freedom"

Huey was still in Louisiana when freedom came. After emancipation, Louisiana didn't fare any better than Mississippi. Like his parents, Huey continued to farm, and spent most of his days picking cotton. One day, as he separated the white fur from the stalk, he thought back to the Lewis plantation in Mississippi. He was very much aware that he was one of the lucky ones. He had been born in slavery, but was now free. His neighbors Green, Harriett, Kitty, and Frank, all shared this bond. They were grateful that their children had not spent a lifetime in slavery. They felt blessed to be able to watch their children grow up in freedom. After six generations of enslavement in the family, Huey's children were born free! He hoped that his parents had tasted freedom. Huey regretted that he did not get back to Mississippi before they died. His grandfather Tom would be well over 80 years old now, if he were still alive. Tom always said that if he lived according to the earth's rhythms that he would live to be at least 100. He went down to the river each morning to pray. He loved to be near streams of water, because he believed that the stream nourished both the body and the spirit. Huey once asked Tom to tell him about the way the Cherokee's worshiped but Tom refused. When Huey pressed further, Tom had become angry.

"Huey," he said. "Don't even let them folks hear you *think* thata way. That's a good way to get me whupped, and you too!" Nevertheless, Huey still wondered about it. He knew that the slavers would not allow any slave worship that was not what they considered "Christian". And he knew that a white person always had to attend or watch over the slaves worship. He understood why Tom had to worship in secret, but he still wanted to know about the Cherokee religion. Tom always seemed at peace after a trip to the river. He spoke frequently about going back to the maroon society to find the people that they left behind when he was captured into slavery. He told of the fellowship with the other Cherokees and Choctaws. Tom always said that the white man never respected God's gifts the way the Indians did.

Huey's grandmother Jane had also refused to talk to Huey about her days in Africa before she was brought over on the slave ship. There was talk around town that Jane had once been whipped for praying and dancing by the river. The slaveholder had accused her of trying to "hex" him. Huey thought about the pouch that Jane always wore around her waist. No one could see it. But each morning before she went out into the fields she would touch the pouch to her lips, and then put her clothes on over the pouch. Once Huey asked her, what the pouch was. She looked at him for a moment before she replied, then she said, "Keeps me safe."

Huey didn't understand "Safe how?" he asked.

"Jes safe." She said. Huey knew better than to press her further. He knew the look that indicated that the conversation was over.

And Jane had that look now. So, Huey let the subject drop. However, his imagination got the best of him. He fantasized that it was a magic potion that only African's knew how to use. Or maybe it was a vial of whisky she hid from the white folks. Or maybe she had some food in there. As he grew older, he found that many of the African slaves that he came to know had similar pouches. Now he wished that he had seen Jane before she died. She would surly tell him what the pouch was for now that they were free. And Tom would tell him the ways of the Cherokee.

Huey had tried twice to go back to Mississippi to see his family. The first time was in late 1863. He decided to travel by night, so that he would not be caught. However, luck was not with him. His shoes were badly worn, and he had twisted his ankle while running through a sparse area of brush. All through the night, he made his way through the dense trees. He wanted to make sure that he was in a wooded area by sun up. . However, he still had a long way to go as the sun came up. The sun was just beginning to peak out over the horizon when he heard dogs barking in the distance. He tried to quicken his step but the barking got closer. There were a few trees but no good places to hide. He ducked behind a tree, but the dogs soon caught up with him. The dogs were on his heels, yapping, barking, and running around him. Teeth bared, they held their ground and awaited the order to attack. Huey hoped that the order would not come. Then he saw the white men on horses closing in on him. There was nowhere to run. The horses surrounded the dogs, and the dogs surrounded Huey.

The white men on the horses looked smug, as if they had just bagged a deer. "Where you think you going, nigger? Who do you belong to?"

Huey had to think fast. He knew that nothing he could say would help him now. But he decided to try it anyway. "I's free, Suh! Muh horse done throwed me and run off. I done hurt muh ankle, and I's looking fuh muh horse."

"Where are your free papers, nigger?"

"They's in a satchel on muh horse. If you jes let me find muh horse, I kin git the papuh's fuh yuh."

"You know you ain't got no papers, boy! And you shore ain't no free nigger! Matter fact, you look *jest* like that runaway nigger that belongs to Master Lott."

"No suh! Don't know nothin about a Massa Lott. I's free suh."

"Well! Lets jes see about that." Under protest, and the whip, Huey was taken to the Lott plantation in Louisiana. Jim Lott, the owner of the plantation said that Huey was his runaway slave. He paid the slave-catchers the bounty, and sent Huey to the overseer. Lott had been pleased at his find. A slave on his plantation had run away a few weeks before, and he had little chance of finding him. His runaway slave was about 10 years older than Huey. Lott rationalized that if he didn't keep Huey, some other planter would. Negroes didn't stay loose for very long in these parts. He figured that if there was a slave on the loose, he might as well keep him. So, Huey was stuck on the Lott plantation. He wanted to run away again, but the overseer kept close tabs on his slaves.

Huey wanted to forget the slave days but the thoughts kept creeping in. He remembered when the slaves began hearing more about the abolitionists, and freedom. They dreamed of going north to freedom. Then the entire slave system came into question, and things in the South became chaotic. However, Huey did not have the opportunity to run away again. He was watched very carefully. He was still on the Lott plantation when freedom came. It was there that he met Arthina, his future wife.

Huey looked over at his friends, Green and Frank. They were busy picking cotton. The sun was hot. It reminded him of that warm day when he heard rumblings about the war. He had heard that Lincoln wanted to free the slaves. But the south was whipping the north. Then Lincoln issued the emancipation proclamation that said that the slaves were free. Several slaves had thrown down their tools and claimed their freedom.

He vividly remembered later that same day, when the overseer dashed all of their hopes. In order to quash any attempts of the slaves to leave, the overseer rode out to the fields to deliver a message from the master. "You all better pick them tools up and git yourself back to work. You's still in the South, and Lincoln can't free no slaves in these parts. Jefferson Davis is the President here, not Abe Lincoln! That proclamation ain't got nothing to do with you! The south ain't part of the Union no more, and Lincoln can't free no slaves in it! Now git back to work unless you' all want to be whipped!" He snapped the reins on the horse's backside and rode back towards the big house.

Huey remembered how heavy the tools felt, when he went back to work. The slaves talked about what the overseer said and were trying to understand if they were supposed to be slave or free. They believed that President Lincoln had freed them with the Emancipation Proclamation. They wouldn't put it past Lott to lie to them to get all the work he could out of them. Moreover, what the overseer said just didn't make sense. Green seemed to understand it better and tried to explain it to them. "Lincoln's jest messin' wit the mind of these southern slavers. The South is whupping them Yankees. Now Lincoln is trying to get mo' people to fight wit them. I hear'd em talkin'. They say Lincoln's goin ta let de slaves fight for they own freedom. And if he gits the slaves in the south to run away an' fight for the North, they has a betta chance of winnin. They say that if slaves fight, Lincoln gonna give em they freedom no matta what happen!"

Frank had heard things too and he spoke up. "I hear'd it that some over on the Ball plantation done left to go fight the wah. They's fightin free now. I sho wud lak to go! I reckon walkin' in freedom be sweet as honey."

Huey would never forget the look in Kitty's eyes that day, when they were talking about fighting for their freedom. She looked at them as if they were from outer space. "You nigga's is crazy! Ain't no white man gonna give no culled man no freedom jest cuz the govenment say so. An' he sho ain't goin' give a nigga no gun. Nigga cain't even get a sharp knife round heah cuz they thank we's gonna cut em up in they sleep. An' ya'll thank they 'bout to put a gun in yo' hand? Humph! You's still a nigga! We's slaves. And they gonna keep us slavin as long as they's able!" With that, she turned back to picking cotton. Huey knew that even though she talked tough, Kitty wanted to believe that they would soon be free. When she got nervous, she sang. And she started singing. *"Gonna lay down my bur-den, down by the riverside; down by the riverside; down by the riverside; Gonna lay down my burden, down by the riverside; down by-eh the riv-er-side."* The rest joined in;

"Ain't gonna study wah no mo-r; study wah no mo-r. Stud—ee-ee wa—hh no mo-r'."

A loud bell brought Huey out of his thoughts. It was the first supper bell letting them know that supper would soon be ready. Huey was ready for some supper! However, he still couldn't get his mind off the slave days. Some days he couldn't get the images out of his head. Mostly he thought about how blessed he was to be free.

His mind returned to the months after the Emancipation Proclamation. The year 1863 came and went. Master Lott had been right. They were still slaves. Finally, one day in 1865, the field hands, looked up and saw the Union soldiers, riding high on their horses. They looked mighty fine up there. The horses were stepping high and proud. Huey looked up, and yelled to the others. "Hey! Look!" Finally, the soldiers reached the big house. A little while later the slaves were all asked to gather in front of the big house. Massa, and Missus and the other white slavers stood on the porch. They were clearly upset. They waited while the slaves came out of the fields and the cabins. Finally, after everyone had gathered one of the soldiers pulled out a scroll and started reading;

"The people of Louisiana are informed that in accordance with a Proclamation from the Executive of the United States, all slaves are henceforth and forever free. This involves an absolute equality of rights and rights of property between former masters and slaves, and the connection heretofore existing between them becomes that between employer and free laborer."

Shovels flew across he fields! Shouts could be heard for miles! There was dancing, singing, and praying. "Thank you Jesus! Thank you Lord! The Lord done set us free! The Lord done lifted us out of slavery!"

The next time Huey went back to Mississippi, he was a free man. He looked forward to a reunion with his family. He would hug his mother. He would pat his father on the back. He would kid around with his brothers and sisters. They would stay up all night and sleep late the next day if they wanted to. However, sadly, when he arrived, the plantation was bare. At the time Huey arrived, his family had left the county to try to find Huey and Emily. Huey went to the door of the big house and knocked. Receiving no answer, he headed back down the trail.

He saw a farmhand passing by the plantation in a wagon. He flagged him down. "Mornin suh. Muh name's Huey Lewis. I be lookin fuh my kinfolks. My Grandpa Tom be bout 80 now, if'n he still livin'. Gran'mama Jane straight African. She bout 70 I reckon. An' my Daddy. His name Harmon. He bout forty-three or fo'. Has a wife name Syntha. She never knowed how ol' she was but she is a right smart younga than my Daddy."

The man looked at him. His eyes looked sad, as if he didn't want to give Huey bad news. "Naw. Don't reckon I know ob them. I live ova in Kokomo. Don't know too much 'bout heah. But they say that after freedom come, most of de slaves heah done left. Dat is, the one's dat wern't broke by slabrey. Ain't too many field hands see 70 or 80 yeahs."

Sadly, Huey headed back to Louisiana believing that his family had left the Lewis plantation. He thought that Tom and Jane might be dead. He wondered if the rest were headed to Louisiana or somewhere else to strike out on their own. He reasoned that they would probably not want to stay on the slave plantation after freedom came.

Huey went back to Louisiana. He settled down near the Harris Plantation. He and Arthina decided to stay there for the time being.

Huey brought himself out of his thoughts and looked over at the others. He had made new friends in Louisiana. The Louisiana plantation was not as large as the Mississippi plantation. During slave times, there were maybe 20 or 30 slaves at the most. Most of them belonged to one of only three or four families. Frank and his wife Josephine lived in the cabin next to Huey's. Frank's mother Kitty lived with them. In many ways, Kitty reminded Huey of his grandmother, Jane. Kitty had also come over on a slave ship. She had five other sons, but all of them had been sold from her. Kitty was a spitfire. She was not a woman who held her tongue. She often spoke of her hellish voyage to America. She had a deep hatred for white men, and spoke often of their Godlessness.

Huey was working next to Kitty. She was singing as she worked. She had a velvety smooth voice, and could carry any tune, high or low. She liked to use both whenever she sang. Now she was singing about the Chariot. *"Swing low, sweet Chariot-at, coming for to carry me ah-home. Swi-ing low sweet charia-at, coming for to carry me home."*

Huey started rhythmically picking his cotton. Without glancing up, he joined in the song with Kitty. *"I looked over Jordan and what did I see-ee, coming for to carry me home? A ba'nd of Angels coming after me-e. Coming for to carry me ho-me."* For the next 30 to forty minutes, they picked cotton as they sang. Soon they both had full bags and the sun was starting to set, casting a red glow on the horizon.

Kitty looked up from her cotton. She looked at Huey and smiled.

Huey started to tie a knot on his full bag. "Look lak we got us a mess of cotton today!" he said. "But if'n da sun be any hotter we melt like the riva. It be like blenden" up the way white folks is always talkin 'bout. Dey be braggin and talkin bout how people all over the wurl wants to come heah to 'Merica and blends up together."

Kitty stood straight up. "Blenden up my eye! White folks ain't neva blended togetha. White folks is always a talkin bout' who they is and what they got!" Kitty started mocking the way she heard white men talking over tea on the old plantation.

White folks youse ta say, *"Wud yew like a spot-uf-tea, Madah'm'?"* (Then changing her voice to a gruff tone). *"Estell, get that tea."* (back to the pleasant voice) *"Yew know my Faatha was British, me Mum was a French Lady-ee'. My family came ovah on thee Mayflaugh-ah. We worked so hard on this here land. I will take you out and show you our fields. We have thirty Negro slaves now. We just started with two or three. America is such a great land of opportunity! Anyone can come to America and blend together in harmony!"*

Kitty pretended to put her teacup down delicately. Then she straightened up and picked up another bag. "Dem white folks ain't done nothin. But you know what I say? I say we Africans is the only ones that blended! Shoot! When we wus took on dat slave boat, they done snatched up all kinds uh African's from they villages. Some of us was Ga. Some was Ibo. Some Wolof. They snatched Mandinka, and Fulani. But I tell you what. Afta all dat time in da bottom ob dat boat, when we gits to America we's like one peoples. I say we done blended into one people at da bottom of dat stankin' slaveboat!"

She slung her bag of cotton over her back. She looked up sadly, "But these days we's jes cullud! Own chillun now cain't even tell you what they is no mo'. Dat's how good we done blended! Maybe

85

dey should call us ' Wolobalani'. Cuz dat is what we is! Wolobalani!"

Kitty's eyes turned dark as she remembered the slave ship. "We was on dat boat, not knowin whey we goin. We done hear'd thangs bout' slav'ry but couldn't nothin fix yo' mind fuh what it were. Den dey put dat hot iron on muh back, and holds it till duh iron sizzle de flesh off! Ah's still got da mark. Dey brand us like we's some kind ob cattle. Den dey sol us on de block and don't eben let us keep our own name. Make us watch our own chillun sol from us!" Kitty shook her head as she remembered her children.

"I had me eight chillun. Frank de onliest one dey didn't take from me. We's sol' togetha — him fo' $1200 and me fo' $800. Rest uh muh chillun sol' to differn't Massa's. All muh chillun got dem differn't las' names." Kitty began to count off the last names on her fingers. "Let's see! We's *Tison, Peterson, Banks, Jordan,* and *Henderson.*"

Huey walked over to Kitty to help her with her bags of cotton. Kitty didn't seem to notice. Her eyes were far away now, in another time, another place.

She didn't look up. She started to gather her belongings. "They tells me 'Yo' name "Mariah" But dey nickname me "Kitty" cause of my eyes. Well, I reckon da name 'Kitty' better en some they give. Dey name one slave Shadow, jes lak he some ol' dog. My daddy be turnin' over in his grave, if'n he knowed my name taken from me. Muh Daddy spent seben days jes a thankin' bout mah name. He'd rise wit de sun and go up to the riva and jes set and thank about it. Back in Africa dey believes dat whatever name they gives you, dats what you goin be like."

Kitty looked at the children running around the fields. "My daddy say I was meant to raise chillun. He say he knowed by the way I come into this wurl I was goin take da time to raise up chillun right. So my daddy name me Coumba. He say Coumba mean, 'Mama who raises children proper.' Kitty suddenly stopped talking and became sullen. "Now I don't eben know where my own chillun is."

Huey looked at Kitty. "We ain't slaves no mo' Miss Kitty. You can always take yo' African name back when you gits ready. Folks been changin' they name to what they wants they own name tuh be." Kitty stopped and looked sadly at Huey. "Been called 'Kitty' so long, 'Coumba' don't even soun' right no mo." Anyway, I cain't get no otha name. Cuz if my chillun be lookin fuh me, dey be lookin fo 'Kitty'. I's be Kitty if'n it mean someday I gits my chillun back. I even named my baby girl 'Kitty', so's I can find her when freedom come. An' when she was sol away, I name the next girl 'Kitty' too. I say if freedom come I goin to roun' up mah whole littuh of Kittys."

As they headed back to the main house, Kitty continued to talk about the slave days. "Slav'ry!" she said deliberately. "The word ain't even good enough. How you gonna kidnap somebody, put em in da dungeon, chain 'em up, brang 'em across da wata an make em work fuh nothin'? It's mo like murderin the peoples! Cuz you done took all they is!" Kitty was clearly agitated now.

"We build de house, an sleep on da flo! We grows de food, den eat dey slop. We suckle dey babies, and dey sells off ours. We does de work n dey gits de pay."

Huey nodded in agreement. "Sho nuf!"

Green and Harriett had reached them now. Harriet saw Kitty's fist pounding the air. She figured that Kitty was on one of her tirades about something. Harriet shook her head and grinned a crooked grin. "Oh Lawd! You done gone and got her started!" Green and Harriet now owned their own plantation. They were Creek Indian, but knew about slavery firsthand. They had been run off their land with a promise for better land in Oklahoma.

Huey picked up a bag and threw it to Green. "She runnin off bout the slave days. But you an Injun, Green! Dem white folks say dat dey done right by you Injuns. They gives you some land ob yo' own."

"Umm Humm!" Green nodded his head. "Dey give us some of *our* land all right. Sho did!" Then he tried to force down a smile and get a serious look on his face. He failed miserably. His eyes twinkled and the end of his mouth curled upwards, making him look anything but serious.

"Well, I reckon if you take a man's fertile land, and march 'im 200 miles into 300 acres of rock, and say 'This heah is prime land!' Then the white folks done us right." Now, Green had laughter in his voice. He started imitating the white man. Massa say, "'Now Green, we's goin give ya'll this here nice treaty to git yo' own lan.' Now this is a fair treaty we wrote up by *ourselves*." (Green winked one eye to show his point). "We jes goin trade yo' nice growin land here in Georgia for some nice little rocks, *way* ova there. We gonna even bring all the Injuns out of Florida. Dat way everybidy gits to live wit dey own kind."

Kitty had put her bag down and now the conversation had her full attention. "We's all one peoples Green. Ain't you heard? We all kin live together and blend up where eva we wants."

Green ignored her. He was just getting warmed up with his own version of the white man. "Massa say, 'Now Injun! It goin tuh be a fair trade! You get yo' own land up in dat nice little rock —er I mean *grand hillside* in Oklahoma wit dat nice green mold —oops I mean grass!" Now Green was moving his right arm up and quickly back down as though he was cracking a whip. "We's even goin to see to it dat you don't get lost cuz we goin take you and yo Mammy Lizzie, and yo' wife Harriet dere our self. Exceppen we don't have nuf horses and wagons. Oh well, I guess you hafta walk."

Finished for the moment, he picked up the sack that Huey had thrown to him.

"Yeah," said Huey, "But dey give you one of dem treaty agreements. You's yo' own kind of country."

"Uh Huh," said Green. "An dey ain't kep one word of it yet. We was here in Luziana when Mama jes lay down. She lay down to die

I reckon. I reckon dey thought she dead cuz dey lef us right here. I hear tell dat dey was dead folk from Geo'gia to Okahoma. Some couldn't walk no mo'. So we jes stay in Luziana. They said we had to move west of the Mississippi Riva. I guess dis was far enough. I hear tell that Luziana's betta farmin den Okahoma, or Arkansas anyhow. So we tries to git some crops outa this here soil. We does cane and cotton. Man always goin need some cane and some cotton. The Lawd gonna see us through!"

Huey looked up. Kitty was heading down the road to meet Frank. Frank was talking to one of the other field hands. They seemed to be having a very heated discussion. When Kitty reached them, she listened to them for a moment and started shaking her head, with disbelief. "Oh naw! Dey cain't do dat!"

Huey headed down the road to meet them. "What's wrong Miss Kitty?" Huey asked.

Kitty looked up at Huey. "Ol Mistah Lott say Frank gotta leave Louisiana! He know dat Frank been piece mealin fo' the cullud Rankins. Now Mistah Lott say dey's a new law. You cain't work fuh no colored lak he been doin. If you ain't workin' fuh a white man, you got to leave the county. Dey done even made new law say colored cain't own or rent no land heah."

"Well, I say!" Huey said. "That there ain't no better than slav'ry!"

"An dat ain't all, Kitty said. "Ya'll member Cyrus from the Lewis plantation in Mississippi?"

"Yeah."

"Uh Huh."

"Well," Kitty continued, "They say ol Cyrus done broke de law. Said he done stole some bread outa Mistah Butla's sto'. Now dey's sayin dat da law is sendin' Cyrus to go back an work for his ol Massa, for da rest of his life!"

"Da rest of his life?" Huey repeated the question to make sure he had heard correctly. "That *is* slavery! They done found a way to make us slave again! About twenty minutes; that's all we had. Jes twenty minutes of Freedom!"

Now Green reached them and joined the conversation. "How is dey gonna take our freedom from us? Day say da 13th mendment outlaws slavery. Dey cain't slave us no mo!"

"I done tol' ya'll you cain't trust dem crackers!" said Kitty. "Dey made sho dat mendment had an 'out' clause. They fixed it so the mendment say you can be slave again if you break de law. Den dey fixed it so anythang we does is against the law!"

It seemed as though history began to repeat itself. The old folks talked about how Africans were enslaved in the olden days. First, they were bound out for just a few years as indentured servants, the same as whites. Then their indentures were extended by no good judges. Then laws were made that made them slaves for life. It seemed as though the same thing was happening now. New laws were rapidly made. With each new law came a new restriction. Laws now said that, "Negroes must be in the employ of some white person," or leave the county. This meant that families were again split up just like in slavery. If a Black man was employed by a white man, but his wife was not, she either needed work for the white man herself, or leave the county. Children were not exempt from this law, either once they were a certain age. Those who had once been enslaved saw very little difference between the slave codes that were in place during slavery, and the so-called "black codes" that were now the law.

That night they all sat around the fire trying to figure out what they were going to do. Frank decided that he would go to Arkansas. Arkansas was just across the border. That way he would be close to his family in Louisiana. Kitty, Green, and Harriet decided to stay on in Louisiana to try to save money, and see how things went in Arkansas. If things went ok for Frank, they would join him later. Huey decided to stay in Louisiana for the time being.

People started to talk about the new slavery. It hadn't been long since the slaves were set free. However, the focus of Congress for the next 20 to 30 years would be to decide how to handle "the negro problem." Kitty was right. They found a loophole by including an exception clause in the 13th Amendment, which virtually allowed slavery to still exist. The subject was bitterly fought over between the southern planters and the abolitionists. Finally, they settled on a compromise. The finished product said;

"Neither slavery nor involuntary servitude, *except as punishment for a crime*, where of the party shall have duly been convicted, shall exist in the United States, or any place subject to their jurisdiction."

The southern planters immediately began to formulate a plan to use the "exception clause" to their advantage. They reasoned that the clause "except as punishment for a crime", would allow them to enslave the prison population. The planters were aggressive in its use. Blacks, who were incarcerated for crimes, became the "new slaves." Moreover, Blacks found themselves incarcerated for every crime *imaginable*.

Soon after they found about Cyrus, the community decided to hold a meeting about the new slavery. Green came out to the fields and told the field hands to come to a meeting at the church so that they could decide what they were going to do. The church, built shortly after emancipation, served as a meeting place, a school, and a place to go to when you needed food or clothes. It even served as a bank for the colored people in the community.

The farmers met a 6 pm. It seemed that the entire Negro community came out to the meeting. Cyrus' brother, Jimmy was among them and spoke first. Jimmy, like Cyrus had taught himself to read in secret during slavery, and was now a very accomplished speaker.

"You all know that my brother Cyrus is in the white man's jail. He was sentenced to 40-years of labor with his former master for stealing food. The only thing that he is guilty of, is being free in a country that would still have us slaves," he said raising his fist in the air. The others stated their approval.

"Yes suh!"

"They sho do!"

"Tell it right!"

Jimmy went on talking. "This State is now reducing Negro men by declaring every little petty offense a crime that is punishable by life. And as punishment for these made-up crimes, we must go back and work for our former masters for the rest of our lives. They are taking Negro men left and right. They are accusing us of crimes that we have not committed and then having us thrown in jail. No Negro man is allowed on the jury. Twelve white men make a mockery of the judicial system. The jury box is full of foxes in a hen house! The jury is nothing but the colored man's old master looking to get his slaves back!" Jimmy shook his head sadly. "I know that I don't have much time left here. I will surely end up at Massa Tom's plantation for daring to speak out. But I pray before God that they will see the error of their ways and set us free. I'm here to tell you that we must find a way to keep them from re-enslaving us. We must..."

Kitty jumped up before he could finish the next sentence. "Don't look like mendment 13 did us no good, do it!? I done tol you niggas that they ain't neva gonna leave us be. Ever since Scott lost that case in '57 dey say that we ain't human, and not fit to tend our own business. Dey say cullud aint civilized, and is jes fit fo' the jungle. They still see's us as animals. Shoot! 'Tween all these new laws and no good white folk, we always be slaves!"

Green spoke up then. "Dey's gettin us all kinds of ways. Dey got it so some had to go back to the Mississippi slave plantation. Dey's saying we owe money for sech & sech a thang. They got men, women and chillun workin' fo' a share of the crop now, but by da time dey pay fo' the tools and sech they owes mo'en dey make. Some done run off cuz it ain't no better den slavery."

Huey agreed. "Yeah. If I had my way I would neva work for nobody but myself eva agin. If you don't have to answer to nobody you can get ahead a little. Til yo' own ground. Set down when you git ready. We got to find us a way to jest work fo' ourself! That what freedom is!"

The next day was Sunday. Sunday was a favorite day for the former slaves. They could worship as they saw fit. And they saw fit to worship all day long. They had early morning worship and then Sunday school. Then they had the morning service. They would sing and pray until early afternoon. After church, they would cook a big dinner and everyone would share in the fellowship. In addition, they always made sure to take a plate to anyone who was sick or shut-in.

However, this Sunday was a little different. Slavery was on their minds. There was unrest among the community. So, that Sunday, the prayers were more intense. The songs were about faith and freedom. Many of the same songs that were sung in slavery were on their lips that day. Song somehow helped to ease the pain. But now there was one big change. They felt that they were on the road to freedom. God had brought them too far to turn back now. Kitty got up and led the Choir that day. She started singing as she walked up to the front of the church and the others chimed in.

".. *Ain't gonna let nobidy turn me around, turn me around, turn me around...Ain't gonna let nobidy turn me around...—my Lawd will walk beside me —to-daay.*"

Worship was a combination of African, American, and slave cultures all blended into one. The sound of the drums that had been outlawed during slavery, drummed a welcome beat. The culture of African spirituality, blended with American Christianity.

After church, there was an aura of peace. Kitty had prayed long and hard. She had asked God for guidance and understanding. By the time she was finished, she felt more at peace than she had for a long time. She decided to turn it all over to God. It was at dinner when she spoke of the understanding that she had come to.

"God delivered us from slavery. And God will show us the way. He won't give us more that we can bear. We jes' need to ask Him to guide us the way he wants us to go. Jest let go and give it to God!"

Faith in God was something that was always present in their lives. So, they simply put their trust in Him and were thankful that they had each other. They would pray for this new America to see the error of her ways, and they felt that soon they would be delivered out of the bondage that they had been forced back into. They prayed a special prayer for Cyrus.

A few years later, they thought that their prayers had been answered. Green learned that they had passed another amendment for colored people. He was sure that they finally saw the error's of the 13th Amendment.

"They done passed Amendment number fo'teen," he reported. "Now they say that we is citizens of America. And get this. This is the most important part. The law says that the States cain't make no mo' laws that ain't fair to colored. Now they *have* to treat us jest as good as white folk."

Kitty rolled her eyes. "They done said that befo'. I keepa tellin' you all that these laws that dey is makin ain't goin change nothin! Po' Cyrus went to jail a long time ago. Cyrus is still a slave! Once a slave, always a slave!"

"You's wrong Miss Kitty," Green insisted. "This one different. They done wrote it all up in sumpin they's callin' a *Civil Rights Act*. That mean they gotta do right and give us the same rights as white men. The Fed'l gov'nment tells all the States what to do now. That mean that the old Massa cain't control da South no mo'."

However, Kitty was not convinced. "Did the Fed'l govenment say they goin send us back home if'n we wants to go? Is they goin put me and mine back on that stankin' ship and take us back to where they brung us from? What if I wants to go back and live with my Momma? That be my Civil Right. Or is you saying that

African's is now Americans whetha or not we want to be Americans?"

"Well, Miss Kitty, I reckon that's the way it go," he said. "Guess they jes cain't figure out who ta send back home. And its better we stay heah anyhow. They's savages in Africa. Who want to go back wit savages?"

"An' now dey got yo' mind too, Green. You don't know what you talkin 'bout!" said Kitty. Now she was mad. "They got all you nigga's thankin' that mess. African's is jes lak you an me. I'm African. AF-RI-CAN. African's is mo civilized den white folk any day of da week! White folk know it. They jes don't want you to know it. Dey thank if they keepa sayin' ain't nothin in Africa, we be beholden to them. And they jes' ain't gonna give up none uh that money they made off our backs by spending it to send us home!" Then she turned and walked off.

Still, most of the former slaves felt that their future now held great promise. The new law said that Negroes now had the same privileges as whites. Those who could read, read the clause to the others, repeatedly. Section 1 of the amendment said;

> "All persons born or naturalized in the United States and subject to the jurisdiction thereof, are citizens of the United States and the States wherein they reside. No State shall make or enforce any law which shall abridge the privileges or immunities of citizens of the United States...Nor shall any State deprive any person of life, liberty, or property, without Due Process of Law."

To most, it sounded like the government was really trying to give colored people true freedom. Nevertheless, others still viewed the new law with suspicion. As Kitty once said, "The government give and the Massa' taketh away." But Huey held out hope that the new amendment would give more meaning to their lives.

Things seemed to move quickly now. Soon after the 14th

Amendment, another civil rights act said that Blacks could even ride alongside whites on ferries and trains. In addition, they could rent rooms any place that whites could.

They were out in the fields one day when Huey mentioned to the others how great it was that the government had finally straightened up the South.

"It been awhile since the 14th Amendment," he pointed out. "And the government still say that we equal to white folk." Kitty opened her mouth to speak. However, Frank, (who was in Louisiana at the time) beat her it.

"You ain't neva tried to rent no room, or ride in the front of no train, is you Huey?"

"Well, no," Huey answered.

"Well, you still cain't." Frank reported. "You try it, and you still may get whipped. All these crackers down here say they still ain't gotta obey the law. Dey's even talk 'bout anotha civil wah. Dey say dey's still fightin' dat law and da Supreme Court is gonna strike it down. The Supreme Court has the final say on dat law! And the Supreme Court ain't neva been the colored man's friend."

The Back of the Bus

The Six Generation

"Jim Crow"
Charley, Sarah, Gertrude, Dan, Willie, Jimmy, Sing, Bud

Photo of JAMES "JIMMY" Peterson
"Uncle Jimmy"

7

"Jim Crowed"

I n 1883, the news came that they had all been dreading. They had heard rumors that their civil rights would be short lived. The news that they heard confirmed it. Once again, the Supreme Court turned back the clock. It ruled that the 1866 Civil Rights Act was unconstitutional because it "trampled" on the rights of the States. Rights were restored to the State governments, which meant that the Negro population was once again at the mercy of the States. The Negro community was crushed. The Jim Crow era was upon them.

Nevertheless, they still had hope. They knew that in 1870 the 15th Amendment to the Constitution had given them the right to vote. They had had some success after slavery in using the ballot box. Although things had gotten tougher on southern Blacks after the Tilton-Hays compromise of 1877, they decided that they would rally the Black vote and make some positive changes in the community. One evening, after they finished their chores, the men discussed the upcoming election. They discussed how they would use their vote to make things better for the Negroes. Huey said that if they got every man to vote, they could make a difference.

Kitty rolled her eyes and shook her head. "What you talkin' 'bout, Huey," she asked.

"Talkin bout votin'. Colored men can vote now. We can have some say round heah!"

Kitty looked at him skeptically and mumbled under her breath, "Colored man get kilt tryin' to vote!"

The men from the old plantation were very excited about the upcoming election. Green and Huey talked about who they would vote for. Their wives looked at them with respect and hope. Their husbands would be able to have a say in the law. Maybe some things would change in the south for the better. They even had the law memorized;

"The right of citizens of the United States to vote shall not be denied...by the United States or by any State on account of race, color, or previous condition of servitude."

The Presidential debates had been going on for months. The colored men held meetings at the church to discuss who should get their vote. Finally, the day came when they could cast their vote for president. They dressed up in their finest clothes and went down to the courthouse. It seemed as though every colored man in the county was there. They proudly waited their turn at the ballot box. Huey was first in line. They had decided that Huey should be the first among them to vote, since it was he, who got most of the information about the election. Huey stepped up, "I'd like muh ballot please!" The white man at the ballot box looked carefully at Huey and the others who were behind him.

"Yeah, I guess you Negroes can vote according to the law. But you still have to follow the voting rules. And the rule in this state is that you can't vote unless your grandfather voted in the last election!"

"What you mean I cain't vote! That cain't be right," Huey said. "My daddy couldn't vote in the last election, because he culled. His daddy couldn't vote neither cuz he was a slave!"

"Well, I guess that's just too bad then. That's the law. We got to follow the law!"

With his head down, Huey turned around, and explained to the others what had happened. There were tears, anger, and frustration. They waited until the last vote had been cast, hoping that someone would come out and correct the mistake. However, it didn't happen. None of them was allowed to vote that day.

Frank also tried to vote that day in Arkansas. When he asked for his ballot, he was handed a "Literacy Test." The test had questions that were impossible even for most educated people to answer even if they knew how to read. Questions like "What date is the President sworn in?" "Who originates bills for raising revenue?" "Who is the fourth person in the cabinet in line for the Presidency?" Frank left without casting his ballot. Scenes like these were repeated throughout the south, and even at some polling places in the north. There were even reports that some colored men were required to accurately guess how many jellybeans were in a bowl or how many bubbles were in a bar of soap before they could vote. The law had failed them again.

It seemed that every time they dared to hope, a new law would move them a step backwards. Nevertheless, chattel slavery finally seemed to be a thing of the past.

By 1885, Huey and Arthina had five children; Leanna, Maggie, Litha, Harmon and Eddie. Harmon was named after Huey's father in Mississippi. His middle name was Charley, and most folks called him Charley. The Harris' had nine children. Their daughter Sarah was a handful. She had a quick wit about her and was very headstrong. Like many children of the first generation in America to be born free, she did not plan to live her life bowing down to anybody. She had not witnessed the whippings and the inhumanity of slavery. She wasn't yet born when her father was marched off his land and across the Mississippi river, because the white folks decided that their "discovery rights" in America were superior to the Native American's land rights. So, to Sarah, it seemed like the older colored folk were too timid around the white folks.

"Paw, don't let them crackers talk to you that way!" she often demanded. "You ain't no slave no mo'. They cain't do nothin' to you!" Green had raised his daughter to be proud. But like most of this new generation, she didn't realize just how powerless the Negro community really was. Green had managed to do all right for himself and he pretty much kept out of the way of white folks. But sometimes he cringed at the things that Sarah said or did. He didn't want her to grow up afraid but he did want her to be realistic.

"Sarah." he said. "You too young to know what white folks is like. White folk still have a way of gettin back at ya. They's trees all up and down heah. It don't take much for a colored man to end up hangin' from them trees! You seen the Klan! You know they lynchin folks jes cuz dey can. You be careful gal! I don't want to be burying yo' body cuz you done said somethin' wrong."

She shook her head. "Oh Papa!" she insisted. "They ain't goin to lynch no woman!"

"Don't kid yo'self gal! They done strung up women too. Don't get to thankin that you cain't be strung up! You watch yo'self now!"

"Well if it be my time, I guess it jes be my time then."

Sarah continued to live her life that way. She said what she wanted and decided that she would deal with the consequences.

Huey also tried to teach his children about how brutal the world could be. His son, Charley had seen the scars on his father's back. He had overheard his father talking to Green one day about the slave days, and when he was whipped. Charley was enraged.

He couldn't bear to think about his father beaten like that. He wondered what kind of animal could do that to a man. From that day on, Charley viewed white men with suspicion. He spent as little time as he could in their presence. Thankfully, there were not a lot of them to deal with in their small community. Most colored folks just kept to themselves and white folks did the same. They lived separate lives unless they had to go to town for something.

One day Huey was cleaning the barn when he heard a horse galloping down the road. He came out of the barn and looked up to see Frank riding high on his horse. Frank had kept his promise and came to Louisiana frequently. Minden, Louisiana was just across the border from Taylor, Arkansas and it didn't take long to get from one town to the other.

Frank had been married twice by this time. He and his first wife, Mary, had three children, Gertrude, Willie, and Jimmy. Mary had died when Jimmy was born in 1898. Frank married Josephine a year later, but she died soon after from a bout of pneumonia.

Frank hitched the horse to a post. Smiling, and hand outreached, he greeted Huey. Huey had made some plans since the last time Frank came. He was very happy to see him so that he could finally share those plans.

"Good to see ya'll." said Huey as he shook Frank's hand.

"I been thankin bout ya'll. We's bout ready to give Arkansas a try now. Been saving a little money," Huey said. "We's movin to Taylor. We's goin ta get us 40 acres of land and farm our own land!"

8

"Migration"

As Sarah and Charley grew up, they were inseparable. Either she was at his house, or he was at hers. Finally, they couldn't stand to be apart at all. They were married in 1898 in Bossier, Louisiana, and were anxious to start a family. Both wanted a large one. By 1908, Sarah had been pregnant eleven times but only three of the children were still living. Each pregnancy was very difficult for Sarah, and each delivery involved extraordinarily long labor. Eight of the children died as infants, or as small children.

One evening, Charley and Sarah were walking up to their house. They had just returned from milking the cows, and Charley had a pail of milk in his hands. It was nearing the Christmas holidays and Sarah was going to begin her holiday baking with the fresh milk and the eggs that they had gathered earlier in the day.

Suddenly Frank came galloping up on his horse. He had his rifle in one hand and he had a scowl on his face that let everyone know that he was angry. Very angry! In fact, it looked like anyone in his way should consider moving very quickly. He was yelling at the top of his lungs.

"Where he at?" You cain't hide Dan McGee!" Kitty came running out of her cabin.

"Frank! Frank! What is it?" Frank pulled on the reins of his horse and spun the horse around in a complete circle.

"I'm gonna kill him Mama. He ain't had no right and I'm gonna kill him dead!"

Kitty was startled to see Frank this angry. She knew he had a temper. However, Frank was a minister now. He was a man of God. He tried very hard to keep God's word. She wondered who could have possibly made him mad enough to talk about killing someone. Frank's horse reared back once and finally stopped. He jumped down off the horse.

"That no good Dan McGee! He done gone and got my Gertrude in trouble."

Kitty looked at him. She had heard the stories about Gertrude and Dan McGee. Everyone had. Dan was married to Bettie McGee but Dan had a wandering eye. Eventually, his eyes wandered towards Gertrude. She was much younger than he was, but Dan had a way about him that Gertrude loved. Frank had raised Gertrude pretty much on his own and he was very protective of her.

Kitty tried to reason with her son. "Frank! Put the gun down! You know that Gertrude had her own hand in gittin that baby." However, Frank was not convinced. Gertrude was his little girl.

"Dan McGee is old enough to be her father!" Frank shouted. "He taken advantage of my little girl." Kitty shook her head from side to side.

"Frank!" she said emphatically. "Yo' baby girl is 23 years old!"

Frank seemed to calm down slightly. He looked thoughtfully at Kitty for a moment.

"Well. She still *my* baby!" With that, he climbed back on his horse and rode off, heading back to Taylor.

A week later, Frank awoke to a loud pounding on the front door. "Frank! Frank! Open the door! We gotta get to Minden!"

Frank recognized his brother Bud's voice and leaped out of the bed.

"What the hell is wrong with you?" he demanded. "You trying to wake the dead?"

"Frank, they gonna hang 'im." Bud cried as he rushed through the door. "They said Chester done killed them white people and they looking to put him to death."

Frank was wide awake now! He knew that any allegation of wrongdoing against whites could lead to a lynching. He grabbed his pants as Bud filled him in on the rumors about their brother Chester. Bud explained that on Christmas Eve, the entire household of a prominent white family, the Reeves, had been killed in their sleep. The police had arrived this morning to arrest Chester and their cousin Mark. They had been taken to jail but there was no guarantee that the lynch mob could be kept at bay. Bud had heard the news from one of their younger brothers, and came to get Frank to try to help.

Frank grabbed his gun. He didn't know what to expect when he got to Minden, and he wanted to be ready to protect himself.

He arrived to find his mother in tears. She tried to calm down enough to tell Bud and Frank what had transpired over the last several hours. The police had come to the door. They said that Chester had used her ax and killed John Reeves, his wife and three of their children. They told her that Chester tried to blame it on Henry Waller and Johnnie Long, two white man who lived in Grove, a community which was adjacent to Minden. The police went on to claim that tracks of blood and other evidence lead them straight to her house! They said that there was a lynch mob headed to the jail to try to get to Chester and Mark.

Through his own fears, Frank tried to comfort his mother. He knew that Chester was in real danger. He might either be killed by the law, or by the mob. It wouldn't be the first time it had happened.

Through her tears and her anguish she told her sons everything that she had pieced together. Early on Christmas Eve, two white men had come to get Chester and Mark on the pretense of a card game at the Reeves. When they arrived at the Reeves, Henry Waller took the ax that he had taken from her property, and hacked the entire Reeves family to death with it! He then threatened to blame the entire thing on Chester and Mark if they told a soul. When the police discovered the crime, bloody footprints lead them to Chester's house and he was arrested. But Mark told the police that it was Henry Waller who committed the crime. Now the jail was surrounded by an angry white mob who wanted revenge for the murders and for Chester and Mark blaming a white man.

Chester and Mark, as well as two of their cousins, Anderson Heard and Larkin Stewart, found themselves on trial a short time later. The two white men were to be tried separately.

Evidence at the trial pointed to Henry Waller, the white man who had come to get Chester and Mark, as the actual killer. According to testimony, he was trying to silence John Reeves from revealing his involvement in another crime. To cover up the murder, his strategy was to round up some unsuspecting "niggers," and use a weapon that could be traced to them. He would then frame them for the murders. Henry knew that the community would much rather believe a white man from a good upstanding family in the community, than to believe a group of lowly negroes. He had threatened Chester, Mark, and everyone who witnessed his actions that the "same thing would happen to them," if they ever told a soul.

Henry Waller's carefully crafted alibi crumbled when Johnie Long, a white man, turned against him. Although everyone who was arrested for the crime was separated and questioned, they all told identical stories that ended with Henry Waller as the person who swung the ax. Johnie's testimony carried a lot of weight because he too was white, and told the same story as the negroes.

Although it was proven that Chester and Mark did not commit the murder, and that Anderson was a developmentally disabled man who was nowhere near the scene, Chester and Mark were sentenced to hang, and Anderson and Larkin were given life in prison. They were sent to Louisiana State Prison, in Angola, Louisiana. Ironically, Angola had previously been a slave plantation.

A few months later the trial was held for the two white men. Although Henry Waller denied any wrongdoing, the testimony of Johnie and the others involved lead to both being convicted and sentenced to life in prison. Even though Henry and Johnie had been found guilty, and given life, many people still wanted Chester and Mark to be hung immediately. But the governor had different ideas. The governor wanted to keep them alive long enough to testify against Henry Waller and Johnie Long just in case charges from other murders materialized.

The hanging of Chester Tyson and Mark Peters was scheduled to take place on August 9, 1918. Kitty was there, in the midst of the mostly white crowd who had gathered to witness the hangings. She wept as she observed the two nooses that hung on a nearby tree. Chester and Mark were beginning their descent from the jailhouse to the platform when the Sheriff came dashing towards the deputies.

"Wait!" he shouted. "Don't do it!"

The sheriff ran up to the deputies and breathlessly informed them that he had just spoken to the governor. Because the actual killer had only gotten life in prison and not been sentenced to hang, the new governor had commuted the sentences of Chester and Mark to life in prison. There would be no hanging!

As news of the stay of execution spread, pandemonium swept through the crowd. Most were angry! They had come to see the negroes hang and they expected to see the hanging. Others were relieved. They felt that Chester and Mark were just pawns that were designed to save Henry Waller's neck.

Kitty was certainly relieved that her son would not hang. She had lost enough children in slavery and seen enough lynching's to last her a lifetime. But the commutations of the sentence lead to more threats and more hatred from those in the community who felt that "the negroes got away with murder." Even though Chester remained in jail, every day she feared that one of her other children would be lynched because of Chester's perceived transgression. She had good reason to worry. Lynching was not uncommon her part of the country.

The toll on the family proved to be too much. The anger against them made each day unbearable, and many in the family moved across the border to Arkansas. Some abandoned their homes and their lifelong possessions as they quietly left town. Some even changed their names to start a new life.

Kitty moved to Taylor with her son Frank, and her granddaughter, Gertrude. Gertrude had arrived in Taylor with a little something from Minden. Dan McGee's child was growing inside of her. Seven months later, Arlie Bertha Lee McGee was born. Everyone called her "Ollie".

Gertrude and Arlie returned to Louisiana the following year to wrap up things at Kitty's house. They stayed for a little over a year. The following summer, they once again returned to Taylor, Arkansas. This time, in addition to Arlie, Gertrude had twins, Essie Mae and Bessie Mae in tow. Their last name was McGee, like their father.

Gertrude's pregnancy had been a very difficult one. She had a very hard delivery with the twins, laboring all day and all night. Finally, the first twin was born on August 28. However, Gertrude had trouble delivering the second one. She became frightened as she remembered that her mother died in childbirth. The midwife told her that she knew she had a long way to go to deliver the other twin. Gertrude prayed that both her twins would be ok. She labored all night long. Finally, on the next day, August 29th, the second twin was born.

Gertrude was exhausted after a rough time in childbirth. Finally, the midwife brought the twins to her. She was all smiles as the midwife laid the twins on her bed. She began taking the covers off her newborn babies. The smile disappeared quickly as she got a look at the twins. She pointed to one of twins.

"This one's not my baby! This one's a white baby!"

"That *is* your baby Gertrude. She just lighter than the other one. 'Cept for color, they look just alike." Gertrude studied them again. "No they don't neither! I had twins and these babies don't look nothin' alike. This white one ain't mine. And I don't want this white baby!"

"Gertrude! Hush up! You know good and well that culled babies are born light-skinned. She'll darken up after a few weeks." Gertrude still didn't quite believe it. Nevertheless, she took both babies home. Weeks passed. Then months. Bessie didn't get any darker.

Finally, Gertrude decided that she didn't want to raise the white baby. She decided that she would give Bessie away. Gertrude's Uncle, Bud Henderson and his wife Josie stopped by the house one day. "Aunt Josie, I don't want this white baby no more." Gertrude stated. Josie looked from Gertrude, to Bessie who was sitting quietly in the corner, dropping a spoon into a little plastic bucket. She would then turn the bucket upside down, and start the game all over again.

Josie looked at Gertrude for a long time. She was trying to figure out if she was serious or not.

"Gertrude you do know that that is your own baby, right? I was right there with the midwife when the twins were born. Bessie jes' look white but she'll darken up. She probably took her color from some injuns in the family way back."

"But she 'sposed to be Essie's twin! But she white! Essie is dark-skinded. I don't think this white baby is mine!" Gertrude insisted.

Josie decided to take her at her word. "Okay, she said finally. I'll go get my place ready for Bessie. I'll come and get her in a day or two." True to her word, two days later Josie arrived at Gertrude's house carrying a small suitcase. She gave it to Gertrude. "You can put Bessie's clothes in here. And I'll put the rest of her things on the wagon."

"What you talkin' bout Aunt Josie? Why you need Bessie's things?"

"You told me you didn't want her cuz she white."

"Aunt Josie! What's the matter with you? You know I ain't gonna give you my baby." She went over to Bessie and picked her up, holding her tight. "If that's all you came for, you might as well leave, cuz you sho' ain't takin' my baby!"

With that, she went into the kitchen and started stirring the pot of beans that was on the stove. Josie smiled. She knew that Gertrude loved Bessie whether or not she believed that she was really her daughter. And besides, Josie had helped the midwife deliver the twins and she knew for sure that Bessie was Essie's twin, although one was certainly a lot lighter than the other. She knew that time would tell. It would get better. Bessie would get darker and Gertrude would realize that the baby she loved was her very own. Neither Gertrude, nor Josie ever spoke about giving Bessie away again. But Josie always had a soft spot in her heart for Bessie and always treated her extra special. Gertrude now focused on raising her girls in the Taylor community.

9

"Still Jim Crowed"

Taylor, Arkansas was a growing community. Some said that there was oil on the land. Others said that the ground was as fertile as Louisiana, and good for growing cotton. Charley and Sarah thought that they might go to Arkansas and buy a farm. Maybe they would get lucky and find oil on it. If things were good enough, the whole family would follow in a year or two. They already had friends and family in Taylor. Frank and Gertrude lived there. Huey had moved there a few years back. Since it was right across the border from Minden, Louisiana, it seemed much as if Taylor and Minden were the same community. The children often spent part of the year in Minden, and part of the year in Taylor with different relatives.

Charley and Sarah decided to make the move. Huey, was thrilled to have his son's family close to them. Huey had saved all that he could over the years. He had saved over three hundred dollars! That was a lot for a Colored man in those days. He had purchased 40 acres of land about 40 miles from Minden. Charley and Sarah purchased land close to Huey's. Soon, both father and son had farms to be proud of. They raised horses and cows. They had a few hogs, fruit trees, and vegetable patches. Huey was living the life that his own parents only dreamed about on the Lewis Plantation of Mississippi. He was proud that he worked for himself, and that he was able to care for his family, and own his own property.

Sarah didn't lose her edge over the years. In fact, she became even more hotheaded as she grew up. She had a salty tongue, and some said she cursed like a sailor. She was always willing to give anyone, white or Colored a piece of her mind. She developed a reputation as "that crazy Indian". But Sarah said that they could call her crazy if they wanted, as long as they didn't mess with her.

Charley and Sarah's family grew larger. They wanted a big family to fill up their 40 acres. Charley was an excellent farmer. Huey had shown him some of his grandfather Tom's farming methods. Huey could pick three hundred pounds of cotton in a day. He would use both hands, adjust the bag on his side, and pick two rows at a time. Soon he had plenty of fruits, vegetables and goods that sold very well at the market. The hogs and cows not only provided additional food for the family, but turned a handsome profit when they went to slaughter. And Charley was proud of his stable of horses. Each of his children had their own horse, and their own cow. Of course, the horse was theirs to ride, but the cows were theirs to milk. Charley thought it was a fair trade off.

By 1923, Sarah had given birth to 16 children, 8 boys and 8 girls. However, eight of them had passed on at a young age. The oldest was Arthina. Then next came William, Della, Henry, Ionnie (Big Baby), and Charley, Jr. The youngest girl was Hattie B. The B. in her middle name didn't stand for anything. Sarah just thought that the initial went well with the name "Hattie". Hattie was born two days before Christmas in 1918. The youngest son was Tommie Tim. Tommie was born in 1923.

Tommie and Hattie were very close. They did everything together. And Hattie was very protective of her younger brother. If you wanted to mess with Tommie, you had to go through Hattie! Of course, Tommie didn't mind that, and frequently got into trouble that Hattie got him out of.

The town of Taylor began to boom. There was indeed oil on some of the land. A few families became wealthy as a result. Roads were cleared as more people got automobiles. Soon they built a schoolhouse and a church. It was a proud day when the children started at Taylor School. Their teacher, Nettie Powell, was a very light-skinned black woman that the students all loved. Students from the first grade all the way through the tenth grades were taught in the same 1-room schoolhouse. Tommie, Hattie, Arlie, Essie and Bessie all went to school together when they could. During planting season, the children often had to skip school to get the planting and the harvesting done. After the school was built, the population grew even more. Soon, a new sign was displayed prominently at the edge of both ends of town. The sign said "Welcome to Taylor. Population 657!"

Bessie was the smallest of the children. She was also the fastest. Even though the school was 3 miles from where she lived, she always ran all the way there. She would jog back at times to see where the others were, and then she would run off again.

It was somewhat of a miracle that Bessie could run at all. She had rickets as a child and couldn't even walk until she was two years old. When she started to walk, a terrible accident sidelined her again. Bessie's stepfather, Willie, had a reputation for being mean. One day Gertrude and Willie were arguing. Gertrude had Bessie in her arms when Willie started for her. Gertrude tried to back away, but as she stepped backwards, she tripped over a rug, dropping Bessie. The argument stopped, but Bessie had a broken back. The doctors were not sure if she would ever walk again. However, miraculously, over time, her back healed and once she could walk again, she starting running everywhere!

It was time to go to school one warm Tuesday morning. Tommie had just started school that year. Hattie was eight years old and in the third grade. Tommie looked all around the farm but he couldn't find Hattie. Finally, he went into the barn. Hearing a noise, he looked over in the corner and realized Hattie was crying. Tommie looked down at her dress and saw the blood.

"Hattie! What happened? Did the horse throw you?" Hattie didn't answer. She seemed to be in pain and was still crying. Tommie tried to pick her up, but he was too small to lift her. "Stay here Hattie! I'm gonna go get Mama!" Tommie ran off to the house. "Mama. Mama! Somethin's the matter with Hattie. She's in the barn. There's blood and she won't quit crying." Sarah put down the potatoes she was peeling and ran out of the house and to the barn.

"Hattie! Hattie! What's the matter? What happened?" Still, Hattie didn't answer. Sarah looked to see where the blood was coming from. Hattie's underwear was on the ground soaked with blood. "Oh Lord! Oh, Lord! Not this! Not my baby!" Sarah picked Hattie up and ran back to the house. She screamed for Charley. They got Hattie on the wagon and took her to Doctor Horn's house, which was about two miles away.

Doctor Horn was shocked at what he saw when he examined Hattie! Sarah's heart was pounding. She feared the worse! Hattie was Sarah's youngest girl and Sarah could not imagine anyone violating her child in such a vicious way. It seemed like both a second and a day before Doctor Horn spoke. When he did, he said the words that changed their lives forever. "Miss Sarah. This child has been raped! Do you know who would do such a thing?"

"Oh my God, Oh my God," Sarah screamed and reached out for a nearby chair. She began to sob, and sank to the floor, still trying to support herself with the chair. She shook her head in disbelief. "No. No. Not my Hattie! Not my child!" It was some time before she could stop crying enough to speak. "Animal! What kind of animal would do this to a baby?"

Doctor Horn finished examining Hattie. "She's hurt pretty bad Sarah. Take her home and put this salve on her every day. Give her this aspirin for the pain. I'll look in on her again in a few days." He opened his mouth again and then closed it. He looked like he wanted to say something but didn't quite know how. Finally, he said, "Sarah. Hattie's not the only one. Gertrude's daughter Ollie was raped yesterday." Sarah could not believe her ears.

"Ollie? Ollie's bout the same age as my Hattie ain't she? She cain't be no more than about seven or eight." Doctor Horn looked at Sarah.

"Ollie was lucky to live through it. She ain't gonna ever have children, though."

Sarah wrapped Hattie in a blanket and took her home. She laid her in the bed, and gently stroked her hair. She sang softly to Hattie until she fell asleep. Then she headed for St. Paul Church. The church had a giant bell in the steeple. The bell was rung to let people know when it was time for church or Sunday school. The Taylor community also used the bell when there was an emergency, like when someone was sick, or when someone died. Sarah grabbed the rope. She began to ring the bell. She rang it hard. She rang it so hard that her back began to hurt. Nevertheless, she wanted to make sure that everyone heard the bell, and would come to the church. She rang it until she was exhausted. The neighbors began to come. As they arrived, Sarah told them what happened to Hattie. Upon hearing the news, Rev. D went over to the rope and rang the bell again. He rang it as loud as he could. He wanted everyone in the community to be aware of this tragic news, before another child was hurt. More of the neighbors began to arrive. Sarah didn't mention that the same thing had happened to Ollie; she would leave that to Gertrude. But she told them that this man, whoever he was, was targeting very young girls. She said that she wanted them to know so that their children wouldn't be hurt.

Some screamed or cried in disbelief. Everyone was angry. Sarah was shaking from both anger and grief. "I'm gonna kill him dead if I get my hands on him! You all better find him before I do! They think I'm a crazy Indian now. Just wait till I get my hands on that monster, and they'll *really* know what this crazy Indian will do to anyone who would dare to hurt me or mine!"

The whole town was enraged. They talked among themselves. Some had heard things about a man who had just moved into

Taylor. He lived alone and usually kept to himself. Some thought that at times he seemed a little odd when he talked to them. Then someone remembered that he seemed very interested in the little girls in the neighborhood. One of the neighbors knew that he had invited some of the girls to his house to get some cane. They didn't think much about it at the time, but now, it seemed suspicious. Several of the men took off with bats, crowbars, or anything else that could be used as a weapon. They began their search. It didn't take them long to find him. They knew him as Clayton. He was at home, in a deep sleep on the porch when they arrived. An empty bottle of homemade wine was on the floor near him. They dragged him off the porch and one of them threw him to the ground. They dragged him away from his house and took him to Sarah's place. Sarah was holding Hattie on her lap when they arrived,

"Hattie? Don't be afraid. Is this the man who hurt you?" Hattie looked up at the man and began to cry.

"Mama!" She screamed. She was clearly terrified of the man. It was enough for them. They took him out to the barn, and beat him to a bloody pulp. Soon the sheriff rode up on his horse and fired a shot in the air in an attempt to stop the fight. "What's going on here, he shouted?" They stopped beating Clayton and screamed back at the sheriff. "This man is going around raping little girls!" They told the sheriff about Hattie. Someone knew about Ollie and told him about her. The sheriff arrested Clayton and took him to jail. He was tried, convicted, and sent off to prison for 20 years.

Hattie's body healed over time, but the rape had affected her trust in men. She became very aggressive, and fought with many of the boys in the neighborhood. It was as if she had decided that she would never be hurt again. She became known as a kid who could whip any other kid, girl or boy.

10

"To Kill a Black Man"

Nineteen Twenty Nine. The stock market crashed. The Great Depression was upon America. However, for Frank and Gertrude nothing changed much. They didn't have much even before the depression. They grew their own food, and made their own clothes, and Gertrude worked at the hospital. During the depression, many people found that food was hard to come by. Most folks in Taylor just tightened their belts, and made do with what they had, or what they could grow. They raised a few chickens when they could, or hunted for rabbit or deer. Gertrude's family was luckier than some. Doctor Hudnall, the doctor Gertrude now worked for, had given the family a cow. They had all the milk they wanted, and they grew plenty of vegetables in their garden. Meals consisted mainly of beans, rice, homemade bread and home churned butter, and vegetables. They lived on the top floor of the hospital, so that Gertrude could help Dr. Hudnall any time she was needed. In return, Doctor Hudnall allowed the family to stay at the hospital rent-free. Gertrude cooked for the patients and kept the hospital clean.

It seemed to Gertrude that more people in Taylor were falling ill lately, and many of them did not have the money to pay for their care. She believed that poor eating and worrying about the depression contributed to the surge in illness.

Most farmers, including the Lewis family, felt the pinch during the depression. Many of their crops, eggs, and meat were sold at the market. Since most people were tightening their belts, and there were restrictions on what they could grow or sell, they cut down on the amount of meat that they ate. Because people ate less meat, they sold fewer cattle. This, in turn, led to less money coming into the household from the sale of the cattle. However, the cattle and the hogs still had to be fed and cared for. It was a catch-22. Charley realized that the livestock were getting too expensive to feed. He decided that he needed to sell off some of his prized horses. He put the word out that the horses and some of the livestock were for sale. Soon he had several offers. Mr. Stuart, a white man from Taylor, arrived one day with cash in hand.

"How much you want for those horses?" he inquired.

Charley was familiar with the price of horses. He had been buying and selling horses, cows, hogs, and chickens for over thirty years. However, it was the depression. Prices weren't what they used to be.

"Ninety-five dollars," he offered.

"Ninety-five dollars? They ain't worth but half that much!" declared Stuart! "Don't you know that we're in a depression, boy? I kin give you $65 dollars for em!"

Charley wasn't surprised. He had heard about the white folks buying up horses, livestock, and even land in Taylor, for next to nothing. But he knew that $65 was almost robbery for his prized horses.

"I kin let em go for seventy-five, but no lower," he offered.

Stuart looked at the horses and then back to Charley. "Charley, we all was hit by this depression. They ain't sellin for no more than sixty five dollars."

Nevertheless, Charley thought he'd hold out for a better price. "No. I'm going to hang onto them till I get a fair price."

"Well Charley, let me know if you change your mind." Then

Stuart turned and walked away.

Two weeks later, Charley counted all of the money that he had left. Six one-dollar bills, 7 quarters, 3 dimes and 18 pennies. Eight dollars and 23 cents! Not enough to live on for very long. He knew that he was about out of feed for the livestock. And he knew what he had to do.

When Charley arrived at Stuart's place, Stuart already had contracts drawn up. Sixty-five dollars! The amount was already filled out. All Charley had to do was sign the contracts, and he would have money to take back home. Stuart put the contract on the table. Charley looked at the space beneath Stuart's signature. Stuart had already written "Harmon Charley Lewis, his mark" on the line that Charley was supposed to sign. Charley looked at the contract and paused as he looked at the signature line. For a moment, he was angry. Dan had assumed that Charley couldn't read or write! Charley could do both, but rather than cause a fuss, he just marked an X above his name. Dan handed Stuart $65, and Charley thanked him and walked out of the door.

The next day, when Charley got out of bed, he felt very tired. He had been feeling tired for a long time now. He usually tried to ignore it and get on with the day's chores. However, Sarah was worried about him. Several times, she insisted that he see Doctor Hudnall. However, each time Charley saw Doctor Hudnall, the doctor said there was nothing that he could do for him. He told Charley that he had "bad blood" which was making him tired, and gave him a bottle of pills. "This should help," he said. "Take two of these every morning when you get up."

Charley did as he was told and soon he felt a little better. He had a little more energy. On the other hand, he thought that the pills were making him moody. He became forgetful. Some days he had trouble concentrating. His vision became blurry, at times. Doctor Hudnall sent Charley to Dr Horn, who told him to just keep taking the medicine, and come in for a check-up each week. It was a warm day in the middle of June, when Charley got some bad news from Dr. Horn. He arrived about two o'clock in the afternoon for his appointment. Doctor Horn gave Charley his check-up. He asked him a lot of questions. "Did he have trouble remembering things lately? Was he tired all of the time? Did he frequently feel confused?" He wrote some things down on a tablet and then looked at Charley for a long time before he spoke. Finally, he said, "Charley, I'm afraid your mind is going. I can't do any more for you here. You need to go up to the hospital in Little Rock. They can probably help you there. I'll call ahead for you."

Charley had been to the hospital in Little Rock before. Doctor Horn had sent him there once to get some tests. He remembered how bad he felt after the doctors got finished with him. They pushed and probed, and some of the tests were very painful. The worst pain that Charley had ever felt was the "spinal tap". They put a needle in his spine to draw some fluid. They told him that they needed to test his blood for diseases. His back had never been the same since that spinal tap. After the test, the doctor at the hospital repeated what Doctor Horn had told him. "Charley," he said, "You have bad blood. We can treat it, but you have to come to the hospital every two weeks for treatment." They gave him some medicine that seemed to help for a while, but now it seemed like his energy just would not come back.

One day Charley was feeling particularly weak. He had a hard time getting out of bed that morning. He felt sharp pains in his back. He went to see Doctor Horn for more medicine. "Charley," Dr. Horn said, "There is nothing else that I can do for you here. You will have to go back to the hospital in Little Rock. I will set it up for the Sheriff to take you to the train. Someone will meet you and take you to the hospital."

It was early on a Wednesday morning when the Sheriff pulled in front of Charley's house. He was on a horse drawn wagon. As Charley climbed on the back of the wagon, Sarah, Hattie, Tommie, and their older brother, Buddy, came out of the house to see him off. Tommie had tears in his eyes. He didn't like it when his daddy had to leave. Charley usually took Tommie with him everywhere he went. Charley looked down at his son. Tommie was nine years old, and tried hard not to cry. He wanted to be a big boy. However, Tommie's life was centered on his father. Charley was the one who taught him how to ride and groom a horse. Tommie had helped his daddy build the barn. Now he was being left behind, and he couldn't control the tears any longer.

"Now Son," Charley said. "Be a big boy now. Take care of your Mama and Hattie, you hear? You help Mama around the farm. This farm is all we got. I never had to work for nobody else 'cause I had my own farm. Now you a big man. You keep this farm going for yo' Mama. This farm is going to be yours one day. You won't ever need to work for nobody but yo'self!" Charley looked at Tommie and smiled as Tommie tried to fight down the tears. "Tommie! You straighten up now. You only nine years old but you got your own shoe business! You a businessman son and you gonna be all right. I'll be back so soon, you won't even know I been gone." Tommie gave him a big bear hug and then stood back with his mother, brother, and sister and watched while the wagon slowly went down the road. They watched until it was gone from their sight. Sarah put her arm around Tommie as they turned and walked back to the house.

"He'll be back soon, Tommie," Sarah said. "Now you and Hattie and Buddy get ready for supper."

Supper seemed very lonely that night with Charley's seat empty. Laughter was missing from the table. They finished eating supper, cleaned up the dishes, and went to bed.

A week later, Ed Rankin, a widower on the next farm, came over to Sarah's house. Sarah was in the garden picking tomatoes. "How's Charley doin?" Ed asked.

"I ain't heard nothin fo' a few days, but I'm sure he fine. He probably be back any day now."

"Glad to hear it. I was a little worried. You heard about Miss Brown's husband, John? They took him up to the hospital in Little Rock, too. They say he was teched in the head. Week later, they say he dead. They brought the man back here to bury him. But when the body get here, it ain't him. Somebody say it was Charley. But it turned out to be another woman's husband from Spring Hill."

"Well I say! Naw, I ain't heard 'bout that. I had Sheriff Fincher check in on Charley jest a few days ago to make sure that everythang was ok. He checked and say he was doin' fine. I reckon they jest got the story mixed up with that other man. That poor woman, them people puttin' her through that. But naw, it weren't Charley."

Two weeks later on a Tuesday morning, Sarah walked over to Ed's house. She looked worried as she walked up to the house. Ed saw her standing at the door.

"Come on in, Miss Sarah," Ed called out. "Have a seat. Sho' is hot today. Kin I get you some water, Miss Sarah?"

"Water sound fine!" Sarah responded. Ed brought her a cool glass of water. Sarah drank some of it, and then sat down on the couch in the living room.

"Ed, I ain't heard nothing 'bout Charley. I thought he be back by now. Sheriff Fincher done gone to Louisiana, so I stopped at the Jacks' house cause they the only ones have a phone. I tried to call the hospital but I cain't get through. I want you to take me up to Little Rock to see about him."

"When you want to go Miss Sarah?" Ed asked. "I kin take you in the mornin'. I know that Bob Jacks will let me borrow his car. Or we can take the train."

The Jacks were one of the few families in Taylor who had a car. It was a 1928 Ford, with a crank in the front.

The next morning, Ed and Sarah made the long, hot, trip to Little Rock. They got to the hospital about two o'clock in the afternoon. Sarah went up to the woman sitting at the front desk. "How do? I'm Mrs. Charley Lewis. My husband was brought up here bout three weeks ago. Can you tell me what room he's in?"

"You say his name is Charley Lewis?"

"Yes, Ma'am. His full name is Harmon Charley Lewis."

The woman pulled the card index towards her. She flipped the cards until she got to the L's.

"We don't have no Negro named Charley or Harmon Lewis."

"Maybe it's not filed right," Sarah offered. "Maybe they put it under Lewis Harmon? Or under the name, Charley?"

The woman looked again, this time under the C's and the H's. "No Ma'am. He ain't here." Sarah was becoming agitated.

"He got to be here. He came here. And he ain't been back."

"Just a moment." The woman looked in another card file that was marked 'discharged.' "He ain't been here."

"He got to be here! This is where they brung him."

"I told you — we ain't got no Charley Lewis!"

"Let me see that box!" she demanded. "I'll see for muh self where he is."

"I cain't give you the box. Those files are confidential. I already checked and he's not here!"

"Give me that damned box! I ain't leaving till I find my husband." Sarah reached for the box. The woman behind the desk moved it out of her reach.

"Ma'am, do I have to call security?"

"Well you better call somebody, cuz I ain't leavin till I see the box!" The woman picked up the phone. She dialed a number, but apparently, there was no answer because she put the phone back down. She got up from the desk and quickly walked towards the back of the room, looking for someone to help her. As soon as her back was turned, Sarah grabbed the box and looked through the L's. Charley wasn't there. She looked through the H's and the C's. Still no Charley. Then she started at the front of the box and went through each card, scanning each one of them for her husband's name. She was about half way through the box when the woman returned with a security guard.

"This Negra is refusing to leave. I told her that her husband is not here, but she is being very unreasonable. Now she has the box and I told her it was confidential."

"Ma'am, that is hospital property." the guard stated. "You need to put the box down and leave." Sarah continued to go through the box. The guard reached for the box, just as Sarah viewed the last card. Charley's name was not among them.

"Here! You take this shit!" Sarah said, thrusting the box at the guard. "Come on Ed, let's go." They went out of the door and around the back to the colored side of the hospital. Sarah looked in each room, but did not find Charley. Finally, she and Ed made the long trip home.

"Ed, I think they done something to him. You know how it is for a colored man around here."

"You may be right, Miss Sarah," Ed answered. "It sho wouldn't be the first time that somethin' happen."

During the next few weeks, Sarah and Ed checked every hospital between Little Rock, Arkansas and Shreveport, Louisiana looking for Charley. However, each time they returned, they had to tell the others that they could not find him.

"He probably dead," Huey said. "They probably done killed my son! Ain't none uh these white folk around heah any good. They treat old dogs better'n they treat colored folk. They probably got my son swingin' from a tree or floatin' in a riva somewheah. I seen it. I done seen it all my life! Colored man ain't neva' been safe around no white folk!"

"Uncle Huey, maybe Charley just lost," said Sarah. "You know his mind ain't been right this year. Maybe he cain't find his way back."

"They don't neva come back!" Huey insisted. "They go up theah to dat ol' hospital and they don't neva come back no mo'!" Then he turned and started walking down the road. He headed straight for St. Paul cemetery where his beloved Arthina was buried. Oh, how he missed her! She had passed away just a year or so ago, and Huey still went out to the grave every single day. Most of the time, he would sit at her grave and talk to her. Then he would lay on top of the grave so that he could feel closer to her. He sometimes stayed there for hours, often falling asleep.

He reached her grave and sat down beside it. He told her about his fear that someone had killed their son. He prayed that God would see the family through this latest crisis. He knew that Charley's children would have a hard time without their father. Especially Huey's grandson, Tommie. Tommie held an extra special place in Huey's heart. When Tommie was about four years old, he would practice shining Huey's shoes. He always laughed at the times that Huey wore his shoes on the wrong foot. But Huey always reminded Tommie that you could get more wear out of a shoe if you switched them around and wore them on the "wrong" feet sometimes. Huey reasoned that the shoes would wear evenly and you would get twice as much wear out of them. Tommie liked to shine his Daddy's shoes too, but Huey feared that he would never get the chance to do that again.

Each day, Tommie would ask for his "Papa." Each day Sarah would tell him that his Papa would be back soon. She tried to get him to play with the other kids. Ollie, Essie, and Bessie came over each day to play with Tommie and Hattie, but Tommie still asked about his Papa every day. The children were outside pitching horseshoes one day when Sarah's oldest daughter, Shug, came to visit. Shug had moved to Louisiana, but frequently took the train to Taylor. Sarah loved it when Shug came to visit. Shug's younger brothers and sisters all perked up and the whole house smiled. Shug had a way with people. Her given name was Della, but a few days after she was born, Sarah took a good look at her and said she was as sweet as sugar. Della had been called "Shug" ever since.

Shug hugged all of the children and pitched a few horseshoes with them. Then she went inside to see Sarah. Soon, Shug and Sarah were deep in conversation. Finally, Shug put her arms around Sarah and gave her a hug. "Don't worry, Mama. He be just fine." They went outside and walked over to the children. "Tommie," Sarah said. "How would you like to go stay with your sister Shug in Louisiana for awhile?"

"Yeah!" Tommie shouted. Tommie loved Shug. She always said nice things to him and she liked to play games with the children. He had been to Louisiana once to visit Shug, but it was only for 3 days, and then they returned to Taylor. He was excited about another trip to Louisiana.

"Run on in and get that little suitcase. I'll be in in a minute to help you pack."

Tommie ran inside. He got his little shoe shine box that he had made from a fruit box. It was the box that Charley talked about when he left. Tommie used the shoebox to earn money. When they went to town, he would take his box and charge a nickel to shine shoes. He had regular customers by the time he was seven. He would dance, and "pop" his shine rag around. Between the dancing and the popping, he could shine shoes better than some of the grown men who shined them in the barbershop. Then he got out his shoeshine outfit. It was really just an old apron with three pockets. But it served its purpose for Tommie. He put his homemade polish in one pocket and his rags in another. The middle pocket was for all the money he would make. There would be lots of new customers in Shreveport! He envisioned that someday the pocket would be full of money! He ran outside with his box.

"I'm ready!" he announced.

"That was quick!" Shug said with laugh. "But you might want to bring some clothes to wear."

"Oh." Tommie went back into the house. About an hour later, they headed to Shug's house in Shreveport. He waved good-bye to the other children. The girls missed him already. He was a lot fun for a boy. He usually kept them laughing with one joke or another. And he liked to show off when he made money, so he always brought them something when he went to town.

Ollie, Essie and Bessie pitched horseshoes for a while longer. Then the sun began to set and it was time to go home for supper. When they got home, they heard yelling. Mr. Willie and their Mama, Gertrude, were having a very loud argument. It wasn't the first time though. They argued a lot! Bessie still remembered the time that it got so bad that Gertrude dropped her while she was trying to get away from Willie. She was only two years old when it happened, but she was old enough to remember being hurt and scared. Bessie could not get up, because her back had broken in the fall. She thought about that almost every time her Mama and Willie argued.

Bessie was always afraid of Willie. She didn't like the way he cussed at her and her sisters and at their mother. He was using that language now. Bessie, Ollie, and Essie walked unnoticed into the room. Willie had a horsewhip in his hands. He pulled his hand back and started to swing the whip at Gertrude. Bessie ran up and grabbed the whip to stop Willie from hitting her mother with it. Willie and Gertrude were both taken by surprise and looked at the girls. Then Willie walked out of the door. Gertrude pulled the girls together in a hug. "It's all right," she said. "Willie won't hurt me." After that, Bessie began to wonder about her *real* father. She knew that her father's name was Dan McGee and that he lived in Minden. She also knew that he had another family. She remembered Gertrude calling Dan and asking him to send some clothes to the girls. Then she heard her mother say, "No, I'm not sending them up there Dan." Bessie thought about her father and wondered why he never came to visit. She had decided that Dan didn't want to see them. However, she still wondered what he looked like, and if he was nicer than mean old Willie.

In 1930, tragedy struck Taylor. Frank was now about eighty years old, and had been sick off and on for the last year. One night in November, Gertrude and the girls were sitting in his room by his bed as he was telling them stories. They stayed up well past their bedtime that night. Gertrude didn't send them to bed. She knew in her heart that this would probably be the last night that the girls could talk to their grandfather. She was right. A little after midnight Frank's speech got slower, and his breathing was shallow. Finally, he stopped talking. A few minutes later, he coughed and then took a deep breath. Then the motion of his chest stopped. Frank was dead! Gertrude cried softly and prayed over Frank's body. She and the girls stayed up for the entire night.

The next morning the church bell rang. As the neighbors found out about Frank, they started to gather at Gertrude's house. The men fashioned a homemade casket out of left over wood from the barn they had built behind the Jacks' house. They prepared Frank's body for his burial.

Frank's funeral arrangements were made. After the funeral service in Taylor, Frank's casket was gently placed on a wagon pulled by a white horse. Frank wanted to be buried in Minden, next to his mother, Kitty, who had died several years before. The funeral procession extended for over a mile, as the Taylor community accompanied his body from Arkansas to Minden, Louisiana.

When they arrived in Minden, it was dark. They lit candles, sang, and prayed throughout the night. The next morning they buried Frank in a plot next to his mother Kitty. After the burial, they went to Shug's home for a meal.

But Gertrude had one more thing she needed to do. She called Ollie, Essie, and Bessie and they all got into a car that was parked outside of Shug's house. They drove for about 2 miles until they came to a house that was set back from the road. It was a small white house, and huge weeds were beginning to overtake the yard. Gertrude knocked on the door. There was no answer. She knocked again, this time louder. A man's voice called out to them.

"Come in." Gertrude went in and the girls followed her. Then Bessie could hardly believe her ears when she heard her mother say, "Hello Dan. Here are your girls." Bessie stepped out from behind her mother, to finally get a look at her father, the man she had wanted to see for so long. She smiled as she looked across the room. He was smiling and his arms were outstretched. His eyes looked kind, and twinkled with his smile. Bessie stepped forward. Then she suddenly stopped. She looked down, and then she saw it. Her father was in a wheelchair! But she wasn't afraid. Her mother worked in a hospital. She had seen plenty of wheelchairs before. She even sat in one once. Suddenly all of the mixed feelings of hurt and anger left her. She realized that her father couldn't come see her because he couldn't walk! She decided then and there that it wasn't his fault. She continued her walk and gave Dan a quick hug. Ollie and Essie finally followed her lead, and went up to hug their father. Dan and Gertrude made small talk for about thirty minutes. Then they got into the car and headed back to Shug's house. From there, they made the long trip home.

11

"Bethlehem Baptist Church"

Sunday morning, Gertrude and her daughters put on their finest clothes, and went to Bethlehem Baptist Church. It was a beautiful, June day. The sun shone brightly as everyone enjoyed the shade beneath the tent. There was a podium near the front of the tent, where the Pastor would speak in just a few minutes. Bethlehem, established in 1868, was one of the first Black churches in Magnolia and had recently been remodeled. Today was the dedication, which would be followed by the first church service.

Almost everyone they knew had come out for the event. Taylor, Arkansas was only 20 miles away, and many people from Taylor turned out for the event. They were all outside, excitedly talking to each other. There was a tent set up with chairs underneath the canopy. Gertrude and the girls took their seats next to Huey and Sarah, and Sarah's children who had also come to the dedication. They greeted each other and spoke with anticipation about the new church. When Pastor finally headed towards the podium, a hush fell over the crowd. He took his place behind the podium.

"Brother's and Sister's," he started, "this is a new day. The Lawd has seen fit to give us this house of worship and we thank you Lawd! We thank you and we glorify yo' name, Lawd for without you, we would not be standing here today."

"Yes Lawd!"

"Amen!"

"We thank you Lawd for keeping us safe as we slept last night, and we thank you Lawd fo' wakin' us up this moanin' to behold your glorious day! We thank you Lawd and we honor your name!"

"Halleluiah!"

"Yes suh!"

"Now brothers and sisters, some of you here today were born during slave times. You couldn't worship without the master controlling your every move." He nodded towards Huey. Huey was a young man when the slaves were freed and he had told him the stories about worship during slave times. "Our own Brother Huey couldn't worship unless the overseer or one of his cronies was present." Then the Pastor turned and looked at Gertrude. "And Sister Gertrude, I know your grandmother was brought here on a slave ship. She was whipped when she tried to worship the way she learned in Africa. They called her a "heathen" and it was against the law for her to worship in her own way. Brother's and Sister's let us remember today that many colored people were punished just for praying. This church was built when freedom was only 3 years old. The Lawd gave us this church so that we could lift up his Holy name. Now we have our own church and we can sing and praise the Lord as we see fit! So just let go, and let God!" A loud round of applause and several "Amen's" erupted from the crowd. When the clapping slowed down, the Pastor began to speak again.

"In this church we blend the old with the new. We have a

drum, and a piano, and we can do our holy dance until God calls us home."

"Praise the Lawd"

"My God!"

"But brothers and sisters, this is more than a church, praise God. The doors are always open to the sick and the poor. We have a food bank for those in need. We will have Sunday school, and teach the children. So we ask God's blessing today as we dedicate this church in his holy name. The doors of the Church are open. Now let's go inside, brothers and sisters, and give God all the praise!"

"Amen!"

"Amen!"

"Alleluia!"

The Pastor walked out from behind the podium and headed towards the double doors of the church. He walked up the four steps to the doorway. A long red ribbon accented by a huge red and gold bow graced the double doors. Sister Henderson handed the pastor a pair of scissors and he ceremoniously snipped the ribbon. Then two ushers held the door open as the rest of the congregation followed the Pastor into the church. As each person entered the church, sounds of "Amen" could be heard over and over again. Upon entering, they stepped onto a red runner, which ran the length of the floor. Newly painted pews sat on each side of the runner, filling the church with a pleasant aroma. At the front of the church, was a beautiful pulpit covered with red and gold velvet. A pattern of red and gold crosses adorned the cloth. Two large, high-back chairs, covered with red velvet sat just slightly on either side of the podium. Behind the pulpit, was the "Choir Pit" made up of three rows of benches, each arranged in a semi-circle.

Gertrude and the girls made their way up to the second row of the church, and took a seat, anxiously awaiting the start of the service. As they waited, the church filled up. The Pastor sat down in one of the high back chairs. He began to clap to the music as a chorus of voices was heard from the back of the church.

"At the Cross — At the Cross — Where I first saw the light— and the burden on my heart rolled a-way-yee-. It was there by faith I received my sight and now I am ha-ppy all the day!"

The choir marched up to the front of the church, singing as they walked. They sang all the way up the steps of the platform and continued singing until they all stood in front of the seats in the choir pit. They rocked from side to side to the beat as they sang one more chorus of *"At the Cross."* Then, everyone except Sister Henderson sat down. She walked down the steps of the choir pit, and over to a microphone on the side of the stage. Everyone knew that Sister Henderson had a beautiful voice, and they were in for a treat! She started slowly, her voice soft and smooth.

".. She-ee used to pra-ay that I- ah-on Jee-sus would rely; and always walk the shining gospel way; aye-aye-aye-aye. So-oh trusting in his love, I-I'm seeking ho-ome above. Oh, if I could he-hear my-ee Motherrr; pray again!"

By the end of the song, her voice was loud and strong. The congregation clapped enthusiastically.

"Thank you Jesus!"

"Yes, Lord!"

"Amen."

With both hands in the air, Sister Henderson walked back to her seat, shouting, "Halleluiah! Halleluiah! Halleluiah!" The drums got louder as a fast rhythmic beat filled the church. Sister Jordan, who was sitting in the sixth row jumped out of her seat, and suddenly she was in the aisle. She jumped up and down to the beat of the drums. Several others in the church were also on their feet dancing and shouting "Thank you Jesus! Thank you Jesus!" Their hands were in the air, praising God. Finally, the drums slowed and finally stopped. "Amen's" and "Halleluiah" continued to be heard as they made their way back to their seats, praising and thanking God with each few steps. The Pastor arose and walked up to the pulpit. He bowed his head.

"Let us pray," he began. "Dear God, we thank you...." The Pastor prayed, and asked God's blessing on the congregation. He thanked God for giving them their House of Worship. He asked for forgiveness for the sinners. He prayed for wisdom, for strength and for health. Next, he opened his Bible and read from the Old Testament before giving a soul-stirring sermon that once again got the congregation on their feet. Then, as the organ played, he walked back over to his velvet-cushioned seat. As he sat down, the ushers walked up to the front of the church, and began passing the velvet lined offering plate, while the choir hummed a tune. After the offering, the Pastor again walked up to the pulpit and asked for God's blessing on the offering: "Dear Lord, we thank you for this offering for the uplifting of your word. We ask that you bless the givers. And Dear Lord, we ask you to bless those who had the desire to give, but could not." Once again, Sister Henderson made her way to the microphone at the front of the choir pit, and began to sing.

"I am on the Battlefield for my Law-aw-aw-awd. I'm on the Bat- tlefield for my Law-aw-awd: And I promised him that I — I'm gon- na serve him till I die, I am on the Battlefield for my Lawd!"

The congregation joined in the song. After the second chorus of the song, Sister Henderson's voice softened and everyone began to hum the chorus of the song as the Pastor walked back to the Podium.

"The doors of the Church are open. If there is someone here without a church home, come take my hand and join our church family. Just come as you are for the Lawd will show you the way. Don't worry about form or fashion; the Lawd has a place for you!"

Several people in the congregation walked up to the front of the church as the pastor stepped out from behind the podium to greet them. The congregation responded with shouts of "Hallelu- iah" and "Amen" as they celebrated the new members who were surrendering their lives to God. Soon, the front row of the church was filled with people who had made their way to take the Pastor's hand. While the organ played softly, the Pastor asked each of them to introduce themselves and say a few words to the congregation.

After all of the introductions were made and the new members were inducted into the Church, the Pastor motioned for the congregation to stand. He raised his right hand and bowed his head to deliver the Benediction;

"Even the youth shall faint and be weary; Young men shall utterly fall; But they that wait upon the Lord, shall renew their strength; they shall mount up with wings as eagles; they shall run and not be weary; and they shall walk, and not faint."

"Amen!"

"Amen!"

Everyone headed back outside to enjoy the potluck meal that had been prepared. They ate country fried chicken, hot biscuits, fluffy mashed potatoes, corn-on-the-cob, and collard greens. Dessert consisted of peach cobbler, banana pudding, and sweet potato pie. They topped it all off with ice-cold sweet lemon tea. Then with a full body, and a lifted spirit, they headed home after the first Sunday at the New Bethlehem Baptist Church

The Back of
The Train

The Seventh Generation

Still..... "Jim Crowed"

Tommie, Bessie, Hattie, Ollie, Essie

COLUMBIA COUNTY, ARKANSAS
TAYLOR TOWN
Population 657

12

"The Color Line"

In the Taylor community, the young people frequently helped their families by doing odd jobs on various farms. Most of the time, their job was picking cotton, or chopping sugar cane. Their pay was about 25 cents per bag. Hattie was faster than any of them when it came to picking cotton. She could pick up to 300 pounds a day. Her grandfather had shown her how to do it. Like Huey, she pulled two rows at a time. Ollie was a close second when it came to picking the cotton. Some days she could pick almost as much as Hattie. Bessie liked to do the plowing. She would work that plow in perfect little rows, all ready for planting. When she wasn't plowing, she liked to chop sugar cane. The farmer that they chopped cane for always gave them a stalk or two to take home. Raw cane was one of Bessie's favorite snacks. She would get a nice big glass of fresh milk from the cow that Dr. Hudnall had given them. Sometimes she liked to eat it with bread and the butter that they churned at home. She would save some of her cane until her butter was churned and clabbered. Then, a little cane in the butter sweetened it just right. One day she took a piece of the cane to school. One of her classmates asked her where she got it. "I chopped some on Mr. Tom's farm, and he gave me a piece of it." she answered.

The girl looked at Bessie. She really wanted some cane but didn't want to ask for it. So she thought of something mean to say. Finally, she shrugged her shoulders and said. "He only give it to you cuz you a high yellow colored girl."

Bessie was still very light skinned and many of the girls hated her for that. They called her "high yellow" and said that she was stuck up. Bessie was always hurt by the comments. She would remember how her mother almost gave her away because her skin was so light. However, she didn't see herself as light skinned. When she looked in the mirror, she saw a nice chocolate brown! In fact, Bessie herself didn't like light-skinned people because *she* thought that they were stuck up. One day she was talking to Ollie about their cousin Tossie.

"Tossie thank she cute jest 'cuz she light skinned," Bessie stated. Light-skinned people always is running around thankin that they so cute. I can't stand them stuck up light skinned people."

"You light skinded." Ollie said.

"I am not! I used to be but I'm darker now!" Bessie countered.

"That ain't what yo' mirror say. Yo' mirror say that you a high yella nigger girl." Bessie started crying and Essie walked up to her sisters just at that moment.

"What you cryin fo' now, Bessie?" Essie asked.

"Ollie keep a callin' me yella!" Bessie cried.

Ollie looked at Bessie and put her hands on her hips. "What you crying to Essie fuh?" she asked Bessie. "Essie yella too!" Essie balled her hand up into a fist. She pulled her arm way back so that she could get the maximum momentum in her swing, and let Ollie have it! Ollie yelled and fell to the ground. She held the side of her face as it was swelling up, and looked up at Bessie and Essie. Essie dropped to her knees in front of Ollie and pulled her arm back again, so that she could deliver another slug on.

Bessie ran over to Ollie to push her out of Essie's path and help her up. "Don't hit her no mo' Essie! Ollie don't mean it!" Bessie shouted.

"If she didn't mean it she wouldn't uh said it!" Essie replied. With Bessie's help, Ollie picked herself up from the ground and started running towards home. Bessie was right behind her, and Essie brought up the rear. Ollie ran as fast as she could. Finally, when the safety of home was only about 30 feet in front of her, she stopped. Essie was catching up fast. Ollie looked around for a rock or something to throw at her. Ollie figured that she could hit Essie with a rock and then run into the house before Essie caught her, but Essie and Bessie were quickly closing in behind her. There was a little white girl standing near the house waiting for Essie and Bessie. The little girl's named was Doris. Gertrude worked for her parents. Doris lived nearby, and came around frequently. Ollie had almost knocked Doris down, in her haste to get away from Essie. But Essie caught up with her before Ollie found her rock. Essie took another swing at Ollie, but this time, Ollie managed to duck out of the way. Then she rose up and pushed Essie hard! Essie stumbled back and almost lost her balance, but she pushed herself off the ground with one hand and managed to keep from falling.

"Uh oh! You in for it now, Ollie!" Essie yelled at her. Bessie had caught up now, and was running towards the door, so that she could tell her mother about the fight. Doris took in the scene, and then apparently had the same idea as Bessie.

"Ooooh, Bes-ss-eee!" Doris said to Essie. Doris frequently got Bessie and Essie's names mixed up, and assumed that it was Bessie that Ollie was fighting with. "I'm gonna tell Miss Gertrude that you're fighting!"

Essie raised her fist and shook it towards Doris. "I'll hit you too, you stupid ol' girl!" Essie threatened.

"You better not, Doris shot back!" Essie walked up to Doris and slapped her hard across the face! Doris ran into the house, calling for Gertrude. "Miss Gertrude! Miss Gertrude! Bessie hit me, she cried!" Bessie, Essie, and Ollie were close behind her, ready to deny it all.

Gertrude quickly came out of the kitchen. "What is it?" she asked.

"Bessie hit me," she said again. Gertrude looked at her three girls and then again at Doris. She knew at a glance what had happened. She knew that Essie was quick to hit, but Bessie wasn't. Bessie would throw something and run.

"Bessie didn't hit you Doris. It was Essie that hit you!" Gertrude sighed and turned to Essie. "Essie, why did you hit Doris?"

"I didn't hit that ol girl!" Essie said. "I shoulda hit her, though."

"Essie, I done told you over and over. It ain't nice hittin' people. Why do you want to fight all the time? It just don't take much for you to haul off and hit somebody."

"Well they shouldn't do stuff." replied Essie.

"Oh Essie, one of these days somebody is gonna get you good. You lucky that God takes care of babies and fools!" When Gertrude turned to go back into the kitchen, Essie balled up her fist and shook it in the air towards Doris. Then she mumbled under her breath, "I'm gonna get you, Doris!" Doris ran out of the door and went home. She had been on the receiving end of Essie's fist more than once, and she didn't want to be hit again. But she took comfort in knowing that Miss Gertrude would probably spank Essie. Essie did get a licking. It was at least 3 days before she hit Ollie again!

***

As the girls began to grow older, they caught the eye of some of the young men in the neighborhood. Russell Jacks took a shine to Bessie. Russ liked to show off because his family owned oil wells, and he could pretty much buy what he wanted. But Hattie's brother Tommie also took a shine to Bessie. He still lived in Shreveport with Shug but he frequently took the train back to Taylor to see his family. When he came back, he would always find Bessie. She often wore a red hat, so he took to calling her Red. Tommie rarely called anyone by their real names. He would look at them and give them a nickname. He had a special name for Russ. He called him "Squirrel," saying that Russ was scrawny. Tommie didn't like Russ, and especially didn't like seeing him with Bessie Mae. Tommie finally decided to come back to Taylor to live. He wanted to spend more time with Bessie, and he wanted Russ Jacks to spend less time with her.

One Saturday afternoon, he arrived in Taylor. He was now 15 years old, and Bessie was 13. He was on his way to Bessie's house when he saw Bessie and Russ walking towards him. They were walking arm in arm. Tommie calmly walked up to them and took Bessie's other arm and walked her the other way. Russ stood there with his mouth open, but Bessie kept walking with Tommie. They walked all the way back to Bessie's house, laughing and talking. When they got to the door, they heard the "talking machine" playing. The talking machine was one of the earlier kinds of record players that played 78-rpm wax records. Bessie thought back to the first time she had seen one. She had seen a talking machine at the Jack's house. Russ would put a record on it and crank it up. Sweet music would come out of the box. When the record slowed down, Russ would crank it up again so that the record played right. The girls never expected to have a talking machine of their own. They asked Russ how much it cost. "Fifteen Dollars," was his reply.

"Fifteen Dollars?" echoed Bessie. "That's more than Mama makes in a month!" She never thought she would see one at *her* house. However, one day Gertrude promised Bessie and her sisters that if they kept the house clean for a whole month, she would buy them a talking machine. True to her word, Gertrude bought the machine after the girls kept the house clean for a month. And she enjoyed that machine just as much as Bessie and the girls did!

Tommie and Bessie went into the house. The record was slowing down, so Bessie walked over to it took hold of the crank in front of the machine. She gave the crank a couple of turns, and the record started back up at the proper pace. Tommie had learned a few dance steps in Shreveport and he showed Bessie how to "cut-a-rug," (dance) and do the "Swing" and the "Lindy Hop." They enjoyed themselves so much that they spent most of their free time together over the next few days. The days turned into months, and they never tired of each other's company. They were listening to the talking machine one day when Gertrude came into the room.

"Bessie," she said. "Getcha thangs togetha honey. We movin' to Magnolia. Ollie and Essie already started packin.'"

Dr. Horn was moving to Magnolia, and wanted Gertrude to come with him. She and the girls would live in a room above the hospital. Bessie was afraid that she wouldn't get to see Tommie anymore.

"I'm not going to let you get away from me Red, no matter how far you move. Magnolia's not far. I can get there in 20 minutes. I'll just ride my horse 'Slick' up there to see you."

"Okay." Bessie said half-heartedly. It seemed like a long way to her. She didn't know if he could manage it. However, true to his word, every few days Tommie rode up to Magnolia on his horse to visit Bessie. Sometimes Bessie or one of her sisters would ride up to the market with him to get some candy or ice cream. Occasionally, Tommie would borrow a car and drive up to see them. One day they all decided to go to Spring Hill. Spring Hill was a town near Taylor where most of the "juke joints" in the area were located. They had been in the place for all of thirty minutes when Gertrude showed up. She pointed a finger at Tommie and said, "Shame on you Tommie! You know better!" She rounded up the girls and herded them to the door. They never found out how she knew where they were, but she whipped the girls all the way home. That was their last trip to the juke joint. She made them stay in the house for a month. That was the last time that they snuck off anywhere.

Bessie was fifteen years old and Tommie was nearly eighteen when they decided that they wanted to get married. They weren't sure if Gertrude and Sarah would let them so they decided to sneak off and tie the knot. They went down to the courthouse in Magnolia and applied for a marriage license.

"How old are you?" the clerk asked.

"Eighteen," was Tommie's reply!

"Eighteen," was Bessie's. Eighteen was the legal age to marry without parental permission. The clerk issued the marriage license and they started to plan to elope. They finally decided that they weren't sure that they should get married just yet. And it just didn't feel right sneaking off! They decided that they would wait until they were really of legal age. But the next day Tommie decided to do the right thing. He went to Gertrude's floor at the hospital and knocked on a door. Gertrude opened the door and looked Tommie over.

He removed his hat and smiled at her. Tommie was "decked out" from head to toe! He sported a dress hat with a feather tucked neatly into the band. His hair was slicked back, and his waves were perfectly even. He had on a dark blue suit, with creases in the pants that were so sharp, you could cut your finger on them. Tucked neatly into the pocket of his suit was a blue striped handkerchief accented with just a touch of silky black trim. A crisp white shirt with French cuffs peaked out from beneath the jacket. The cuffs on the shirt were held together with gold-toned cufflinks with faux diamond centers that sparkled in the light. Tommie's pants were just high enough above the ankle, so that his socks peaked out from beneath them. His socks were made of fine silk, and had shiny flecks of blue that matched his suit perfectly. And his shoes! He had on black patent leather shoes that shined so bright that you could see your face in them!

Gertrude tried to keep a straight face but began to smile in spite of herself.

"Hello, Tommie. What can I do for you?" she asked.

"Well," Tommie began. "You know that I been around Bessie Mae for a long time!"

"Yes Tommie," I know.

"Well I guess you know how I feel 'bout Bessie Mae. Miss Gertrude, I'd like permission to marry your daughter!"

Gertrude looked squarely at Tommie. She wasn't going to

make this easy for him. The clerk at the courthouse had already come and told her that Tommie and Bessie got a marriage license. But Gertrude didn't let on. She decided to see what Tommie had to say.

"Are you sure you can take care of my daughter, Tommie?"

"Yes Ma'am. I been workin' since I was seven years old. I got my own business now. I can take care of her, and I promise you that I will."

"Do you love Bessie Mae, Tommie?" she questioned further.

"Oh, yes Ma'am!" Tommie said emphatically. "I love her very much!"

"You think you can make my Bessie happy?" she continued.

"She'll be happier then you've ever seen her," Tommie promised.

"OK then," Gertrude finally answered. "If Bessie Mae wants to marry you, then you have my blessing." Tommie broke into a big grin then.

"Thank you! Thank you very much Miss Gertrude!"

"You're welcome Tommie. Don't let me down, now. I'm counting on you to keep your promise."

Tommie went outside to find Bessie. He found her in the garden pulling weeds.

"Red!" he shouted.

"Yes?" Bessie looked up from her gardening.

"I just asked Miss Gertrude if I can marry you. And she said 'yes'!"

Bessie looked at him. She was a bit startled. She thought that they had dropped the marriage talk for now.

"I don't remember you asking me if I would marry you right now!" she accused. "What if I don't have a mind to marry you now? You go ask Mama, but not me?"

Tommie knew she was just mad because he didn't tell her what he was going to do. He looked her squarely in the eye. "Bessie Mae," he demanded, "Are you going to marry me or not?"

She looked at him carefully and finally she spoke. "I'll marry you on two conditions, Tommie," she said. "One is that you never raise a hand against me! And the other is that you never cuss at me!"

"I can most certainly keep that promise!" Tommie laughed. Then with his 5'4" frame, he picked up all 5' of Bessie and gave her a kiss. Then they began to play their future.

They were married on April 22, 1939. Tommie had just turned 18 years old. Bessie was 15. Bessie wore a beautiful blue flowered shirtwaist dress, with a matching leather belt. She wore navy blue patent leather shoes with neat little bows on top. Tommie wore a dark blue suit that matched it perfectly. They got married at the courthouse in Taylor. They thought that they were going to have a small wedding with just their parents, but when they arrived at the courthouse they learned that the court clerk had been very talkative about their marriage plans. Almost all of the neighbors had turned out for the event. They happily said their vows and went back to Sarah's house to begin their new lives.

A few months later, Tommie's sister Hattie married a man named Marion Kelly. Marion was Bessie's cousin, so everyone already seemed like "family." Hattie and Bessie both marveled in the fact that they were newlywed "women." Hattie was the first to have children. In the back of her mind, she always wondered if she would be able to have a child. Later that same year she got her answer when Golden T Kelly was born.

Then a little over a year later, Tommie and Bessie brought a new life into Taylor. Stella T. Lewis, weighing in at a whopping nine pounds was born with the aid of a midwife. Hattie and Bessie were as close as sisters, and they were thrilled to have their children so close together.

Soon Tommie became restless. He wanted to see more of the world. His sister Shug still lived in Louisiana, and he had enjoyed the time that he spent there. He decided to take Bessie and see if she would like living in Louisiana. Hattie was ready for a change too, so she and Kelly decided to go with them. In early 1940, they made the move to Shreveport.

Shreveport, Louisiana was very different from Taylor. Next to Taylor, Shreveport seemed like a huge bustling city. Then in October 1942, Tommie and Bessie welcomed another child, a girl, into the world. Brandy Joyce was a happy baby and a good-natured one. However, because she was born with a genetic heart disease, she was small for her age and was not yet crawling or doing some of the other things that babies did in their first few months. Brandy, (who Bessie nicknamed "Martha") contracted pneumonia when she was just nine months old. On July 22, Bessie took Brandy Joyce to Charity hospital with a cough and a fever. But the fever skyrocketed and the cough became worse as the day wore on. As Brandy became weaker, Bessie frantically tried to get word to Tommie about the baby's deteriorating condition. But sadly, just as Tommie arrived early in the morning on July 23, 1943, Brandy Joyce took her last breath. The next few days were the worst days of their lives as Tommie and Bessie, overcome with grief, watched as Martha's tiny casket was lowered into the ground at Star Cemetery, her final resting place.

The country was in the midst of World War II. Many of the young men in Taylor and Louisiana were being drafted to go into the army and fight the war. Tommie knew that he didn't have long before he was called to go. The military was calling almost every able body to serve. Then one day an official looking letter arrived in the mail. Tommie opened the letter and began to read it. "Greetings," he started. As soon as Bessie heard that word, she began to cry. She knew that the draft letters always started with "Greetings." The words brought up images and memories of some of her friends husbands who had gone to Germany, and returned in body bags. However, they both knew that there was no choice. Tommie had been drafted and he had to serve. Bessie went back to Taylor to stay with Miss Sarah until he returned. Hattie and Kelly joined her.

Bessie was a great help to Miss Sarah on the farm. After Tommie left for Germany, she turned her attention to her sister Ollie, who had gotten married to a man named Glover several months before. Ollie and Essie now worked at the bakery in town. Ollie was a cook and Essie did various jobs at the bakery. Ollie loved her job. She liked to roll the pastry and cut the dough into various shapes and sizes. She baked cakes and rolls from scratch. Many of the families in Taylor, and even in Magnolia loved to treat themselves to one of Ollie's pastries. Mr. Johnson, a white man from Magnolia owned the bakery. He hired colored and white, and unlike many others, he gave the colored the same pay as the whites. He even came to Essie's rescue one day when Essie became ill, and needed to go to the hospital. The colored part of the hospital was full, and Essie was turned away and told to go to the hospital in Little Rock. But Mr. Johnson became angry after hearing this, and took Essie back to the emergency room at the hospital. Mr. Johnson told the staff that they "Will not turn Miss Essie away." He insisted that her money was just as good as everyone else, and if they turned her away he would see to it that whoever had a hand in it would no longer have a job. The staff at the hospital knew that Mr. Johnson had a lot of pull around town, and they knew better than to cross him. They found a place for Essie, and after she recovered and left the hospital, she reported that she received just as good care as many of the whites. Ollie and Bessie were grateful that Mr. Johnson had stepped in. They knew that Essie probably would have died if Mr. Johnson hadn't intervened.

Ollie was happy about Essie's recovery, and she always seemed happy when she was working at the bakery. However, her eyes seemed sad when she was at home, or visiting any of the neighbors. Bessie's daughter Stella was a toddler now, and Bessie thought that Ollie was depressed because she wanted children, and couldn't have them. However, Bessie began to suspect more when Ollie showed up at Miss Sarah's house one day with a big bruise on the side of her face.

"What happened to you Ollie?" Bessie asked.

"What you talkin' bout, Bessie?" Ollie answered as Sarah and Hattie walked into the room.

"I'm talkin about yo' face, Ollie," Bessie replied. "Who hit you

149

in the face?"

"Oh." Ollie took a big breath before she spoke. She didn't look at Bessie when she answered.

"Didn't nobody hit me! I was shoeing the horse when he kicked back and caught me on my cheek."

Sarah walked up to Ollie. She ran her hand over Ollie's cheek. "Turn around Ollie." she demanded. Ollie slowly turned around, trying hard not to let on how painful it was just to move. Once she had her back turned, Sarah unbuttoned the top three buttons on Ollie's dress, and pulled it open.

"And I suppose that after the horse kicked you in the face, you turned around and he kicked you in the back, huh?" she asked.

"Well, after he kicked me, I fell backwards, and hit my back on something," Ollie explained.

"Was it Glover's fist that you fell on, Ollie?" Sarah inquired. She knew the answer. This wasn't the first time that Ollie had turned up with scrapes and bruises. Ollie always had an excuse that she had fallen, or something had fallen on her. Just last week, Ollie had even gone to Dr. Hudnall's office. Glover had stabbed her deep in the chest, but thankfully missed any vital organs. Dr. Hudnall had warned her about six months before, when she arrived at his office with several broken ribs. She lied to Dr. Hudnall, after he inquired about how she got her ribs broken. But he knew better.

"Ollie," he said, "One of these days that husband of yours is going to kill you."

Now Sarah was staring at her, with a knowing look in her eyes. However, Sarah wasn't likely to drop the subject like Dr. Hudnall did. Ollie could tell that Sarah wasn't through with her yet. Sarah had decided that the situation needed her full attention!

"Ollie," Sarah said gently. "You know you can tell us the truth. That man been beating on you, ain't he?"

Ollie began to cry. She knew that it was no use denying it anymore. Sarah knew! Probably everybody knew! "He don't mean it! He just drinks too much sometimes. I want to leave, but he'd kill me if I leave!"

"He's gonna kill you if you stay!" said Miss Sarah. "You come around here all the time making excuses for him! You fell! The horse kicked you! Frying pans with hot grease falling on you! I guess you stabbed your own self too, huh?"

Now Ollie was sobbing great big gulping sobs. She thought that she had covered her tracks well. But Miss Sarah knew about all of it, including the knife. Sarah went up to Ollie and put her arms around her. Ollie felt herself gaining strength. It was as if a huge weight had been lifted off her shoulders. As Sarah spoke, Ollie felt her anger against Glover increasing. She remembered the pain of the hot grease, her blood on the floor from the knife, and the awful bruises that she hid for weeks. She also knew in her heart, that Miss Sarah would understand her anger. Finally Ollie spoke. "Miss Sarah, I don't know what to do! You know I'm a Christian woman, but I even asked God to give me the strength to stab Glover in his sleep!"

Ollie was clearly relieved to get the truth out. Sarah listened while Ollie told of the many times Glover had beaten her, and how she didn't know what to do. She didn't want to tell because she was afraid of what would happen if she did.

Finally Sarah spoke. "Ollie, you don't have to do nothin except let Ed know you ready. Don't you think we all know when something ain't right? Ed knew. We all knew. Now Honey, we put together a little money. Ed's gonna take you away from here. We'll make sure that when Glover comes looking for you, that you'll be far away from here."

Just then, Ed walked in the door. "Ed," Sara said. "Ollie is hurt. It's time to take her away from here!"

Ed looked at Ollie. He knew that this day would come. "I'm ready whenever you are, Ollie!"

Ollie looked at Hattie, and all of a sudden, shame washed over her again. She had hoped that Hattie would never find out about Glover, because she knew that Hattie would have never put up with that kind of behavior from any man. Ollie remembered being near the barn one day. Hattie was married to Kelly at the time, but had packed up her clothes and left him. Kelly had come looking for her and found her near the barn with Bessie and Ollie. He went over to Hattie, pulled a gun out of his waistband, and pointed it at her. Hattie didn't flinch. She looked squarely at Kelly and said, "You ain't gonna shoot me cuz you ain't got the nerve! Go ahead. I dare you! I double dog dare you!"

Ollie remembered how scared she and Bessie were for Hattie. Kelly had gotten out of jail not long before, for shooting someone. He was bad news around Taylor. Kelly was Ollie's cousin and Ollie remembered that just a year before, Kelly, (who they called "cousin Mim"), and several of his friends dug a deep hole and buried someone that they were mad at in several feet of dirt. The only thing that they left uncovered was his head. Some said that Kelly wanted to finish the job but the others talked him out of it. So they just left the man buried there for a few days to teach him a lesson.

Kelly was clearly someone who had the nerve to shoot, and there was Hattie taunting him. But Kelly knew that Hattie had ways of getting back at him if she really wanted to. Hattie had told him about a cousin of hers who was in an abusive marriage. The cousin waited until her husband went to bed and then calmly untucked the sheet from under the mattress. Then, while her husband was in a heavy, drunken sleep, she calmly sewed the sheet all the way around him. That done, she took a crowbar and (literally) beat the life out of him! Because he had a lot of enemies, and many girlfriends, the authorities could not prove who did it.

Hattie kept a sewing basket by her bed and frequently reminded Kelly that she was "an excellent seamstress."

Kelly put the gun back in his waistband. He muttered something about "Crazy witch," and walked away. Hattie went back to her work like it was nothing! It was Ollie and Bessie who were afraid. Bessie had spoken. "Hattie! Are you crazy? You know Cousin Mim could have shot you!"

"Well if it's my time, it's my time!" Hattie had retorted.

Ollie's thoughts returned to the present, and she looked at Hattie. Hattie was looking back at her. She knew what Ollie was thinking. "Ollie," Hattie said. "You got to get away from here. Don't be like me. I know I take stupid chances sometimes, but I don't want nothin to happen to you."

Ollie let out a sigh of relief. She didn't want to be looked at as weak. However, she also knew that Miss Sarah would not take "no" for an answer. Ollie did not go back home that day. She quickly and quietly said her goodbye's to her sisters and her mother, and then came back to Sarah's house. There was a bag there waiting for her. She took the bag, and climbed into the car with Ed. Two hours later, they arrived at Shug's house in Louisiana. Shug was expecting her and gave her a warm welcome.

Sure enough, the next day Glover came around looking for Ollie. No one admitted to seeing her. He came around for several days after that. Still no Ollie. Finally, he stopped coming around. Sarah heard that he had been drafted into the army. It would be the last time anyone heard from Glover.

The following year Tommie returned from the military. World War II was over, and he rejoined his family. When he returned, he seemed somehow different from when he left. Of course, he was older, and more mature. Nevertheless, there was a kind of quiet anger that seemed to bubble just below the surface. His friends and family were glad to see him. But when anyone wanted to talk about the war, he would change the subject, and steer the conversation towards hometown talk. Then on one chilly winter night, Tommie appeared to be having a nightmare. He cried out in his sleep. "No! No! Please! Don't do it! Don't do it!" He woke up with sweat pouring down his face, a look of panic in his eyes. Bessie woke up too. It was a long time before either of them spoke. Finally, Bessie said, "Honey, I know it must have been bad over there. But like you always told me, 'There's more room out than there is in'!" Tommie tried to stifle a deep sob, but the tears began to flow.

"Red, I have never seen so many horrible things in all my life. But the worst was the kids! Kids without food, or clothes. Kid's without parents. Kid's shot and laying..." His voice trailed off, and Bessie knew he couldn't continue. She knew that she could never envision the horrors that he saw. All she could do was hold him and be there for him. And that's what she did. Finally, Tommie settled down a bit. But neither of them slept much that night.

The following day, Tommie told Bessie that he wanted to get away from Arkansas for "a little while." He was planning to go to Houston when he was drafted into the army. So he told Bessie that he would go to there and find a job. After he found something, he would send for her. About 4 weeks later, he sent word from Houston. He had found a job. He wanted Bessie to meet him in Houston, and he wanted his sister Hattie to come too. He thought that Hattie would enjoy the change, and that she and Bessie could keep each other company.

About a week later, Hattie and Bessie packed up their clothes, and the two children. They boarded a bus for Lufkin, Texas. From there they would transfer and take another bus to Houston.

Tommie had a job working in construction as a bricklayer. The three of them found a home in the 3rd Ward section of Houston. It was hot, and to Bessie and Tommie, it seemed a lot less friendly than Arkansas. It helped that they had settled down near Shug, and a few other cousins who had moved to Houston. Their first son, Calvin, was born there in 1944.

Shortly after Calvin's birth, Hattie and Bessie were looking out of the window about 9:00 am and saw a Western Union agent coming up to the door. Hattie opened the door as Bessie looked on.

"Telegram for the Lewis Family," the deliveryman announced. Hattie signed for the envelope and thanked him. She sat down and nervously opened the long yellow envelope. The message inside was short and to the point.

"Huey Lewis ....passed away....../stop/...Funeral on Friday...../stop/ ....please come home if you can...."

The next day, Tommie, Bessie, Hattie and their children boarded a bus for Taylor, Arkansas. They were subdued as they boarded. They all loved Huey. He told funny jokes, and told them sad stories about slavery. They remembered how devastated he was after his wife, Arthina, died. They recalled how much he loved her and how he'd made a ritual of going to the cemetery. He would lie on top of her grave so he could be close to her. Miss Sarah had written to them and told them that had never missed a day going to the cemetery, unless he was too sick to get out of bed. Now Huey would take his place in St. Paul cemetery right next to Arthina.

Tommie knew that Huey had been sick a lot lately. He wished he had gone back to Taylor for a visit before Huey died. Instead, he faced going back to the place where his father had disappeared, never to be heard from again, and now, where his beloved grandfather, who had practically raised him, was gone too.

The bus rumbled to a stop outside of a small diner in Lufkin, Texas. They got off the bus. Tommie and Bessie took the children and walked past the "white only" sign that was displayed prominently on the front window of the restaurant. They headed around the back to find the "colored" bathroom. There wasn't one. There was only a sign that said "colored" and pointed to an outhouse. Bessie sighed and carefully opened a hinged door that had most of the screws missing. A few minutes later, they rejoined the others in front of the diner. They waited while the white passengers re boarded. Then Tommie stood back while Bessie boarded with the children. Then he attempted to board the bus. However, before he could get a foot on the step, the bus driver stopped him.

"You can't get back on this bus, boy," he stated. "A white man needs to leave here to get up to Texarkana. We don't have no more seats for colored." Tommie looked over at the bus driver. His mind flashed back to the war. He had served as an American soldier for the past two years. He had served his country along with the others who talked about "freedom." He had traveled the world, riding on buses in many other places. Then he came back to America. He marveled that only in America did he have to give up his seat to a white man. He thought about his grandfather. He didn't want Red to have to go to Taylor without him at her side. He wanted to be there to comfort her.

He decided to appeal to the bus driver's sense of decency. "I just got back from the war a few months ago. Now my grandfather just passed away, and me and my family are on the way to the funeral. I just got off this bus. I paid good money like everyone else. Don't you think I should be allowed back on the bus?"

"What I think doesn't matter," the driver said. "Law around here says I can't take no colored when a white man needs to ride. There will be another bus in about five hours. Your wife can wait for you in Shreveport. There's a colored restaurant near the next bus stop."

There was another Black man behind Tommie who had also gotten off the bus in Lufkin. He'd heard what the bus driver said, and became very upset.

He pushed his way in front of Tommie so that he could talk to the driver. "My name is Willie Henderson," he said. "I have a ticket for this bus. I really need to get back on this bus," he pleaded. "My mother is real sick and I have been trying to get home to her for two days. I already gave up my seat on the last bus!"

"I done told you, boy!" the bus driver shouted. "I don't have no more seats for colored."

Just then, a white man and a young boy came out of the restaurant and headed to the front of the line, taking "their" place in front of the colored people who were standing outside. Tommie didn't recognize them as passengers from Houston. He figured that they must be the white passengers that the bus driver was giving their seats to.

"Step back please!" the bus driver said to Willie.

"But I...," Willie started to say something, and the bus driver got angry.

"Look here, nigger!" he shouted. "Who do you think you are?" I told you—you ain't gettin' back on this bus." He shoved Willie towards the bus, and Willie fell into the white man's son, who was standing near the door of the bus. The white man became angry and shoved Willie up against the side of the bus. Then some white men came running out of the restaurant to see what was going on.

"Get him!" the bus driver yelled. "He hit that white man!"

Suddenly the white men armed themselves with sticks and started swinging the sticks at Willie. Those without sticks began using their fists and their feet as they beat and kicked Willie who was now on the ground. The restaurant owner came running out of the diner yelling, "Stop — stop — you're gonna kill him!" But it didn't matter. They continued their melee, kicking and punching Willie with zeal.

Suddenly they heard a gunshot. The sheriff had arrived and fired a shot into the air to stop the mob from beating Willie. Willie lay on the ground, blood spewing from his nose and mouth. His entire face was swollen and black and blue, and his lips were split and bleeding.

Bessie had gotten off the bus when the altercation started and was horrified to witness the scene before her. She was afraid that Tommie would lose his temper, and that he would end up being beaten, or worse. With her eyes, and a slight tilt of her head, she pleaded with Tommie not to say anything.

The sheriff handcuffed Willie and arrested him for assaulting the white men. Despite Willie's protest that he did not hit anyone, and his assertion that he was the one who was shoved and thrown around, they dragged him to the police car, which was parked in front of the diner. The sheriff slammed Willie's head into the car and demanded his silence. Finally, he put Willie into the police car. The bus driver, who had given the police a statement about the events headed back to the bus. The crowd began to disperse as the patrons from the diner went back inside.

The bus driver got on the bus followed by the white man and his son. The other white people who had gotten off to see what the commotion was about followed next. Finally, the colored passengers took their place behind the whites. As Bessie stood near the steps of the bus, she tried to assure Tommie that everything was okay. They knew that they needed to get everyone that they could to the next town. They decided that Tommie would wait for the next bus while the others went on ahead.

"It's okay, Honey," Bessie said. "Me and the kids will wait at the next stop for you. We stopped there before, on the way here, remember? It's gonna be all right!"

Tommie looked at his family as they re-boarded the bus. In that moment he felt enraged at the Jim Crow system in America. He was ashamed to have Red see him belittled like this. But most of all he didn't want to put her through any additional pain. So, he agreed to let them go on ahead. The place in Shreveport was a better place for her to be until the next bus came along. The bus slowly pulled away from the restaurant. He watched as it rolled down the road. Seven hours later, he joined the rest of his family in Shreveport. Then the five of them boarded another bus and arrived in Taylor later that evening.

13

"Westward Bound"

It was quiet when they arrived in Taylor. Sarah met them at the door. They went into the living room and joined the others. Everyone was awake, and sitting around the fireplace.

"How did it happen?" Tommie asked.

"We really don't know what happened." Sarah said. "You know, Huey been sick off and on. Sheriff Stuart said he took him to the hospital in Little Rock. But when we went up there to see about him they said that there wasn't any room in the colored part of the hospital, and that they had sent him up to the jail in Magnolia. We went up to the jail two—maybe three times, but they wouldn't let us see him. They said he couldn't have visitors because they don't allow it at the jail. Then a few days ago, a truck pulled up and three white men got out of it. They pulled a box out of the back of the truck and threw it in the yard. I wondered what the box was because it was only about three feet across. Then they got back in the truck and took off! I went and opened the box, and ...," Sarah's voice trailed off as she remembered the sight she saw when she opened the box. She unsuccessfully fought back the tears that were rolling down her cheeks. Her whole body shook in anger and in grief! "It was Uncle Huey," she said. "How could they do that to a man? How could any human being do that to a man?" She sobbed uncontrollably as she remembered her ordeal. Then she took a deep breath and continued to speak.

"It remind me of Charley. He been gone over ten years and we still don't know what happened. Now it's Uncle Huey. Nobody told us they moved Uncle Huey from the hospital, we just found out from somebody who worked there." Sarah's voice trailed off as she wondered what Uncle Huey had gone through before he died. But she vowed to give him a nice burial. They would bury him next to his beloved Arthina at St. Paul Cemetery. They would mark the grave with a wagon wheel as a way of showing that he was brought back by wagon when he died. They would plant flowers around the wagon wheel to make it beautiful.

"You know that Cousin Willie spent time in that jail." Sara continued. "He say that somebody told him that Uncle Huey died at least three months ago. Why would they keep his body for three whole months? He got family here worried about him. No tellin' what they did to him!"

Huey was buried two days later at St. Paul Cemetery in Taylor. The wagon wheel was polished and surrounded by beautiful flowers. A colorful sash was tied around it and it was laid on his grave. Next to the wagon wheel, they placed a decorative iron sculpture, which was about nine inches square. The piece was the same design as the one that lay above Arthina's grave.

Tommie stayed at the grave long after the others left. Like Sarah, he wondered about his father, Charley. "He must be dead now," he thought. "My daddy never came back, and now my granddaddy comes back in a little box." Once again, Taylor didn't seem like a place that he wanted to be. He had seen to many things in here. Colored men and boys swinging from trees or disappearing in the night. Fourteen-year-old boys, lynched. And it was too much to ask a man to stand ashamed, and mute while a white man disrespected him in front of his wife and children. Jails were filled with colored people convicted of crimes that they did not commit. He shuddered as he thought of the multitude of things that might have happened to his father Charley, and his Grandfather Huey. Tommie was a proud man. Too proud to subject himself to the drama of the south. The following day, he and Bessie went back to Houston.

However, they didn't stay in Houston long. Neither of them liked it much. It was a lot like Arkansas. It was still the south. They heard that many people were moving to Denver, Colorado. The west was supposed to be a better place for colored people. They thought that maybe they should try it. So, about six months later Tommie went to Denver and found a job as an elevator operator. He sent for Bessie and Hattie. Two weeks later they boarded a train with Stella, Calvin and Hattie's son, Golden, and joined Tommie in Denver. They heard that Denver would be a good place to raise a family. The only thing they missed about Houston was some of the relatives that still lived there. They hated leaving Shug, and their cousins, and friends. So, after staying in Denver for about a year, they decided to try Houston again, but they didn't like it any better the second time. They stayed there for about nine short months, just long enough to have their third child, Tommie Tim Lewis, Jr. They called him "Little T." After Little T was born, everyone began to call Tommie, Sr. "Big T" or "T.T." Soon after Tommie's birth, they went back to Colorado. They settled down in Denver in the mid 1940's. Tommie, Sr. reclaimed his job at the Kenmark Hotel.

The job as was never boring. Celebrities stayed at the hotel often. And oh! The stories they would tell while riding the elevator! Tommie discovered that the people who rode the elevator usually forgot that he was there. Or maybe they considered him part of the equipment. They would get on the elevator, and usually give him a little nod. "Going up?" he would say as he took them between the first and the 12th floor. Once they got on the elevator, they would talk as if he was invisible. More than once, he heard people planning all kinds of things, some of them clearly illegal, and others simply immoral. Occasionally out-of-towners would ask him for suggestions on where to eat, or where to go for entertainment. He quickly learned the best places downtown, and was always ready with a suggestion. In addition to the tips he made from operating the elevator, he often received good tips for his suggestions.

Denver was steadily growing during those years. The Black community was still segregated, primarily in the northeast section of town called "The Points," but there was a sense of family, and it held its own. The southerners tried to forget the horrors of lynching, and other wrongs in the south, and brought their children up to believe that they were just as good as anyone else. Other whites occasionally tested this theory. Although Denver was not as racist as most places in the south, it still had its own problems, and brand of racism. It was well known that Denver had a rather large Ku Klux Klan membership. Ben Stapleton, Mayor of the city during the forties, was proud to be associated with the Klan. There was even an airport in the Black community named "Stapleton Airport" after him. Many Blacks felt that this was a slap in the face. However, it was still better than the south, because the city was bigger, and there were more places to move about. More jobs were available to sustain the family. There were also many things that the south required of Blacks, that northern Blacks refused to do. Tommie decided to test the system one hot day in July. It was late in the day, one Thursday afternoon when he climbed on a bus and took a seat up front. There were no other seats. A white man got on the bus and looked at Tommie, expecting him to give up his seat. Tommie looked right in the white man's eyes and didn't budge. Later, Armstrong, one of Tommie's friends who had witnessed the event said to Tommie, "You've got a lot of nerve, T.T.! That cracker looked at you like he wanted to hurt you!"

"Well, all he can do is 'want'. We not in the south no more." Tommie retorted. "I got a right to sit where I want on any bus! I'd a busted that man in the head, if he da tol me to move!"

"Yeah, more like busted yo' neck trying to get off the bus if he'd a said something!" Armstrong laughed. "I saw you in the 'Crows' Nest' (balcony) at the picture show with all the other colored folk yesterday! You ain't crazy, T.T. You know when to hold 'em, and when to fold 'em!" Tommie laughed too. Armstrong was right.

They knew that even though Denver didn't have "colored only" signs like the South, you still had to stay "in your place." And when colored people went to the movies in Denver, there was an unwritten rule that they sit in the balcony while the white patrons sat downstairs in the main part of the theatre.

The elevator business lasted for about two years. Then someone came up with a bright idea of making elevators run automatically, and Tommie was out of a job. However, it was summertime, and he quickly found a job laying bricks. Bricklaying was a good job during the springtime and summer, but the weather in Denver was cold and snowy in the wintertime, and work was scarce. One day after a hard day laying bricks, Armstrong, came up to Tommie after work.

"T.T.," said Armstrong. "A few of us are going to get together and play a little poker after work. You want to come?"

"Sure," Tommie said. He had played a little poker when he was in the army and found that he was good at it. Of course, he didn't tell the others that he was good. That night he won $50 playing poker. The week after that he won $100. Tommie found that poker was a good way to make extra money for his family. Some days he lost, other days he won. Nevertheless, he played poker until he started to lose more than he won.

Tommie finally gave up the bricklaying job, because the weather so unpredictable. He had just come through a winter where it snowed more than usual, and it had been very hard to make ends meet. And there was another reason he needed to find something that paid better. That reason weighed six pounds, eleven ounces, and was 19 inches long. That reason was me.

***

I was the fourth child. Daddy (Tommie Lewis) named me Mary Jane. I was born on a cool day in February, at Denver General Hospital. Seven days later, I went home to Downing Street. Bessie, (who the kids called "Madea") had always wanted four children, and I made that wish come true. Two boys and two girls.

Daddy decided to go back into the shoe business. He and Ted, a long-time friend, opened a shoeshine shop on Welton Street, which was sometimes called "Black Wall Street," of Denver. In the 1950's, Welton Street was also the Black Cultural district in Denver. The area was called "Five Point's" because five streets came together at one intersection. Most of the community just called it "The Points." A club called the Rossonian headlined many of the popular colored singers like Sam Cooke, The Staple Singers, The Platters and others. Daddy even had a gospel group, the Golden Crown Gospel Singers who occasionally sang at the club. People from all over Denver came to hear them sing. They cut a record, and sang at most of the Black churches in Denver.

The shoe shop did a good business. Daddy taught his partner all about the business. Daddy put up most of the money for the shop. The agreement called for him to receive a higher split than Ted. But funny things started happening to the money. One Saturday in March, Daddy went down to the shop to pick up his portion of the split.

"I don't think I owe you any money, because you haven't been here enough," Ted stated.

"Ted, we been friends a long time. I *know* you are not going to try to cheat me!"

Ted squared his shoulders and looked directly at Daddy. "Ain't no 'cheat' about it, T.T... I sold your part to my brother and you are out!"

"We'll see about that!" Daddy went directly out of the shop and downtown to 16th street to see his attorney, "King" Trimble.

"Did you have a written agreement?" Attorney Trimble asked.

"Yes we did." Daddy showed him the writing and pointed to the notary seal on the document.

"Tommie," Trimble said. "We've got a problem. The notary seal was expired at the time that this contract was notarized! Now, T.T.," he continued, "I can represent you. But I don't think you have a leg to stand on by the looks of this contract." Tommie was not one to look back instead of going forward. He marched down to the shop and confronted Ted.

"Ted," he began, "I just went to see my attorney. And I guess you got away with cheating me this time. But I want you to know this. Until you do right by me, you won't have no peace of mind."

"With that he walked out of the door, and didn't look back." He started shining shoes again at the barbershop and made pretty good money from the celebrities who came to the shop. He also made a lot of friends while working in the shoe business. He collected autographs from many of them, such as Jack Benny, John Wayne, and Sammy Davis Jr. He bought a home on Larimer Street, and spent weekends with Bessie and the kids. The house was a small frame house that at one time had been a one-room house, but was now sectioned off to hold two bedrooms. A bathroom had been added inside the house. Well not exactly a bathroom. A tiny toilet was sectioned off in the kitchen. But it was ours! We had many good times at that house on Larimer St. I loved to watch Madea cook on the big coal stove. Then the home decorating bug got a hold of Daddy. When he got bored, he wallpapered the house or painted his old Cadillac. The neighbors loved to come over to see what crazy color the car was that week, or what crazy pattern graced the living room walls. He had his own way of painting the car. He would go to the store and get about ten cans of spray paint. Then he would cover the chrome, and spray away. Soon he had colors like no one had ever seen. Then he would go inside the house and get that week's rolls of wallpaper. Once he papered the house with such a crazy stripped pattern, that I thought the room was full of tiger's and couldn't go to sleep. Daddy changed the wallpaper to a nice beige pattern the next week, and decided to let it stay that way for a while.

Daddy continued to play cards occasionally. We were always excited to see the weekend coming because we knew it was time to do something fun! We went on outings frequently. We went to the mountains, or to the parks. Daddy and Madea loved to fish, and often piled all of us, and several of our friends into the 1949 Buick that he had bought. Sometimes we went on fishing trips for three days at a time, in Ogallala, Nebraska. We would make a campfire and have a great time.

By the early 1960's, the shoe business had slowed down considerably, forcing Daddy to go into another line of business. He heard that a family on Monaco Street, which, at the time was one of the most exclusive areas in Denver, was looking for a chauffeur. Daddy had never had a chauffeur's job, but he considered himself a quick study, and he liked to drive. When he got to the house on Monaco, a maid came to the door.

"Hi, I'm Ophelia." she said. "You must be T.T. Lewis."

"I am."

"Come on in. Mr. Friedman will see you shortly." Ophelia led Daddy down the hall to a parlor. There were four other men in the room, all waiting for an interview for the chauffeur's job. All of them were talking about their previous chauffeur's job. Tommie listened carefully, thinking to himself. "Well, I don't have any chauffeur experience, but I've got more class than these guys. I have a good chance of being hired."

Finally, Ophelia came and took Daddy back for his interview. Mr. and Mrs. Friedman were sitting at the end of a long oval table. They asked Daddy to take the seat next to them.

"Hello, (Mr. Friedman looked down at the paper), T.T. How much experience do you have chauffeuring?" asked Mr. Friedman.

"None." was the reply.

"Do you have a chauffeur's license?"

"No but I can get one."

"Okay." said Mr. Friedman. "Tell me about yourself."

Daddy and the Friedman's talked for a long time that day. They talked about chauffeuring, but they talked about many other things too.

Mr. Friedman was having a good time, because Daddy could be funny and could talk about almost anything with anybody. But he remembered that other people were waiting for him and decided to get back down to business. Finally, he said, "T.T., the job pays $60 per week. If we were to hire you could you work six days a week, and sometimes come in on a Sunday?"

"I can certainly work six days a week, but on Sunday, I spend the day with my family. I can't work on Sunday."

"Can't work a Sunday?!" Mr. Friedman was incredulous with

this bit of news.

"That's right," said Daddy "I just want to be up front with you, Mr. Friedman. I can work hard, I can work long, and I am a good driver. But I can't work on Sunday."

"Ok," said Mr. Friedman. "You can take a seat back in the parlor with the rest of the men. Me and Mrs. Friedman will make a decision in just a few minutes."

Ophelia took Daddy back to the parlor, and he sat down. Then she disappeared again through the double doors. The four men sat in the parlor and talked about their interviews. Rufus, the big one on the chair near the door said, "Boy! That Friedman is sure a tough nut to crack. The man doesn't even smile."

"That's right," the man on his left, said. "He's all business. He one stuffy old man! What'd you think T.T.?"

"Well, I didn't think he was bad." Daddy said. "I might even hire him!" They all laughed at that.

Finally, Ophelia returned and told the other men that they could go. Then she turned to Daddy. "T.T., Mr. Friedman wants to see you again."

Daddy walked back to the table and sat down. "T.T., I'll tell you the truth." Mr. Friedman said. "I have never had anyone come in for an interview that impressed me like you did. You seem comfortable in any situation, and you have a class. I know that you don't have any experience, and won't agree to working on a Sunday. But I like you, T.T. You're a good, hardworking man. I appreciate a man who puts his family first. Can you start on Monday?"

"Sure I can! Thank you." Daddy answered. Mr. Friedman showed Daddy the two cars that he would be driving. Both were black cars. One was a Chrysler, and the other was a Cadillac.

Then Mr. Friedman gave Daddy a list of things that he needed to do. He would have to get a chauffeur's license, and buy a suit. Tommie looked at the list. "Black suit. Black tie. White shirt. Black shoes. Black hat."

He went home and gave Madea the good news. "Red, I got the chauffeur's job," he announced. "They want me to buy a black suit, black tie, black shoes, a black hat, drive a black car, and *oh*, by the way, the Friedman's are *white* folks." They both got a good laugh at that!

For the next few years, Daddy drove for the Friedmans. They settled into a routine. Mr. Friedman would start each day with a trip to downtown to Denver's "Wall Street." Several times a week he took his toy poodle "Bon Bon" to the dog groomer (and everywhere else), and almost every evening, he went to the *Mile High Dog Track*. Daddy enjoyed the driving. Most of his time was his own. After he dropped Mr. Friedman off, he sometimes went home for the day or took Bon Bon for a walk in the park. Bon Bon loved to see Daddy coming, and he hated to see him go. Sometimes he whimpered and kicked up such a fuss when it was time for Daddy to leave for the night that Daddy would bring him home with Mr. Friedman's blessing. We all loved playing with Bon Bon.

Daddy grew bored one night while he was waiting for Mr. Friedman at the dog track. He had about four hours until it was time to pick him up. He parked the car in the special area that they had for chauffeur's and then he wandered into the dog track. He looked at the board and one of the flyers that "handicapped" the race. On the flyer, he noticed that one of the dogs had a very interesting name. The name was "Dumb Luck." He looked at the dog's statistics. The dog had a horrible record and was listed as a 20-1 favorite. But Daddy couldn't get over thinking that this was a lucky dog. He went up to the window and placed his bet. "Give me four dollars on number 12 in the 5th." The man behind the counter handed him two tickets on dog number 12. The fifth race was up next, and Daddy went out to the bleachers to watch it. A gunshot rang out and the cages opened up. A mechanical rabbit hopped in front of the dogs and the dogs began to chase it. The rabbit rounded the first corner. There were eight dogs chasing it. Number 3 was first. Next number 7, then 11, 17, 5, 14, 2, and finally Dumb Luck, number 12, brought up the rear. Daddy shook his head and mumbled to himself, "Oh, well, I guess there goes 4 dollars." Then the dogs rounded the second corner. Number 3 was still first then 11, 7, 17, 14, 12, 2, and number 5 was now bringing up the rear. Daddy watched while the dogs approached the third corner. Dumb Luck was gaining, and had pulled up to second place behind number 3! Daddy got real excited then, as the dogs rounded the third corner and headed into the home stretch. The beginning of the home stretch saw Dumb Luck running adjacent to number 3's hind legs. Mid-way on the home stretch it was Dumb Luck and number 3 neck and neck. At the finish line, it looked to Daddy that Dumb Luck had pulled in first, just about a nose ahead of number 3. Daddy looked excitedly at the scoreboard to see who had won the race. Under line number 5, where the winner of the 5th race was supposed to be posted, were the words "photo finish." Daddy was tense, now! He would have to wait for the judges to look at the film of the race in slow motion to see which dog had won. Finally, over the microphone, the judge announced, "We have a winner in the fifth race! The winner — by a nose — is number 12 — Dumb Luck!" Daddy clapped his hands and did a little dance. Dumb luck had sure been lucky for him tonight! He took his tickets to the counter, and watched the cashier count out eighty dollars to him. He put $60 in his pocket and got three tickets for the next race. He won the next race and turned those tickets in for the Twin Quinn, which was a good payoff if you could get back-to-back wins. The "Twin" paid off for Daddy. At the end of the evening, as he waited for Mr. Friedman back at the car, he smiled as he thought of the $786.00 he had won that night!

It was past midnight when Daddy strolled into his door at home. Madea heard him come in, and as she always did, she met him at the door and said, "Hi Honey. How was your night?"

"Fine! Just fine," said Daddy. He tried to keep a straight face, but after almost 30 years of marriage, Bessie knew that he was excited about something. She also smelled barbeque, and noticed the greasy brown bag that he was holding in one hand.

"Oh, Honey!" she smiled. "You stopped at Big Chef's!" She clasped her hands together. She loved Big Chef's barbeque. Daddy would frequently bring her a sandwich from Big Chef's or a Pig-ear sandwich from T.K.'s (Tamale King) which was a tiny walk-up stand on the "Point's." T.K.'s was famous for its hot dogs and pig-ear sandwiches in the 5 Points community.

She took the bag and noticed that it was full of sandwiches. "Honey, why did you get so many sandwiches?" she asked.

"Red, you know how much the kids like Big Chef's."

"I know, Honey, but there must be ten sandwiches in here." She followed him into the bedroom, still clutching the bag as he emptied his pocket on the dresser the way he did every night. But this time, what she saw made her jaw drop! "Honey!" she finally managed to find her voice. "Where did you get all that money?"

"Just Dumb Luck I guess!" he chuckled.

"Dumb Luck! What do you mean, Dumb Luck?"

Daddy laughed at her obvious confusion. Then he told her about the dog track and how Dumb Luck came in first. Madea was so excited that she forgot about the sandwiches until about half-hour later. She was too busy counting the money, and spending it in her mind. It was a good night! Tomorrow they could catch up on the bills, and have a little extra to do something with the kids!

Daddy went to the track again the next night. He took the "green sheet" with some dog's names that Madea had circled. "It looked to him like she picked all the wrong dogs! When he asked her why she picked them she just said, "I don't know. I just had a dream where a dog with a name like that one came in." Daddy shrugged his shoulders and played her numbers at the track along with his picks. All of her picks except one came in. None of his did. After that, Madea would do most of the picking. And Daddy tried to get her to sleep a lot more after that, so she could dream up a winner. He "played the dogs" two or three times a week after that. He would drop off Mr. Friedman at the track, and then park the car. Then he would go up to the south end of the stands and play the dogs. He would be at the car waiting when it was time to drive Mr. Friedman home. The four of us kids were old enough to stay at home now, so he would take Madea along with him on Saturday nights. By the end of the week, their winnings were often more than their losses and they came out ahead. Then one day, they hit it big at the track. $2,000 was a lot of money in those days. It was time to celebrate! They caught up on all the bills, and the next evening they went out for a nice dinner. When they returned, they parked in front of the house and noticed that the front door was wide open.

"Why is the door open?" Tommie asked Bessie? "Didn't you say that the kids all went to Lake McConaughy with the Phil?"

"Yeah." Bessie was clearly as confused as Tommie. "They won't be back until Monday."

Cautiously, they got out of the car. Tommie's first instinct was to protect his wife. "Stay back, Red!" he ordered. As Bessie stood back, Tommie went into the house. A few minutes later he emerged, and broke the news to Red. "They tore up the house pretty bad, but they're gone now." They went inside. The back door had been kicked in and was standing wide open. The kitchen window was broken. Glass littered the floor. Furniture was turned upside down. All of the mattresses were flipped over and strewn about. Dresser drawers had been tumbled over and lay in a heap on the floor. But the T.V. and stereo were untouched. Tommie and Bessie looked around but could not find anything missing." I wonder what they were looking for?" Red was obviously puzzled.

"Money, Red!" Tommie stated emphatically. "They thought that there was money laying around here and they were looking for money. A lot of people know the numbers that I play and figured out that I hit it big last night. They wanted to help themselves to some of that money."

"Well they sho' didn't find anything!" asserted Bessie.

"That's right, cuz there aint nothing here!" retorted Tommie. Tommie shook his head in disgust, and Bessie again looked at her disheveled home. Tommie headed for the telephone and dialed the police. Ten minutes later an officer came to the door and filled out a report on the break-in. Tommie boarded up the door and the window while the police surveyed the mess. After they left, he took Bessie by the hand and headed for the door.

"Come on, Red!" We can't stay here tonight. We're goin' down to the Stouffer's Inn, and get a room.

The hotel was just about a mile down the road on Quebec Street. A few minutes later, they arrived at the Stouffer's Inn. Their choices were $43.00 for a room without a bath versus $47.50 for a room with a bath. They opted for the latter. They were silent as they got settled into the hotel for the night. Finally, Bessie spoke.

"I sho am glad that we weren't home. What if we had been in there sleeping? They could have knocked us in the head!"

"Yep, they could have did that!" Tommie conceded.

"Red, I been thinking. Playing those dogs ain't helping us that much anymore. And it's just not worth it to have to watch my back whenever I get ahead a little. I'm getting a little tired of the dogs. I think I'm going to slow down some. I'll send the bookie with money every now and then, but maybe we can play bingo a little more just for fun.

"That sounds good to me!" Bessie replied.

The very next week, instead of heading for the dog track, they headed for the Bingo House. After playing bingo for a few months, they began to really enjoy it. They discovered that the volatile nature of playing the dogs was stress that they could do without. Bingo proved to be a relaxing time out, and almost as profitable as the dog track when averaging wins against losses. Bingo proved to be their new outlet.

A few months after the break-in, Tommie arrived for his regular shift at the Friedman home. When Ophelia answered the door, Tommie noticed that she seemed visibly upset, and had been crying. "Mr. Friedman died in his sleep last night. Mrs. Friedman is sending most of the staff home today.

Tommie continued to drive for Mrs. Friedman for a few months until she decided to move back to Oregon with her family. Her move to a new city meant the end of a job for him. But because Mrs. Friedman could not take Bon Bon to the apartment complex with her, Tommie was asked if he wanted to keep the dog that he had grown so fond of. Bon Bon became the newest addition to the Lewis family!

TEN GENERATIONS OF IMAGES

GREEN AND HATTIE HARRIS
MINDEN, LOUISIANA

HARMON CHARLEY WILSON LEWIS
CIR ABT 1900

SARA (HARRIS) LEWIS RANKINS
(mother of T.T. Lewis, and Hattie (Lewis) Mason

HUEY LEWIS
CIR ABT 1935

Tommie and Bessie 38th Anniversary, April 22, 1976

Stella, Calvin, Tommie Jr., Mary
Tommie Sr., Bessie Mae
25th Anniversary

GERTRUDE (PETERSON) CURBY

MOTHER OF BESSIE (McGEE) LEWIS

Dan McGee
Born 1871

Aunt Naomi

Aunt Hattie

Aunt Arlie

Aunt Essie

Favorite Aunts

Naomi Lewis Rice, Hattie Lewis Mason (Mama)
Arlie McGhee Glover, Essie McGhee,

The Lewis-Green Family Tree
2008

Family Cruise, 2012

*Andrew, Samuel, Nemo, Stan, Niecy,
Ojo, Johari, Phyllis, Dennis, Maxie, Dot, Zuton, Olisa
DJ, Brianne, Naomi, Andrew, Ashantay, Monye
Maxwell, Aina, Modupe, Elijah, Stanley, Monye*

The Green Family
Denver, Colorado, December 2003

Raisha

Kiante

Brianne

Aina, Monye, Ojo, Modupe

Phyllis, Zumante, Andrew, Samuel
Niamani, Ashantay, Naomi, Elijah, Stanley, DJ, Maxwell

The Murray Grandkids (top)
The Tolokun-Ajinaku Grandkids (center)
The Lucero-Mills Grandkids (bottom)

14

"You Can Go Home Again"

It was September 1962 when Western Union again came to the door with a telegram.

Madea opened the door. When she saw the deliveryman holding the long yellow envelope her heart sank. She knew that it was a telegram, and telegrams rarely brought good news.

"Yes?" she asked, trying to keep the panic that was building up from taking over her thoughts.

"Are you Mrs. Lewis?" the man asked. "I have a telegram for the Lewis family."

"Yes, I'm Mrs. Lewis."

The deliveryman pushed a clipboard and a pen towards her. "Please sign here."

The man was pleasant enough. However, the sense of panic was still bubbling beneath the surface when she closed the door and nervously tore open the envelope. Her knees buckled beneath

183

her as she dropped onto the sofa. The words on the page began to blur as she read them. Slowly the words sunk in.

"Sarah.....Lewis.....Rankin.....passed....this.....morning...../stop/ Please come home....."

"Oh, No!" she screamed as she put her head in her hands. "Not Miss Sarah! Not Miss Sarah!" She began to sob uncontrollably. She loved Miss Sarah very much. Miss Sarah was almost like a mother to her. Now she was dead. Finally, she managed to pick herself up off the sofa and she called Daddy. He came home immediately. When he opened the door, he called out to his wife. "Red!" She ran to him with the telegram still in her hands. As he realized that the mother he loved so dearly was gone, he began to sob. He had been very close to his mother, and the news of her passing hit him very hard. Daddy called Aunt Hattie who lived on Race Street, which was about two miles from our house. Aunt Hattie was overcome with the shock of her mother's death. Through the tears, she quickly threw some things into a suitcase, and was waiting when Daddy picked her up. The following morning at the first sign of daybreak, the three of them and my brother Calvin piled into the car for the 15-hour drive to Taylor. Calvin was now 18 years old and could help with the driving. They drove straight through and arrived in Taylor at about 9 o'clock that night. It was September, and they were fortunate that the roads were good and it didn't get dark until about 7:30. Everyone was still up when they got there. Daddy's knock at the door was answered by his brother, Henry. Henry was several years older than Daddy was, and had never moved from Taylor. He hugged Daddy and took him into the living room. Shug had driven in from Houston, and other family members had come in from Minden, Louisiana. All of Daddy's brothers and sisters were there. They talked long into the night. The following morning everyone gathered at St. Paul Church.

The entire community came to Miss Sarah's funeral. She was loved by all. She commanded the kind of respect that came from of being a strong but kind woman. Her funeral service went long into the afternoon as everyone took their turn telling about how much she had impacted their lives. They told fond stories about the "Crazy Indian," who could cook up a storm, and had a "salty tongue!" They told of her strength as she tried to find her husband Charley who had left home one day and never returned. And they told about her marriage to Ed Rankins, and how Ed and Sarah had helped each other get through the death of their spouses while building a new life together. They talked about her devotion to her family and to the Taylor community. After the stories, the singing, and the tears, six pallbearers picked up Sarah's casket and took it out of the back door of the church. St. Paul Cemetery was right behind the church, and within a few minutes, they reached the grave that had been dug for her. Her tombstone was grand in style, but simple in words. The gray granite stone was a large one. It was shaped like the hills of a mountain, and the face of it shone like diamonds in the sun. The stone simply said "Sarah Lewis Rankins 1875 - 1962." All the words that were needed had already been said at the service. Sarah was buried there, in the Lewis section, at St. Paul Cemetery on a crisp fall day in September.

On the way back to Denver, Madea and Daddy talked about all of the years that they had been away from Taylor. It was good to see everyone, but bittersweet because of it took Sarah's funeral to get everyone together. They talked about the other relatives who had been buried at St. Paul Cemetery while they had been away. There were a few cousins, and other relatives buried right there in the cemetery, who had died, and they had not even known about it.

Madea would have liked more time with her mother Gertrude, and her sisters Ollie and Essie. Madea and Daddy vowed not to stay gone so long next time. They decided that they would go home at least once per year, to see everyone during the good times. Mother's Day was a day when the families tended to get together, and was almost like a reunion. It would be a good time to go home every year. Mother's Day was about eight months away. They vowed to return and spend two weeks during that time. They kept that vow. After Grandma Sarah's funeral, they returned "home" for two weeks each May.

When Grandma Gertrude passed three years later, they were glad that they had made the decision to go back every year, because the decision had allowed them to spend time with Grandma before she passed.

Daddy would always try to save a lot of money to take back to Arkansas. When he arrived, he would delight in driving up in "his" shiny new Cadillac. Mr. Friedman usually let him use one of his credit cards, so Daddy would also have the "plastic" to throw down. That was something special because the *BankAmericard* was still in its infancy. The notion of a single credit card that you could use at many different stores was very unique at the time. The relatives in Arkansas, were proud of Daddy because he had "made it" in the big city! He and Aunt Hattie always went to Magnolia first to see Aunt Ollie and Aunt Essie. Daddy, Aunt Ollie and Aunt Essie would go to Lake Columbia in Arkansas to fish. Sometimes Madea would go too, but most times, she would stay in and watch "her stories." She especially liked "The Edge of Night," and "The Secret Storm." She had been watching them for years, ever since they stopped playing them on the radio and started playing them on TV.

Other times they would go to Taylor to fish. Taylor had some nice ponds where the catfish were so big that they would almost break your line. They would fill up the ice cooler, and head back to Magnolia.

Mother's Day was always a good time. Bethlehem Church and St. Paul Church always had a big crowd on that Sunday. They looked forward to hearing Daddy, Madea and Aunt Hattie sing. There was always plenty of local, and out of town, Gospel groups that "brought it home" on Mother's day. It seemed like the two weeks always went by quickly, and they would be on their way home to Denver.

The drive to and from Arkansas was part of the fun. One time they stopped at a church in Oklahoma. There was a preacher there who people came from near and far to see. It was there that

Daddy had an experience that really surprised him. The services that night were intense. The minister was known as a "healer," and many people that evening claimed to be cured from various illnesses. Daddy was skeptical until it came time for him to rid himself of his aching back. He went down to the stage and took the minister's hand. Before he knew it, his tongue felt heavy in his mouth. Then suddenly it felt light as a feather, and a string of words that he had no control over, came out of his mouth. He was speaking in "tongues!" He had heard, and seen many people speak in tongues, but it was the first time that it happened to him. Now he was a believer, and his back was healed.

Daddy and Madea continued on their journey stopping at various yard sales, antique shops and roadside markets along the way. They took their time, and stopped frequently to shop or just to look. By the time they got back home, they usually had a trunk full of stuff. They had so much stuff, that Daddy decided to try to sell some of it at the flea market in Denver. Daddy was the kind of man who could sell a man the Brooklyn Bridge in the desert. The flea market was a profitable business for them.

Sometimes me, Stella, or some of our children went to the flea market to see them. It was not unusual to look up and have 10 or 12 family members who just "popped up" at the market. Madea and Daddy loved it when we did that because we all had our own homes now. It was always like an impromptu reunion.

Black
Power

The Eighth Generation

The "Black Power Movement"

Stella & Bobby, Calvin & Carol, Tommie Jr., & Brandi, Mary & Dennis

OLYMPIC GOLD MEDALISTS
Peter Norman, Tommie Smith, John Carlos
Black Power Salute

15

Black Power"

"**W**hat do we want??!!"
"When do we want it??!!"
"Now!!"
"WHAT DO WE WANT??!"
"JUS-TICE."
"AND WHEN-DO-WE-WANT IT??!!!"
"NOW!!!"

Me, Ladana, and about thirty other teen-agers marched in a circle around the Denver Police building. Last night the police had broken up a party in the neighborhood. They had thrown a tear gas grenade into a house to break the party up. The party had been a peaceful one. But the practice of stopping teens from gathering had become the main focus of the Denver Police Department. Any gathering at a home in Park Hill was sure to bring tear gas raining down on its participants. And teens gathered frequently. Sometimes aspiring musicians had parties and charged 25 cents to raise money for band equipment. Other times people held "rent parties" to help someone raise money to pay that month's rent. The word was out that you had better have your fun early because the "pigs" were going to "turn it out" with their tear gas by eleven o'clock. But at about 9:30 last night a 6-month old baby was caught in the crossfire and taken to the hospital. The baby had become very ill from the effects of the tear gas. As the ambulance arrived, people began to gather outside the home on Jasmine Street. As they heard that a baby was hurt in this latest attack, the whole neighborhood was enraged. It was bad enough that others had been hurt in the past. However, this time, a child lay sick in the hospital. Very sick. The party had been a private birthday party, attended by mostly young parents and their children. However, to police in a Black neighborhood in 1965, "thou shalt not gather" was the eleventh commandment. The civil rights movement was in full swing. And that meant that there was always a standoff between the police and the Black community.

Picket lines, sit-ins, and protests were commonplace in the 60's, especially in the Black community. However, the civil rights movement had been gaining momentum since slavery. Before 1865, the movement was about abolishing slavery. Between 1865 and about 1875, reconstruction brought on a multitude of new challenges. The first challenge was "just how free, is free?" The fight was on between the southern planters who wanted to find ways to keep their "property in slaves," (mostly by using loopholes in the new laws) and the formerly enslaved Africans who wanted to obtain equal rights with whites. Then there was a tug-of-war between Blacks who wanted to hold political office, and whites who still viewed them as too intellectually inferior for such an honor. Then in 1896, after years of the "color line," "separate but equal," (Jim Crow) was solidified, after Homer Plessy, a man who was 7/8ths white, lost his bid to legally integrate train cars. Many felt that the "separate but equal" doctrine contributed to the many lynching's that followed over the next years. Blacks were hung for numerous "so called" infractions. It seemed that almost daily, there was a Black man lynched for (supposedly) looking at a white woman.

The practice of lynching came to a head in 1955 when Emmett Till, a 14-year old boy, was lynched in Money, Mississippi for whistling at a white woman. Emmett's beaten and bloated body was found floating in the Tallahatchie River. Enraged, and overcome with grief, Emmett's mother decided to have an open viewing at the funeral, so that everyone could see the "face of racism." Jet magazine and National T.V. were instrumental in helping to get the story and the images out. 1955 was a tumultuous year that would see the end of the bus boycott, and the fight over school desegregation. The Supreme Court finally struck down the "separate but equal" mandate and ordered the schools to be desegregated. However, it wasn't over yet! There were still serious problems with social equality. First, when the Supreme Court required that schools be desegregated, they mandated that desegregation would take place with "all deliberate speed." "Deliberate speed" meant different things to different legislators. To some it meant the schools could start with kindergarten children and integrate the schools one year at a time until all the grades were desegregated. Others interpreted the term to mean that they could allow one or two "negroes" per year until racial balance was achieved. Some governors outright refused to obey the law, prompting the President to send the military in to enforce it. I tuned to the news one evening just in time to see a re-run of part of Governor Wallace's inaugural address. He was standing on the portico of the Alabama State Capital, at the same place where Jefferson Davis had previously been sworn in as President of the Confederate States. Wallace had an angry, defiant look on his face. It caught my attention because Wallace was no friend of the Black race and his presence on the news could only mean trouble for the Black community. Wallace was outraged at the mandate to desegregate Alabama schools. With a finger in the air and shouting to the masses he declared, "Segregation now! Segregation tomorrow! Segregation forever!" The white crowd went wild! They clapped vigorously and shouted their approval, thankful that he would not allow Black children in "their" schools. At that moment, I vowed to never forget Governor Wallace's treatment of Black children. I knew that the day would come when Wallace would have to eat his words! We were determined to integrate the schools. I knew that one day, Wallace would have to apologize, and admit that he was wrong!

Black people still had trouble exercising their right to vote, especially in the South. And even though segregation in *schools* was no longer legal, that did not mean that there could not be segregation in *other places*, such as housing. So, there was still a call for equality. Now it was the 60's. And that day in 1965, the protest at the police building was picking up speed.

The picketers marched around the police building, circling it repeatedly. We wanted someone in authority from the police department to come out and talk to us about last night's attack. Questions needed to be answered. People were asking why the Black community was under attack even in their own homes. We wanted to know why the police were so trigger-happy when it came to Black teens.

"Come out!" we shouted. "Face us! Face us!" we chanted repeatedly.

Things had been especially bad in the Black communities across the nation for the past few years. John Kennedy, the president who many Blacks viewed as their hope for the future, had been gunned down during the height of his Presidency. Many Blacks who took to the streets were hosed down with fire hoses. The hoses had enough power to tear the bark off trees. Others found themselves fighting the teeth of German Sheppard police dogs. Television had become commonplace by this time, and the actions of the police had created a backlash nationwide.

Sure enough, after Kennedy's assassination, some of the hard fought rights in the new civil rights bill seemed to be under attack. We held out hope that the voter's rights bill would be passed. It had been almost one hundred years since Blacks got the right to vote, but America (primarily the South) still used different methods to prevent us from casting our ballots. Poll taxes, literacy tests, intimidation, and various methods were used to disenfranchise Blacks from the ballot box. Today's youth were determined that they would make a difference. Gone were the days when we would sit idly by and let the "white devil" take over!

The picketing went on until late in the day. Finally a police officer came out and announced that a community meeting was planned for the following Friday. Satisfied, we went home to plan our next move. But it was not to be. On Thursday, the police department announced that they were still "reviewing the situation" and would postpone the meeting until they could come up with a "workable solution." Two months later, the meeting was scrapped.

Many blamed the police inaction on the fact that Blacks had little power in Denver. Denver did not have a large Black population. The population was about 10% Black. Most lived in the Cole area, which was about a 2-mile square area. It was prior to the Fair Housing Act and segregated neighborhoods were the norm. Neighborhood housing codes could prevent Blacks from moving into any given neighborhood. There was much discussion about Blacks moving out of the Cole Area, and into the Park Hill area, which was just east of Cole. Park Hill was a newer development. Most of the homes had been built in the mid-fifties, and the homes were built from brick. They were sturdy, beautiful homes. Many were large, and had huge basements and back yards for the children. The greenery was very beautiful, and most streets were named for a tree, a bush or a shrub. The streets all had flowery names like Albion, Birch, Cherry, Dahlia, Elm Street, and Holly Street. Trees in the area were planted when the community was first built, and now, many of the shade trees made a majestic canopy over the streets in the neighborhood. There were a few Black families who managed to obtain housing in the area, even though it meant facing the wrath of whites, and sometimes bodily injury. They were the warriors. They were willing to stand their ground even in the ugly face of racism. But it would be a few more years before Blacks would, under the umbrella of law, move to "The Hill" in large numbers.

Ladana, Janiqua, Demetria, and I, were always picketing for one thing or another. We called ourselves the *Posse*. Ladana and Demetria were 14 years old at the time. Janiqua and I were both fifteen. We went to school together and tried to "look out" for each other. We had made a pact that our kids would not grow up and be second-class Black citizens. We were sitting in the park one day, talking about what we would do when Black people got their "due." James Brown's hit single, *"Say it Loud, (I'm Black and I'm Proud)"* was playing on an 8-track tape in a car that was parked at the curb. The song always motivated the *Posse* to make plans for the next protest.

The 60's era had taken the music world and turned it on its head. We got rid of the Big Band music of the 40's, and Poodle Skirts of the fifties. When I was little, my sister, Stella taught me how to do the "Texas Hop," and how to appreciate Nancy Wilson. After she taught me how to "hop," I loved to dance. Then the Elvis generation took over for a while until the Beatles, those four British hellions hit it big. I even listened to the Beatles before Diana Ross and Motown popped up. But once *soul songs* evolved, there was no looking back! Music defined our world. *"Say it Loud – (I'm Black and Proud)"* signified a new awareness of our race. Curtis Mayfield and Gil Scott Heron rapped about discrimination, power, and the Vietnam War. Up and coming trio's and quartets could be found on any neighborhood corner and in garages that served as local recording studios.

Out went the pressing combs in favor of the Afro. Dashiki outfits added an array of color to the neighborhood attire. Pro-Black jewelry like afro combs and Black-Power fists became an unspoken statement that we were indeed Black and Proud and "down for the cause." Armed with our music, our Afro, and our new attitude, we were always ready for the next protest!

"We need to get everybody in the neighborhood to march down to that police department and stay there until they listen to us!" I said. "Last week they beat poor Bosco 'til he was almost dead. Every time we do *anything*, they're on us like white on rice!"

"Mary, they don't care 'bout nobody marching!" Ladana was clearly agitated as she spoke. "We need to string one of em up — then they'll listen. I bet if it was one of those little white kids who got beat up or tear-gassed, they'd listen to us. That's what we need to do. Tear gas one of those little white kids."

Even though Ladana was only 14 years old, she always added a year to her age to make herself seem older. She said that she was fifteen, and most people believed it. Especially since she *seemed* much older. Ladana did what she wanted. Sometimes she would leave home for 3 days at a time. She would hang out at the park, or sometimes stay at someone's house. When she got tired of that, she would go back home. It didn't seem like she ever got in trouble for running away. She lived a street life and was usually more aggressive in her suggestions about how to protest. But now, everyone nixed snatching a white kid and tear-gassing him.

"Oh, please," said Janiqua, "Anyone who looks crossways at those white kids will end up in jail for life!"

The meeting between the teens in the neighborhood, and the Denver Police Department never materialized. Soon the last picket line was just a memory in everyone's mind. The use of tear gas did seem to decrease a bit. The baby's health improved. Even the white people in the Community took notice of a baby getting hurt, and many joined in the protests. Finally, the neighborhood went back to being calm and peaceful and the Posse settled down a bit. That is until one day, we met at the park and Ladana made her big announcement.

"I'm pregnant!" she announced flatly.

"Pregnant?!" Janiqua said. "You ain't even 15 yet. How can you be pregnant?"

"Robbie Willis got me pregnant." Ladana sat down on the grass and began to fiddle with imaginary lint on her pants. "But he don't believe it's his. That's 'cause Mrs. Willis told him that it better not be his!" She tried to make light of it, and smile through her pain. But somehow, the smile never reached her eyes.

Mrs. Willis had a reputation in the neighborhood for being "High Falutin." She usually worked very hard to make sure that her son's stayed away from girls who she considered low class. As far as Mrs. Willis was concerned, Ladana was one of those girls.

Janiqua looked at Ladana in disbelief. "Did you tell your Grandmama?" she asked.

"I told her," Ladana answered.

"What'd she say?" Demetria and I asked in chorus.

Ladana let out a big sigh before she spoke. She was trying to decide whether or not to tell us what her Grandmother had said. Then she got the kind of crooked little grin on her face that she always got when she was going to say something sarcastic. She decided that she might as well tell us what her grandmother had said. It really didn't matter to her whether we knew or not.

With her hands on her hips, she imitated her Grandmother. "She looked at me and said, 'I didn't think you were old enough to even know what your coochie was for. And now you saying you're 'pregnant'? That's all she said." Ladana went back to picking at her imaginary lint.

We fell quiet for a long time. Finally, Demetria broke the silence. "You keeping it? You know you can take some Quinine or drink a bottle of castor oil and get rid of it. Or you can do like Marcella did and get an abortion. I know of a lady that they say will do you an abortion for $200. Make Robbie pay it!"

"Ain't nobody taking my baby!" Ladana got angry by the very mention of the word "abortion."

"I wasn't raised up like a normal kid! I just *grew up*, period! My baby is going to be raised up like it should. Besides, Marcella almost died from that back-alley abortion. It ain't worth it! It just ain't worth it!"

By Christmas of that year, Ladana had a beautiful baby girl. She named the baby Trisha. Trisha was tiny, and a very happy baby. Ladana took Trisha home from the hospital, vowing to take good care of the baby, at least as good as a fifteen-year-old could. But soon, Ladana left home again. One cold day she rang my doorbell. Madea went to the door and saw Ladana standing outside on the porch, holding the baby in her arms and looking like a lost kitten.

Madea looked down at Ladana and the baby. "Ladana. Hi." she said. "Come on in. Mary's back there somewhere." Madea pointed to the back of the house.

Ladana knew that I had told Madea about the baby. She wasn't sure if Madea would even let me even talk to her again, much less invite her in. Many parents in the neighborhood considered Lanada a "bad influence" on their children because her family was not as strict as most other families in the neighborhood. But Madea didn't bat an eyelash. "Oh Ladana! What a beautiful baby," she said.

Madea had seen Ladana sitting over at the park for the past few days. She figured that she had either run away, or had been kicked out of the house. Either way, she knew that she could not turn her back on a child. Especially a child, *with* a child. She went into the bedroom and came back with a large empty drawer. She lined the drawer with blankets and a tiny pillow, and took the baby from Ladana. She put the sleeping baby in the makeshift bassinet, and put her arms around Ladana.

I looked at the scene unfold before me. I wasn't surprised by Madea's actions. She always watched out for the kids in the neighborhood. Our house was a favorite place among them. She always listened to them, and she never judged them. But Ladana was pleasantly surprised that Madea genuinely cared about her. She listened intently while Madea helped her mix the Karo syrup with the canned milk and water to make the baby formula. Then Madea pulled the baby bottle sterilizer from under the sink, and helped Ladana load the bottles into carrier. She placed the sterilizer on the stove and turned the burner on "high" and instructed

Ladana to let the water boil for about 25 minutes to sterilize the milk. She was very careful to make sure that Ladana knew how to cool the milk and test it by dropping a few drops onto her wrists to make sure that it wasn't too hot for the baby.

After that day, Ladana came over every day, and we adopted each other as sisters. We felt that now, more than ever, we had a reason to make the world a better place. Ladana was determined that Trisha would not grow up in a world where Blacks were relegated to second-class citizenship.

By 1968, the Fair Housing Act was passed and many more Blacks began to move into the Park Hill neighborhood. We moved to Ivanhoe Street. Ladana was one block east, on Ivy Street. Demetria and Janiqua lived on Cherry Street. We frequently walked to each other's homes. The entire Park Hill neighborhood was our back yard. However, when Black people began to move into the Park Hill area, most of the white people promptly moved out. It only took a few years for the neighborhood to go from almost all white, to almost all Black. This phenomenon was repeated all over the United States. It was so common, that one phrase became well known for the practice. They called it "White flight." Nevertheless, the Black people who moved into the neighborhood were proud of their accomplishment. The neighborhood took shape as a nice, new Black community. Many of us felt that we had finally "arrived."

I was now in the eleventh grade. Ladana had stopped going to school earlier that year, and wasn't sure she wanted to go back. Most of girls who got pregnant, had babies or got married while they were in school were promptly kicked out. Most of them just went to school and didn't tell about their situation, but Ladana didn't want to hide the fact that she had a child.

Then came the day that changed the face of the neighborhood. The announcement came over the PA system at school. "Martin Luther King Jr. has just been shot." Manual was a Black school, and many of the teachers were crying, and overcome with anger and with grief. The principal let school out early that day. I rushed home and found the *Posse* at my house staring at the TV. Martin Luther King had been killed. Everyone watched the news in shock, and disbelief. Suddenly we heard gunshots coming from outside the window. From the back window, we could see the shopping center that housed a King Soopers grocery store, a five and dime store, a bank, and other small shops. The shopping center was on fire! Fire trucks started arriving as people were looting and trying to get food and other items out of the stores. Finally, hours later the fire was extinguished. Nevertheless, the stores in the shopping center were burned down, and gutted out. There was also a shopping center on Dahlia Street about five blocks away. Safeway and other shops anchored the Dahlia Street Shopping Center. By the end of the day, both shopping centers were completely destroyed. The face of Park Hill was changed forever!

At the time, people talked about rebuilding. The *Posse* and many others in the community were angry that people had burned up their own neighborhood. In the end, it was the Park Hill neighborhood that suffered by its own hands. Most of the white and Jewish people, who ran their businesses in Park Hill, lived elsewhere in the city. Now they were gone, and the businesses were boarded up! Ladana and I looked at the burned-out, water soaked ruins. It seemed like all of our marching, and sit-ins and singing "we shall overcome," had been for nothing. It seemed as though every time there was a leader, who pledged to help Blacks get ahead, that leader was killed. Medger Evers. Malcolm X. John Kennedy. Robert Kennedy. And now, Martin Luther King. Dead! We felt that we were assassinated by the bullets that went through these men, because they shattered the Black neighborhood in their wake.

As I watched the ashes simmering, my mind flashed back to the wood-burning stove in the kitchen where I grew up. I remembered being 5 years old and living in our old house on Larimer Street. I thought about the baths I took in the big metal tub that sat next to the wood-burning stove. The house had just cold running water. Bath time or washing dishes meant that big pots of water would be heated on the stove, and then poured into the tub for a hot bath.

I remembered the fun that the 35-or-so kids on Larimer Street had together. Everyone loved Madea, and my house was the place to be. We played games like "kick the can", and "hide and seek. We played "ring around the rosies" and the song always ended with, "the last one down is a nigger baby." Not knowing at the time what a "nigger baby" was, I always made sure that I was not the last one to fall down! I had mostly fond memories of Larimer Street. However, as I stared into the burnt out buildings in the shopping center, a few bad memories crept into my mind. I remembered sitting on the step next to my house one Saturday afternoon. Most of my friends had gone to the Little Flower center to play. I had been there before, and I knew how much fun it was. I loved to play games, tap dance, and make crafts at Little Flower. However, that Saturday, I couldn't go. There was a "new lady" at the door who wouldn't let "coloreds" inside. So I sat on the step and wondered why I couldn't go. Madea had always told me that I was as good as everyone else, so why wasn't I good enough to go to Little Flower? A few months later, someone else was at the door and they started letting Blacks in again. Nevertheless, sitting on the step, all alone, because of the color of my skin, was something that I never forgot.

School was another bad memory. Not school itself. I just hated the first part of every school year. At the beginning of each year, I was put into a remedial class which was called "the developmental class." These classes were always reserved for the kids who were thought to be slow or "retarded." The classes were mostly Black. Whereas the schools of 10 years ago were completely segregated, the schools in the late 50's and early 60's had "in-school" segregation. This phenomenon was repeated all over the country. School segregation was no longer legal. But many schools compensated by putting Black children and white children in different classrooms." My school was no different from the rest. Most of the white kids were automatically placed into "accelerated" classes — away from the Black kids. Like the majority of the other Blacks,

I was automatically placed into "developmental" classes. But every year, after about the second week, they moved me out of the "developmental" class and placed me into "accelerated classes." I loved to read. And I could read better than almost anyone in my class. I recalled how I read so much that in second grade, my teacher sent a note home to my mother, telling her to stop letting me read so much, because I was too far ahead of the other (Black) kids. They didn't want to keep putting me into classes where I was "out of place." Madea angrily tore up the note and told me to keep on reading as much as I wanted to.

I had one favorite book at home. It was called *Beezuz and Ramona*, by Beverly Cleary. I read that book over and over again. One of my favorite times was when the Bookmobile came to the neighborhood and we were allowed to borrow books. I would get two books, and I usually read both of them the same evening. Then I would wait impatiently for the next Bookmobile.

My mind snapped back to the present. It seemed to me that things hadn't changed much since I was 5 years old and sat on that step while my friends went other places. We still had a long way to go to "overcome."

Now, Ladana was saying something about going to the Swamp that night.

"You're going to the Swamp?" I asked. I loved to go to the Swamp. I loved to dance and I could dance all I wanted there.

"Yeah," Ladana replied. "We're going to have a meeting and then were gonna jam!" Ladana did a little jig, previewing the dance that she would do that night. The Swamp was the local teen hangout in the Park Hill neighborhood. It was a club that was decorated like a murky forest, and that's where it got its name. The Swamp was known for a drink called "swamp water." Swamp water was a combination of a bunch of different kinds of soda, with a little extra cherry juice mixed in. Everyone went there after school and sometimes on weekends. At least they went when their parents let them. Ladana and Demetria went any time they wanted. They had no curfew, and frequently stayed out very late. For Janiqua and me it was a different story. Janiqua had to be home before midnight. And I only went when my brother Tommie agreed to go and look out for me. But the Swamp was always a good time. Everyone drank swamp water and "jammed" to whatever song was on top that week.

The *Posse* hit the club at about 6:00 that evening. When we hit the door, Junior Walker's song *"Shotgun"* was floating through the room. I jumped on the dance floor. I liked dancing to that song. Everyone was doing a dance called the "shotgun." Soon my good friend Bosco started dancing with me. Then the song changed to the "The Jerk." Ladana and Janiqua hit the floor then. Everyone was doing the "Jerk." Before the evening was over, we had danced to the Supremes, Aretha, and the Temptations. Motown had arrived! Ladana could dance the "dog" better than anyone else on "the Hill," and closed out the evening with everyone in a circle around her while she "dogged," and then "walked the dog." The meeting would wait for another night.

The next year, I graduated from Manual high school. It was the end of an era. 1969 was the last year that all-Black schools were supposed to exist. Bussing was to start the following year in an attempt to finally integrate the schools, almost 15 years after *Brown vs. Board of Education,* struck down the "Separate but equal" doctrine. Other methods for desegregating the schools had not worked, and bussing was the last ditch effort. After graduation, the *Posse* went in different directions. Demetria had a baby and moved to California. By now, Ladana had two children, and was often homebound. Janiqua and I were both 18 years old, which was old enough to get into the NCO club at Lowery Air force base.

Janiqua loved the NCO club. Servicemen with money! It was practically her motto. We got dressed to the 9's on Saturday nights and "made the rounds" at the club. One night Janiqua was particularly happy because there were a lot of "new" men at the club. It was the 1st of the month, which meant "payday" for the servicemen. Janiqua and I were sitting in a booth having a drink when Dennis Green walked into my life.

A band was singing Aretha Franklin's song *Respect* when he walked into the club. People began to jump on the dance floor. Respect was one of my favorite songs to dance to, and I jumped on the dance floor too, hoping that some nice young man would join me on the floor. The "bump" was in that year and it was no fun to bump alone. I bumped to the left, and then jumped up, turned, and bumped to the right. As my hip bumped right, Dennis appeared with a welcome left hip. Then we danced the "double bump," and then the "foot bump." By the end of the evening, we had "bumped" the night away. I had found my match on the dance floor. Dennis could do the splits, ease on up, and flow into a bump without missing a beat.

We were the last to leave the NCO club. Neither of us wanted the evening to end, so we headed for a local restaurant and had a late meal. We passed Janiqua on the way out, and she linked her arm through her serviceman and waived. She had found herself a serviceman, who had stripes and more stripes. Janiqua was in hog heaven!

After the meal, Dennis and I reluctantly said goodnight, and each went our own way. Before our goodbye's, I gave Dennis my phone number, and he promised to call me the next day. "Yeah. Right!" I sarcastically muttered under my breath. I was almost sure that although we had both enjoyed the evening together, I had better not wait by the phone, because "I'll call you," usually meant squat at the NCO club. Besides, Dennis had said that he only had about two more weeks before he had to go to the Air Force Base in Arizona. I didn't want to emotionally invest two weeks in someone who was leaving town. Servicemen were not reliable for long distance relationships. They blew in and out of town like a south wind. Sometimes they left babies in their wake. I didn't want any part of that.

Nevertheless, the following day, my phone rang at 12:37 pm, the exact time that Dennis said he would call. We spent that day, and every single day of the next two weeks together. When I drove him to the airport, I couldn't seem to stop the great big tears that ran down my cheeks as Dennis boarded the plane. I thought that it would be the last time that I would see him. Before he boarded the plane, he promised me that he would call often. but I doubted it. I felt that just because *I* thought that I couldn't live without Dennis, it didn't mean that he felt the same way. But I was wrong. Four days later, my phone rang. "Hey Babe." Dennis' voice was a welcome surprise. "Whatchu doing?" he asked.

"I'm just sitting here listening to some music," I said.

"Stay right there!" Dennis said. "I'm in Denver. I'll be there at 3:42." True to his word, Dennis walked into my apartment at 3:42 that afternoon. Two days later, he went back to Arizona. But we wrote each other every day and visited each other whenever possible for the next two years. We were married the following May, over Memorial Day weekend, because it just seemed like the perfect time for a wedding.

***

The 1970's era was a volatile time for the civil rights movement. Bussing was now in full swing, but no one really seemed to like it. It meant getting up at the crack of dawn to go to a school far away from home. I always thought that they should just "bus the books," and leave the kids alone. I didn't think that Black kids needed to sit next to some white people to get smart. Just bus the books, good teachers, and materials that were needed in the classroom. That was my theory.

16

"An Oral History"

In 1977, the mini-series *Roots* ran for 6 nights on television. The series would prove to be a major turning point for many Black's and a wake-up call to both Blacks and whites during that time period. The series was about Kunta Kinte who was born free in Gambia, West Africa, and then enslaved in the American Colonies in the 18th century. Kunta made sure that his family history was passed down to each generation that came after him. Finally, his 4th great-Grandson, Alex Haley, researched the story, found his way back to Gambia, and then wrote the book, *Roots*. Later, the book was made into a mini-series.

Many of us watched the series in groups. I watched all six episodes. We found it riveting. By the last day of the series, it seemed as though the nation got a much-needed lesson in Black History. Many Blacks adopted new names for themselves. No longer, were we Negro, or Colored. Now we were Afro-Americans, or for the truly enlightened, African-Americans. Roots brought a new sense of pride, identity and validation for everything we were attempting to accomplish from the civil rights movement.

Prior to *Roots*, many people had a distorted view of slavery, if they knew about it at all. Most of the schoolbooks that were written after emancipation carefully left out any mention of slavery. They might refer to "servants on the grounds," but the ugly truth was always distorted. The few books that were published on the subject were usually written by whites, and typically portrayed Blacks as either "uncivilized heathens," or "meek and grateful" that they had been "rescued" out of Africa. *Roots* changed all of that. Even though some "Afro Americans" were angry that *Roots* didn't go far enough in showing the true horrors of slavery and the period immediately after emancipation, most were truly enlightened, and happy that a piece of their history was finally revealed. Some felt vindicated, after being told for years that "Blacks had no history."

But *Roots* brought something else. Not only did some African-Americans change their names, and rid themselves of their "slave name," many began an intense search for *their* roots. I was one of those people.

I started asking questions of Madea and Daddy. Every day I had a new question.

"Where were you born, Daddy?"

"I was born in Taylor, Arkansas. The population was only 657!" Daddy loved talking about his past. He told about growing up on the farm. They raised hogs, and cattle. They had a fruit orchard and grew plenty of vegetables. He had a lot brothers and sisters. I asked some of the questions many times. And he would always answer.

Madea chimed in with *her* version of Daddy's upbringing. "Yes, honey, "THEY — raised hogs and cattle, but that doesn't mean your Dad did any of that work. Your Dad was really spoiled. Miss Sarah cussed up a storm and boy, would she tell you off if you made her mad. But she never even spanked your Daddy. He got anything that he wanted. And he never had to work like we did.

His family had money! They owned their own ranch. All the kids had their own horses. *We* picked cotton and walked wherever we wanted to go."

Daddy didn't appreciate being called spoiled. He was quick to deny it. "I worked just as hard as the rest of em."

"Honey, no you didn't." She looked at me. "We didn't have it as good as your Dad did. We didn't own our house. Your Grandma Gertrude worked at the hospital. The hospital was in Doctor Hudnall's house. We lived in a room over the hospital. Mama cooked and cleaned the hospital and did what she could to help Dr. Hudnall and take care of us. We had to pick cotton and sell it for 25 cents a pound. Your Dad didn't do that, but we sure did! We picked cotton and cut cane. Sometimes they would give us some of that cane. Boy was it good, too!"

"Madea, where were you born?"

"I was born in Minden, Louisiana, but I was raised up in Taylor. We lived with my Grandfather Frank. He was a Methodist preacher. Your Grandpa Frank married seven times. Miss Ola was the last one. She was a lot younger than your Grandpa though. We called her "Aunt Sis" Her and Mama were about the same age."

"Did you get to know your grandmother?" I asked Madea.

"No. She died when I was real little. But I remember they called her Kitty."

"Did you have any other uncles besides Uncle Jimmy?"

"Oh yeah, but they weren't raised up together. They got separated as children. And your Grandma Kitty's kids weren't raised together either. They say that some of em got separated in slavery. Let me see!" Madea began to count them off on her fingers. "Now, Uncle Willie was raised a Jordan but he kept the name Peterson too. He always did tell people his name was 'William Peterson Jordan.' I guess he liked the way it sounded. Then one of your Uncles was a Henderson, and he lived in Stamps. You got some Tyson cousins too. Your Uncle Sang was a Tyson. He was your grandpa Frank's brother, so that would make him my great uncle."

They went on for hours. I was delighted to witness this exchange. Soon Madea and Daddy forgot that I was even there as they rehashed the past. I furiously took notes, trying to keep up with their conversation. It was quite a task figure out who was an Uncle, and who was a Great Uncle. But now I had enough information to start putting together the family history. I drew a chart with what I knew: Daddy's parents were Sarah and Charley. Charley's parents were Huey and Arthina. Sarah's parents were Green Harris and Hattie Harris. I put down the chart. That was as much as I knew that day. I would continue another day.

My next step was to question Aunt Hattie. Aunt Hattie was my father's sister. She was about three years older than Daddy, and a lot more blunt. She never pulled any punches. When you went to Aunt Hattie's house you could be sure that there would always be a pistol and a bottle of Chivas Regal in full view. A half-empty glass of whiskey usually sat on the coffee table.

But I didn't dare call her Aunt Hattie. Since I was a little girl, I called Aunt Hattie, "Mama." When we got out of line, she disciplined the four of us just as much, if not more than Madea. And I knew that Mama would tell me the unvarnished version of the family history.

Mama did not disappoint. A few weeks later, I went to her house on Race Street. When I was little, our family lived with Mama for a while. She worked at General Rose Hospital in the kitchen. She had bought the home in the 50's. The house was on Race Street, because that was as far east as most Blacks were allowed to buy at that time, and Mama always "pushed the envelope" as far as she could.

I went into the house and she put a plate of collard greens and hush puppies in front of me. She knew that I loved her greens. She always kept some in the freezer. When someone came over, she made fresh hush puppies and heated up the greens. For a moment, I forgot that I was supposed to be getting information on the family. I was so involved with the greens that it was a long time before I got around to the questions.

"What was Grandma Sarah like, Mama," I finally asked.

"Your Grandma was a character," Mama started. "Boy would she get on you when you did her wrong! Your grandma cussed up a storm too!" Mama suddenly jumped up. "Oh shit!" she hollered. "I forgot to turn off the damn greens." Then she looked over at me. "I mean 'oh, shoot." she corrected the bad word. I just smiled. It wasn't the first time I had heard Mama curse. But now I knew where Mama got it. Grandma Sarah cussed! It was a strange thought. Until now, when I thought of Grandma Sarah, I thought of a sweet little old lady, in the kitchen, stirring a pot of chicken soup. I had only visited her a few times as a child. I remembered seeing her in the kitchen with her apron on. I never envisioned Grandma cussing people out.

Mama turned the greens off, and came back to the table. "Now, what was I saying?"

"You were telling me that Grandma cussed a lot."

"Oh yeah," she said! "I'm glad I never picked up that bad habit." She grinned a sly grin and winked at me, amused at her own joke.

"Yeah! Right!" I laughed back.

"They called your Grandma, 'That crazy Indian.' That's what white folks say when you talk back to them. They call you 'crazy' then!" She stared off into space and then began to talk. "Boy, those were the days! Yo' grandma could get away with cussin at white folks cuz she didn't need nothin from em. We had everything we needed. This white man almost killed yo' Daddy one time. You see, yo' Daddy came up here and fugot what it was like in the South. He went down there and a white man said something wrong to him. Yo' Daddy hauled off, and hit that white man right in the head! That man took off running, and everybody was so scared. We thought Tommie would get strung up on a rope that day fo' sho'!"

"Was there a lot of trouble between Blacks and whites in Taylor?"

"No, they kept to themselves, and we kept to ours. They had their own school in the same town. Of course, they had good books and stuff, and their school was better than ours, but we didn't mind. We just did the best we could with what we had. But they hung a cousin of yours one time. They called him Manny and they say he raped a white woman. Manny wasn't no more than 14 years old at the time. He didn't rape that white woman. They know who did it. Rupert was the one who did it. But Rupert was a white man and they wanted to blame a Black man."

"Did Grandpa Huey talk much about when he was a boy?"

"No, he didn't like to talk about it very much. But some say he was a slave. And I guess he was, now that I thank about it, cuz he used to talk about the plantation and how he ran away. They used to tie his hands and feet to a stake. They would leave him out in the sun, all day long. He said they pert near killed him one time."

Mama talked for a long time. She told about being raped when she was about 9 years old. She told me about seeing two thirteen year old boys from Taylor, lynched and hanging from a tree.

"Did Bessie ever tell you about the time a little boy almost shot her Grandpa Frank?" she asked. Without waiting for an answer, she told me the story that I had heard from Madea, but I gladly listened to it again.

"Your Grandpa Frank was riding on a wagon with his cousin. There was a little white boy who was about eight years old, riding in the wagon with his Daddy, and he had a rifle. That little boy looked at his Daddy and then back to yo' Grandpa Frank. He pointed that rifle right at Uncle Frank and said, 'Daddy! You said it would be my turn to shoot the next 'coon.' But they finally rode off without firing a shot. Boy! Uncle Frank said that he was really scared that day! He knew that boy could kill him dead and it wouldn't be nothin!"

Mama told me lots of stories that day, and other times when I went to visit her. Then, when I would go to visit Madea and Daddy, I would mention something that Mama had said and it would trigger many more memories for Madea and Daddy. It was a joy to hear them talk about the old days.

One warm spring day I went to visit Madea and Daddy. They

had just returned from their annual trip to Arkansas. Daddy had just hung some pictures on the wall and was checking to make sure that they were straight. "Who's that?" I pointed to a photograph on the wall. The man in the photograph looked a lot like Daddy. In fact, if Daddy had been several years older, and had a long beard, it might have been Daddy!

"That's my grandfather. Huey Lewis! He was about 4 feet tall and a full blood Choctaw Injun!"

I looked at the pictures. Huey did indeed look like an Indian. But he had dark skin. I looked over at Daddy. He had high cheekbones, and straight-but-wavy hair. All this time, I had believed that Daddy "conked" his hair to make it straight. But then I realized she hadn't seen him conk it for a very long time — and it was still straight. He would put water on it and comb it straight back. Then he would push it forward and it would form little waves that looked like black ribbons. I surmised that maybe his Indian blood made his hair straight.

I pointed to the picture next to it. "Who's that?" I inquired

"That's my Daddy. He's your Grandpa Charley. His name is Harmon Charley Lewis. He's your Grandma Sarah's husband."

As usual, Daddy was in the mood to talk about the family. I continued my inquest, so that I could add to the family history.

"Where was Grandma Sarah born?"

"Your grandma was born in Russet, Louisiana. Her full name was Sarah, Katie, Katherine, Emeline, Harris. Her mother and your great-grandpa Green Harris had their own plantation. They had 300 acres. Your grandma and grandpa were full blood Creek Injuns."

Madea decided to join the conversation. She wanted to make sure I wasn't confused. "You remember that picture that we showed you of the Harris'. They are real light-skinned. That was your Grandma Sarah's parents."

I thought back to a picture that I had seen when I was about 8 or 9 years old. I remember being told that those were my grandparents, but I didn't believe it because their skin was so light.

"You mean those white-looking people?" I was incredulous! "They really were my grandparents?" I had almost forgotten about the picture.

Daddy laughed at the shocked look on my face. "Yep! Those white-looking people were my mother's grandparents. I remember when your Grandfather Harris died. I was about 10 years old, I think. He was laying there in the bed, and next to him was a big bucket full of feathers. They say that Injuns like to have feathers near their deathbed to help them go to heaven."

I began to realize just how little I knew about my ancestors. I became very interested in finding out more. It had never occurred to me to ask these questions before.

"You had eight brothers and sisters, Daddy. Right?"

"Well, no. I had eight brothers *and* eight sisters. There was sixteen of us, but Mama raised eight."

"What happened to the other eight?"

"Most of them were real young when they died. Mama had trouble birthin' a lot of her babies."

Suddenly I wished that I had gone back to Taylor more often with them when they went back in May of each year. I began to realize all that I had missed by not knowing my grandparents. I hadn't been to any of their funerals. I didn't even know how they died.

I pointed to the bearded man in the photograph that looked like Daddy. "How did Grandpa Huey die?"

"Well, we really don't know. All we know is that they brought his body back one day on a wagon in a small box. They just threw the box off the wagon. We buried him at St. Paul Cemetery. I know exactly where his grave is because it's marked by a wagon wheel. He is buried right under that wagon wheel. All of your relatives are buried at St. Paul cemetery."

Then I asked the question that would really get me motivated to step up my search. "How did grandpa Charley die?"

Daddy took a deep breath and let out a sigh as he remembered the past. "I remember the last time that I saw my Dad. I was about eight years old. Papa was sitting on the back of a wagon and they were getting ready to take him somewhere. I remember that I was crying cuz I didn't want him to go. I don't know why, but I was afraid for him to go. Now they said he was sick, but he didn't look sick to me. He was sitting up real good and talking jest as good to me like I'm talking to you. Papa looked at me and said, "Son, you a big boy now. Don't cry. You have to take care of your Mama while I'm gone. Now you remember everything Papa told you. Always be your own man. You only eight years old but you have your own business. Keep up your business son. It's important to work for yourself and not for anyone else."

Daddy looked back up at the picture of Grandpa Charley. "That wagon rolled down the road, and I looked at it until it was out of sight." Daddy shook his head slowly, as he remembered the scene. "That was the last time I ever saw my father."

I couldn't quite grasp the enormity of it all. I thought that I might have missed part of the story. "Is he buried at St. Paul too?"

Daddy looked at me and shook his head. "We don't know where he is buried or even when he died. Nobody ever saw him again after that."

I couldn't believe what I was hearing. "You never even got his body back?"

"No. We never got the body back. We never had a chance to bury him. Your Grandma Sarah searched high and low, but she never did find him. But you know, that wasn't that uncommon in those days for Black folks. There is a saying in the south. They say 'The trees cry'. It means that many people who die were hung or just put amongst the trees."

Then I started thinking about the rest of my Aunts and Uncles in Taylor. If Grandpa Huey and Grandpa Charley both died in mysterious ways, were the "trees crying" from some of my other relatives?

"What about Aunt Shug?"

"She's still living. Lives in Houston."

"Uncle Bud?"

215

"They say he lost his mind. He died in a mental home, I think."

"What about Uncle Henry?"

"He wandered off. Found him dead in the woods."

"What happened to Aunt Arthina?"

"She died from Old Timer's disease. But she was pretty young when she got it."

"Is Uncle Charley still living?"

"He died about ten years ago. Some said his liver gave out from drinking too much. But you know, he has a son that is still in Arkansas. His son's name is Charley, too. Just like his Daddy."

"Does Big Baby still live there too?"

"No, she was in a mental home. They said she died when a table fell on her. We didn't really believe it though."

Then Madea spoke up again. "Most of your Dad's brothers and sisters ended up in mental homes. Old Timer's disease runs in the family. Most of them got it before they were old. I don't know why, though."

"You mean *Alzheimer's* disease?" I wanted to know exactly what she meant.

"Yeah, I heard it called that too." Madea replied.

Fear began to grip me around the throat. "Mental disease" running in the family? Daddy seemed perfectly fine. Then I thought about Aunt Hattie. She seemed fine until my cousin Golden died in 1971. He was only 32 years old. Aunt Hattie was about 53. She started acting strangely right after his death. She didn't want to get in the car with the rest of us, because she thought we were going to "get her." We put her paranoia down to stress, but even years later, she seemed to sometimes lose track of things that happened. Other times I noticed that there were things that only happened in her head. I began to think that her condition could be more than just stress. She could have whatever mental condition ran in the family!

I asked many other questions that day. Hours later, I had a lot more information to add to my genealogy. And I was still puzzled by Grandpa Charley's death. I could not imagine how I would feel if one of my parents walked away, never to be heard from again. I imagined what a horrible time an eight-year-old boy, his mother and other family members must have had after Grandpa's disappearance. I made my father a solemn promise that day;

"Daddy, I'm going to find out what happened to Grandpa Charley. When I find out where he died, we can have a memorial for him."

"Okay, honey." Daddy said. I knew he didn't believe me. But I was determined to keep that promise. I knew that Daddy needed to know what had happened to his father. And I needed to know what happened to my grandfather.

Over the next several years, I spent all the time that I could, asking questions and making notes. Sometimes the stories that I heard brought tears to my eyes. Like the time Madea tearfully told me that her mother almost gave her away because she was so light-skinned. To this day, Madea remembers the pain of being a light-skinned Black girl and being called "high yellow" and "stuck up." And sometimes the stories brought knee-slapping laughter. But at the end of the day, the stories brought realization that the Black family in America had endured a "Hellacoust" all their own. Race was a factor in the beginning with the slave trade. Race was a factor for my parents and my grandparents with the color line. And race was a factor for my generation, which was in the midst of fighting for civil rights.

17

"A Past Reclaimed"

Soon, Dennis received his honorable discharged from the Air force. By 1980, we had three children, and our kids were old enough to walk a picket line. By the time Lisa was eleven, Niecy was nine, and Zuton was three, they were walking around the Denver Police building, chanting, "What do we want?"

"Justice!"

"When do we want it?"

"Now!"

The reason for that particular protest at such a young age stemmed from an incident at "Skate City," a skating rink near Denver, during "family night" when both older and younger children were skating. A fight broke out between two of the older kids. The police were called. By the time they arrived, a melee had broken out. One of the police officers used his bullhorn to shout directions to the other officers. "Grab all the niggers!" the cop bellowed. The white kids were left alone, while the police officers grabbed and roughed up some of the Black children. A six year old child who had been hurt in the scuffle had to be taken to the hospital. I was outraged that my children were targeted just because their skin was black. But even at the age of 9 and 11, they had had enough experiences with racism that they knew that they were discriminated against. So we made signs and we marched around the police building. More meetings were promised to the community. More promises were broken. Nothing changed except that many people in the Black community stopped going to Skate City, because we were clearly not welcome there.

A few years later, I began working for Continental Airlines. I loved the flight benefits because of the opportunity to travel all over the world. One spring day in May, Dennis and I decided to make our pilgrimage to Africa. Originally, the plan was to go to Ghana. We knew that the primary language spoken in Ghana was English, and we thought that we would have an easy time understanding the language. Also, Ghana was known as a "Black Utopia." But soon I discovered that World Airways flew non-stop from Newark Airport directly to Senegal, West Africa. They also allowed Continental Airline employees to travel with passes. It would be easier to get to Senegal than Ghana. Moreover, we had friends who had been to Senegal several times and knew some of the locals there. They gave us a few names and phone numbers of people to call when we got there. They wanted to us to say "hello" to their friends for them. Many of our friends gave us lots of tips for our trip to the Continent.

"They like to trade a lot!" we were told.

"Take lots of t-shirts and socks!"

"They need school supplies like pencils, ink pens, and paper."

We packed carefully. We had t-shirts and athletic shoes. We had made little packs of lotions, soaps, and toothpaste to trade. We packed a box of school supplies to give to the school on Goree Island, because we heard that the children had few school supplies to work with. We were ready! Finally, on a hot day in August, we boarded World Airways from Newark Airport, and flew directly into Senegal. We landed and walked down the steps to go into the terminal.

Security clearance in Senegal was different from anything I had ever experienced in the U.S. They unpacked *all* of our bags and looked through *everything*. The security agent seemed to be amused when he looked at all of the packages of t-shirts and toiletries.

"Doing some shopping?" he inquired with a big grin on his face. We didn't answer. It was obvious that we brought things to trade. We got through security, and went out to the main terminal. Because I lived in Denver, I had never seen so many black faces in my life! We had made hotel arrangements to stay at the Novatel Hotel in Senegal. We thought that we would grab a taxi and head for the hotel. But first, we looked at all of the merchandise that the venders were selling in the airport.

The prices were wonderful! Never had I seen African goods priced so low! Drums for $20! Purses for $3. Miscellaneous jewelry for less than $1. We picked up a few pieces and headed outside to hail a taxi. Suddenly we were surrounded by six or seven drivers yelling at us.

"Hey! American! Taxi!? I will take you!" One of them came over to us and took my bag from me.

"I take you!" he announced. He started marching towards his car, and I ran behind him, trying to catch up to my bag. Finally, we reached his car, just as he was trying to open the trunk and put my bag inside it. I looked at the car. It just looked like a regular car, not a taxi! I peeked inside. A blanket partially covered the back seat to cover up the coils that were poking out of it. I was not positive that this person was a taxi driver, and I refused to get into the car with him.

"Give me my bag back!" I demanded. "I don't want to ride with you!"

"Just 12 dolla! Twelve Dolla!"

"No! Give me my bag!" I shouted.

"Okay, ten Dolla. Only ten dolla for you."

Just then, another driver came up and confronted the first one. "It's *my* American! I see them first!" Then they started yelling at each other in a language other than English. I recognized a few words from my notes. Wolof! They were speaking Wolof, one of the African tongues common to Senegal. While they were yelling at each other, Dennis retrieved my bag and we headed for a taxi that had the *Taxi* rider on the top, and the logo on the side. We quickly hopped into the taxi.

"We're going to the Novatel Hotel." Dennis said to the driver.

"Sixteen dolla, Ok?" the driver asked the question instead of stating the fare. I pointed to the meter.

"Turn in on!" I demanded.

"Don't work." he answered.

"Twelve dollars," I offered.

"Twelve dolla American, okay?" He sounded happy.

"Twelve dollars, American." I agreed. He started the taxi and we headed for the Novatel.

The Novatel was a beautiful Hotel. Nice and shiny. It was also expensive. We had heard that Senegal was an inexpensive place to stay, but the Novatel, had prices similar to the U.S. The hotel was $89.00 per night. Breakfast was $12 each guest. And the exchange rate, from U.S. Dollars to CFA Francs was exorbitant. When we arrived at the hotel, one of the locals was playing an instrument that looked like a guitar. But it was round, and looked to be hand made. Someone pointed to it and called it a "Ko." While we were in line waiting to check in, the musician played beautiful music for us. After we checked in, he followed us as we looked around the hotel. Then I noticed that there were dollar bills sticking out of the opening in the instrument. I finally realized that he was looking for a tip. I put a dollar in the opening, and he gave us a little bow and a smile, and started following another couple.

We hadn't had much sleep and after we had eaten, we went directly to bed. We decided that we would rise early, and try to reach

222

Popes'. Popes' was a local. A friend had given us his phone number before we left the States.

We reached Popes' on the first try. We explained that we were from the U.S. and told him that a friend had given us his number, and wanted us to say "hello." Popes' was very pleasant and spoke English very well. It was comforting to have a phone number for someone who spoke English, and now knew us through a mutual friend.

"Welcome to Senegal" Popes' said. "Where are you staying?"

"We are staying at the Novatel Hotel."

"The Novatel?" Popes' stated, obviously upset at this bit of news. "You can't stay at the Novatel! It's too expensive for you! I come and get you. I show you where you can stay!"

We had no argument with that! We told Popes' what we would be wearing, and agreed to meet him in the lobby in an hour.

We got down to the lobby early, and decided to go outside and see what some of the street venders were selling. As soon as we came out of the door, a crowd of venders surrounded us.

"American!"

"Sister!"

"Brother!"

"Over here, American!" Some of the venders ran over to us and started laying out their wares on the ground in front of us. I noticed the cab driver from last night.

"American! I take you all day! Forty dolla! All day!" he shouted to us.

We were overwhelmed by all of the activity in front of us. Some of the artifacts were really beautiful. And the prices that they were yelling out were "dirt cheap."

Finally, one of the locals came up to us. He had nothing in his hands so we knew that he was not a vender. He seemed to be walking purposefully towards us, like he knew us, so I figured that it was Popes'.

"Dennis, and Mary?" he asked. "I'm Popes'. I come for you."

We were relieved to see him. It seemed like the crowd kind of dispersed, and we had room to think.

We joined Popes' as he began to walk down the street. "How far is it?" I asked.

"Not far," he stated. We walked slowly, stopping along the way at various venders. I was saddened by the poverty that we saw. Senegal was a very poor country. Medical care was very hard to come by, and many of people had various deformities, such a fused limbs, or blindness. I was touched by the elderly women who sat on the sidewalks, some with a few pieces of jewelry to sell, others with nothing except a bowl that they hoped someone would put money into.

"Hey my Sister."

"My Brother!"

"American!" People called out to us as we walked along. We put change in some of the bowls. There was a woman with a huge bowl of dolls on her head. There was something about her eyes that touched my soul.

"How much are your dolls?" I inquired.

"For'd you, three dolla." she answered, pulling one of the dolls out of the bowl.

I reached into the pouch around my neck for the three dollars. I pulled out a $2000 CFA bill, which was the equivalent of about four American dollars.

She reached back into the bowl on her head and pulled out another doll.

"Or, two for five dolla." she smiled

I pulled out another $2,000 bill. She had me then! I'm sure she recognized the glint in my eyes. The dolls were beautiful. And they would cost at least ten dollars each at home.

She looked at the four thousand CFA (which was about 8 dollars), and continued to bargain.

"Three for seven dolla!"

About five minutes later, I had ten dolls. They cost me ten dollars. She was happy, and I was happy. Dennis and I quickly caught on to the bargaining in Senegal. Popes' was very patient. By the time we walked through the vender's area and arrived at the hotel, we had a bag full of dolls, masks, and African Bobo's. We had traded some of the t-shirts, toiletries, and shoes. My prized purchase was a ceramic handmade piece of an old man and old woman dressed in white, and playing a game. I had traded two t-shirts and some socks for the piece. It was probably worth about $60 in the states. I really loved how the artist had captured the unique expressions on the faces of the man and the woman. I decided that I would hand-carry it back to the States. We were very happy with our purchases.

We checked into the Ganalee hotel and walked up a flight of stairs. The hotel was nice, and clean, although not nearly as fancy as the Novatel. We looked at a room and decided that it would suit us just fine. It was only $35 per night. What's more, it was away from the tourist district and was in the heart of the local community. We looked out the window to the street below. Some of the locals were doing an African dance, taking turns to "show their moves" in the middle of a big circle. It felt like home!

There was no restaurant inside the hotel, but there was a little cafe right next door. We were excited by our find. Both Dennis, and I preferred being around the local community rather than the tourists. We wanted to get a better "flavor" of the "real" Senegal.

We dropped off our bags, and then decided to get something to eat at the cafe. The menu was in French. I remembered dinner last night. I had something called "Poulet," and I was told that it was chicken. It tasted a little like chicken, and I remembered seeing some people in the community carrying chickens that appeared to be ready for plucking and cooking. We both ordered something with poulet', and asked Popes' to let us buy breakfast for him. We were grateful to him for helping us, and sticking close by us. Popes' ordered an interesting looking rice dish, and had eaten about half of it when he spoke.

"Where do you want to go today?" he asked

"We thought we'd go to Goree Island." Dennis answered. "Goree is the main thing that we wanted to see."

"Ahh, Go-ray," Popes' said with his French/Wolof accent. "African American must make pilgrimage to Go-ray! I take you!"

We arrived at the Port of Goree at about 10 o'clock in the morning. We looked at the price list. Citizens of Senegal — four dollars. Foreign Nationals, — six dollars. Popes' went up to the window with us. The cashier looked at the three of us.

"One Citizen and two foreign nationals?" he inquired.

"No." Popes' corrected him. "These are my friends. They make their pilgrimage today. They are Af-ri-can — just like you and me. Af-ri-can!"

"Yes of course!" the cashier said. "Four dolla today for our African brother's and sisters from America!"

A feeling of peace came over me. Yes, these people were African, just as I was before someone snatched my ancestors and took them across the water. Suddenly I felt grateful to be acknowledged as an AFRICAN.

We got on the houseboat for the short trip to Goree. We could see the Island in the distance. It was a big round brick building surrounded by water. As we got closer, we noticed that there was a huge beach, and many adults and children were swimming and playing in the sand. As we got nearer to the island, some of the children jumped off the boat and into the water. They swam the rest of the way to the shore.

We got off the boat, and walked across the bridge to the beach. "You want to go to the beach museum first?" asked Popes'. We went to the beach museum and then walked around the beach. A couple of hours later it was time for lunch. We stopped at a cafe and had fish sandwiches and coke. We toured the Catholic church that was on the Island, and noted that in Senegal, even at a Catholic church, all of the saints, including Jesus himself, was Black!

Finally, it was time to go to the slave castle. We stopped at the big, green, double doors of the castle and looked at the sign above our heads. It was in French, but I understood part of what it said, "Enslaved Africans." We opened the doors and went inside. There were two curved stairways leading to the upper level of the castle, one on the right, and one on the left. We walked up the right stairway and into the castle. The upper level of the castle was clean, and well lit. Popes' looked at us and explained. "This is the part where the slavers lived. They held the slaves in the dungeon below."

I nodded. I knew that we would be going to the dungeons, and a big lump had started to form in my throat as we walked around the upper level. The upper level of the castle had been turned into a museum. We looked at replicas of slave ships and big iron chains that were used to chain the enslaved together. We made our way through each room, looking at various apparatus that were used for the capture and control of the enslaved.

Finally, we went downstairs to the dungeons. We came to the first small cell. "This is where the men stayed. They kept the men and women separate." I thought about my ancestors who might have been held here. Tears began to well up in my eyes and I wiped them away with the back of my hand. We went to the next dark cell and looked inside. It was about four feet in height, and about 8 feet long. I doubted that this would be a holding cell for anyone. No one of average height would be able to stand up in that hellhole.

"This is where they held the women." Popes' announced. "Behind it is another cell called a "fatting house." They held women there until they were big enough to get a better price."

An incredible sadness came over me. How could anyone who called themselves human, be so inhumane. Four bare concrete walls with a tiny opening surrounded the cell. The dirt served as a toilet. There was complete darkness. Unbearable gloom hung in the air. It was inconceivable that people were held here for days or even months only to be taken to a greater hell.

We came to the next cell. It was about the same size as the women's cell. I looked at the sign above the door. I recognized the first two words. "Innocent enfant's." This was the cell for children! I looked down, and a puddle of blood appeared before my eyes. A huge sob forced its way out of my throat as I turned to leave. I couldn't breathe. The fish sandwich that I had eaten earlier threatened to move back up towards my throat. I looked for a way out. I ran back into the hallway, and slumped to the ground. I couldn't stop the tears. Popes' and Dennis came and helped me up. I saw the tears in their eyes too. After a while, I felt a bit stronger, and regained my resolve. I had to see it! My ancestors had come through this God-forsaken place. The least I could do was acknowledge their pain by facing what they had endured. Feeling a little stronger, I followed Popes' and Dennis through another hallway. Soon I saw some light coming through an opening in the wall. We arrived at the opening and looked out at the ocean just on the other side of it.

"This is the Door of No Return," Popes' said. One at a time, Dennis and I climbed inside the door and looked out at the ocean. As I climbed inside the doorway, I heard wailing sounds and awful screams coming from the water below. Men, women, and children were crying, screaming, fighting and struggling with their captors. I looked down into the ocean and saw a human figure swimming up to the top of the water. It was a Black woman. Her face was thin and worn, and her cheeks were streaked with tears that looked like blood. She swam away and then another figure swam up to the top. The figure stayed there for a moment, and then another swam up. One after another, these, figures seemed to want to reveal themselves to me. Perhaps they wanted me to acknowledge those who had perished in the water. Or perhaps they were thanking me for my return. Finally, there was one big wave, as the last body swam away.

Feeling like we were in a dream, Dennis and I climbed down from The Door of No Return. Popes' was waiting for us. I knew he was concerned for our well-being.

"Many African Americans come here," he stated. "Many fall down. Some faint. They call this the 'Door of No Return, because they say that once they take you through that door, you never come back. But that's not true because you did come back. You came back today for all of your ancestors who went out that door."

I nodded, still overcome from what I had seen and felt. I realized the enormous meaning behind Popes' words and I felt that my presence had somehow helped my ancestor's transition by acknowledging their struggle and paying homage to them.

We made our way back up the steps and out of the door. I felt almost guilty for being able to breathe the fresh air while the spirits of my ancestors were trapped below. When we got outside, there were three drummers and about seven or eight young girls dancing and singing to the beat of the drums. We stopped to look at them. Dennis pulled out his camera and started to photograph them but Popes' gently put his hand on Dennis' shoulder and shook his head.

"Please. No pictures. This is a ceremony. They are doing a dance of mourning for their ancestors who were taken across the water, and they welcome you back!"

Dennis nodded as more hot tears rolled down my face. Then I got angry!

I thought about all of the lies that African Americans were told about Africa over the years. I remember that as a small child, we would laugh and make fun of Africans, believing that they were "uncivilized jungle people." We would be ready to fight if someone called us "an African." I had overheard heard my father relate what he had been told as a child — that Africans lived wore no clothes, were savages and ate each other for dinner. He even seemed surprised when Dennis and I told him we were going to Africa.

"Why," he inquired? "There's nothing but jungles in Africa, is there?" I felt sad that our people had fallen for such obvious brainwashing! Even people who knew a little something about Africa usually likened it to little more than a safari. The rich culture and unique history went un-noticed. I was embarrassed that I, too, had poked fun at "Africans." And I was angry that we had been mis-educated about the entire Black race.

I thought back to one of Malcolm X's speeches. "I say you been had! Tricked! Hoodwinked!" No greater truth was ever spoken.

We were silent on the way back to the hotel. Popes' understood. He had seen African Americans stand in The Door many times before. He understood the pain and the sadness that comes after the experience. And he let us grieve for our ancestors.

We stayed in Senegal for four days. We went to Goree each day and talked to the locals and the children. We also went to the village where Popes' lived and we had a meal, Senegal style with his family. It was in this village that one of the elders gave us African names. Popes' had explained to the elder that we were making our pilgrimage. "Yes, I see." the elder said. Then he looked directly at me.

"You have the heart of a mother, and the grace of a Queen. You are to be called Coumba Johari Ade." Then he turned to Dennis. "You are strong but kind. You are to be called Abdulai Momadou".

That evening, after the four o'clock tea, we went back to the village and had a naming ceremony to celebrate the giving and receiving of our African names. We were humbled by the good wishes and the dances that were done in our honor. The next day, we reluctantly left Senegal. Senegal felt like home. In the four short days we had been there, I learned more about our culture than had I learned my entire life in the United States. We hailed a taxi to the Airport.

"How much?" we asked the driver.

"For my brother, six dolla."

As we left the taxi, Dennis handed the driver twelve American dollars. He gave us a big grin, and a little bow, and then he was gone.

We boarded the World Airways flight for home. I was so deep in thought, that the six-hour flight seemed more like 6 minutes. I thought about all I had done and seen in the last few days. By the end of the trip, I was more determined than ever to find out what had happened to my Grandparents, and I wanted to find out about my ancestors who had gone through *The Door of No Return* in Senegal, or in Ghana, or other ports in Africa.

Generation
X
The Unknown

The Ninth Generation

"Generation X"

OLISA YAA
Florida A & M University

18

"A Grave Uncovered"

After I returned from Senegal, I tried several times to get Grandpa Charley's and Grandpa Huey's death certificates. I knew that the information on the certificates would answer many questions that I had. I mailed requests to Arkansas, then to Louisiana. I even tried Mississippi and Texas. Every request came back with the reply "Unable to locate the death certificate for the above named person."

I began to get very frustrated. I thought that either Arkansas *or* Louisiana **had** to have the death certificates. Grandpa lived in Arkansas, but was close to the Louisiana border. I had narrowed down the date of death for Grandpa Huey. Madea remembered that Calvin was a baby when grandpa Huey was buried, and I checked 10 years on each side of 1942. I also narrowed down Grandpa Charley's date of death by using my father's statement about being about 8 years when his father was taken away on the wagon. I asked the vital records office to check between 1929 and 1960 for Grandpa Charley. Three times, I requested the certificate. And three times, I got back a form that said, "No certificate found." Finally, in frustration, I flew up to the Arkansas department of Vital Records. I had a gut feeling that Grandpa Charley was buried in Arkansas. I got off the plane, and took a bus to the Vital Records department. I was dressed in business attire, which was required for airline employees traveling on a pass.

I walked into the office and filled out two forms— Huey Lewis on the first form and Harmon Charley Lewis on the second. I walked up to the desk and presented the forms.

"I have been trying to get these certificates for three years." I announced. "I just flew in from Denver for the day. I know the certificates here. And I'm not leaving until you find them!"

The clerk looked curiously at me. Not many people flew into town just to get a death certificate. The waiting room was sprinkled with customers who were very casually dressed in shorts or jeans, and t-shirts. She looked at me as if she was trying to figure out who I was and why I was dressed in a business suit. She must have decided that she should cooperate because suddenly she became very helpful! She disappeared through the door behind her. I sat down, and opened a book. I thought that I was in for a long wait. However, about ten minutes later, the woman emerged from the back room. "Ma'am?" she called to me. I walked up to the desk. "Here is a death certificate for Harmon Lewis. But this one died in 1928, and he is a white man. Is the man you are looking for a white man?"

"No," I said sadly. I knew that Grandpa Charley was still alive in 1928. And I was pretty certain that my grandfather was not a white man. The clerk went back through the door. About 15 minutes later, she emerged with two death certificates. I looked at the first one. Harmon Charley Lewis. Date of death, July 5, 1932. Last known residence: *Taylor, Arkansas*. This was it! I had found my grandfather's death certificate. Then I looked at the other death certificate. "Huey Lewis," it read. Date of death January 29, 1940. Last known residence, *Taylor, Arkansas.*

I tried to keep calm, and said to the clerk, "Yes, these are the ones." I slowly walked out of the office, walked over to a bench and sat down. I quickly tore open the envelope that held Grandpa Charley's death certificate. I read every line of the death certificate. "Last date seen alive: July 1. Date of Death, July 5. I realized that my grandfather had died just 4 days after he entered the hospital. And he probably entered the hospital that same warm day, when Daddy was eight years old and waived "goodbye" to his father as he rolled away in the wagon. The enormity of this find after all the years of searching suddenly hit me very hard. I had kept a very important promise to my father, and I held part of my history in my hands. I put my head in my hands and sobbed until there were no more tears.

Finally, I got the strength to dry the tears and take another look at grandpa Charley's death certificate. "Place of death, Little Rock Arkansas. Place of internment: Little Rock State Hospital cemetery!" Suddenly I looked up and realized where I was. I stood up and stared at the big building across the street. I was looking right at Little Rock State Hospital! Grandpa Charley, I reasoned, was buried just across the way! I picked myself up off the bench and marched across the lawn, clutching the death certificate as if the wind was going to sweep it away any minute. I walked up to the information desk.

"I need some information about the cemetery," I began. "My grandfather was buried here in the 1930's. I need to know where the cemetery is, and what space he is buried in!"

The woman behind the desk looked at me almost the same way that the woman at Vital Records had. However, the words that she spoke brought me crashing back down to earth.

"Ma'am, they moved those graves about 20 years ago to make

way for this building. I think they are somewhere in Benton, Arkansas, now." I was shattered! I was so close, yet I had hit another brick wall.

"Well what about hospital records?" I asked. "Can I request hospital records?" The woman looked at me a long time without answering. Then she said, "I'm sure that all of those records were destroyed a long time ago. They wouldn't have much on them anyway! You can fill out this form though and leave your name, and address. If records are available, we will notify you." She pushed the form at me, looking like she had more to say, but thought better of it. I looked at my watch. I had one hour to get back to the airport, or I was going to miss my flight. I quickly filled out the form, caught a cab, and headed for the Airport. I spent the next two hours on the flight reading the death certificates over and over again. I could finally tell my father what happened to Grandpa Charley!

About four days later, a thick envelope arrived in the mail. It was from Little Rock State Hospital! I quickly ripped open the envelope and dropped to the couch. The first page was a sheet of paper with the name Harmon Lewis typed on it. Next to the name, it said, "space number 32" Underneath the name was a little note written on a yellow sticker. "This is where your Grandfather was buried." the note said. The note was unsigned. I turned to the next page. It was a newspaper article from the early 1980's. The title of the Article said, "Serene Cemetery Final Setting for Bodies Donated to Science." I read the entire article. Then I read it again! It talked about bodies being unclaimed and then being buried in the hospital cemetery. The article said that all efforts are made to find the families of the bodies, and if they fail, then the bodies are buried at the cemetery. The bodies are then used for research! The end of the article said something to the effect of, "Wouldn't it be a shame if the hospital stopped donating bodies to science?" I was incredulous! A shame to stop donating bodies? My family hadn't donated anything, especially not my grandfather's body!

Then the full realization hit! Grandpa's body was used for science! He was then buried in a pauper's grave. He was later exhumed and most likely studied again for science! But there was also something else. I got the death certificates and looked at them again. The certificate also had the next of kin, (Arthina) in Taylor. It had a Taylor address! I put the pieces together. The death certificate stated that Grandpa had died from "Cerebrospinal Syphilis!" I knew enough about human biology to know that some disease had affected Grandpa's brain. That disease appeared to be Syphilis. Suddenly I remembered the Tuskegee Syphilis Experiment. Hundreds of Black men in the south, primarily in Alabama who had Syphilis went untreated to facilitate an experiment. The goal of the experiment was to allow the men to believe that they were being treated for an illness, and then when they died, they would be dissected to study the disease. The goal could only be accomplished by "bringing them to autopsy" — (i.e., let them die from the disease, and then study their bodies). When the men moved, they continued to be part of the experiment. The study began on a small scale prior to 1928, and was stepped up in the 1930's. A Black nurse, who was involved with the Government in gaining the trust of the men, finally blew the whistle. The experiment was so well known throughout the south that military recruiters were aware of it and declined to take men who were "flagged" as being in the experiment. They would tell them that they had another condition that prevented them from joining the military. Those behind the experiments knew that a shot of penicillin could cure the disease. Even before the development of penicillin, there were drugs that were effective in fighting the disease. If the men went into the military, they would have to get medication and the result would be that the "subject" was no longer useful because they would no longer have the disease! This went on for over *forty years*! I wasn't aware of it at that time, but in 1998, President Clinton would finally pay some of the families a token sum for the horror that the men were put through.

Now I was looking at what appeared to be something similar. The document was a lie! My grandfather had been to the hospital many times. Someone who knew him well took him there! They had his address on file! Moreover, even if they didn't know his exact address, they knew that he was from Taylor, Arkansas where the population was 657! How hard could it be to find a dead man's family in a town of 657 people, so that he could have a decent burial? Grandpa Charley died when the experiment was just getting underway. He was dug up and dissected years later, probably at the height of the experiment.

Then my thoughts turned to Grandpa Huey. I knew from my father that both Grandpa Huey and Grandpa Charley had spent a few years in Alabama. They moved back to Taylor but traveled back to Alabama on occasion. Grandpa Huey had died when the experiment was in full swing! His body went missing for at least three months and possibly a lot longer, according to Madea. We couldn't even be sure if his body was intact that awful day when Grandma Sarah opened that "small box!"

I carefully re-read both Grandpa Charley and Grandpa Huey's certificates. They had died from the same disease. Both certificates had numerous marks as if someone had changed the information on them several times. The dates of death appeared to be changed. There were discrepancies between the dates when my family *thought* that Grandpa Huey died, based on when his body was unceremoniously "dumped" on the family property; and the date stated on the certificate. ` What were they doing with the body for all of those months?

According to my father, the hospital officials were probably the ones who came and got Grandpa Charley. Family members who tried to visit him were given conflicting information and not allowed to visit. The death certificates were very disturbing. Each certificate held numerous "facts" that were in conflict to what I knew to be the truth!

In my heart I knew that the information that I held in my hands was just the tip of the iceberg. I wanted to make sure that I had as many details as possible before I told my father the awful truth.

The following week, Dennis and I were on a plane back to Arkansas., headed to the Arkansas State Hospital of Medical Sciences building. There was a clinic in Arkansas for syphilitic Blacks that had started as early as 1908. The State Hospital Library housed information and documents about the clinic. Doctors at the Arkansas clinic often did double duty at the Tuskegee clinic. According to research that I conducted prior to the trip, I found that not only were Arkansas and Tuskegee involved in these inhumane practices, they also took place in other towns and even in the Black prison systems, (most notably Leavenworth prison), which were segregated at that time. After a bit of research, I found that Doctorr Wenger, who was tied to the Tuskegee Syphilis Experiment, was actually based in Arkansas, at the same hospital where Grandpa Charley died! Several boxes of his papers were available in a collection at the library and we were able to view the collection.

We arrived at the library at about 9:30 in the morning. The librarian placed several boxes in front of us and by noon, I had uncovered much more than I bargained for. There were medical records and information about various Syphilis "studies" from Alabama, Mississippi, Arkansas, and numerous other places in the United States. There were also boxes of photographs of men, women, and children in various stages of the disease! It sickened me to read the accounts of how the "negroes" were perfect targets for the "study" because they were "trusting" and "immoral." The terminology used made it appear that the "subjects" were no better than animals. But several pages in particular caused me to sit straight up in my chair!

Looking through the documents and the doctors notes, I

found that not only did doctors allow Black men to die so they could study their bodies, but in some cases, the men were given drugs to "hasten" the death.

This could explain why Grandpa Charley appeared to be so healthy, but was dead just days after he left home. It was nothing less than murder! Numerous photographs told the story of not only Black men, but also of women, children, and fetuses that were dealt the same cruel fate. There was one photo that bore a striking resemblance to Grandma Sara, and brought tears to my eyes.

I felt physically ill! I couldn't believe that the "study" was even more horrible than I thought. Line after line of clinical terms describing killing, studying and then burying bodies with graves marked by nothing more than a number. It appeared that some didn't even rate a grave! I had seen enough! I made copies of some of the documents to review at another time – when my heart could stand it. I left the Medical Center shaken to the core over the historical treatment of my ancestors.

Dennis and I flew back into Denver that same evening, armed with the additional information that told the whole story. The following morning, I spread all of the documents out on the table and reviewed them again, to make sure that I had not dreamed the entire, awful scenario. But the documents were just as sickening the second time.

Not only was Grandpa Charley's burial place discovered, and the gap between Grandpa Huey's date of death, and date of burial revealed, an ugly piece of history was discovered right along with it! Blacks were still treated worse than animals, more than 100 years after slavery. Even as late as 1972 – it was acceptable to use Black people as guinea pigs in the name of science!

A flood of memories flashed before me, as I thought about all of the names that were listed in the documents. I remembered my mother saying, "Most of your father's brothers and sisters had Old Timer's disease."

"Of course they did!" I thought. "That's what happens when you have untreated syphilis and the woman has children! The disease is passed on to the children!" Then I thought about my father. He did not appear to have the disease. Of course not! Daddy was in the military. Because of that, he had most likely received a shot of penicillin and medical care. He might have received penicillin even before that time. It occurred to me that moving out of Arkansas might have saved my father's life!

My entire body was tense from the anger I felt. At the same time, I was relieved that I had found the information. I would finally be able to tell my father how Grandpa died, and where he was buried.

With a heavy heart, I finally picked myself up from the table and made myself a cup of tea. Then I sat down and read the articles again, letting the full weight of it finally sink in.

I pondered President Clinton's "apology" to the survivors of the Tuskegee Syphilis Experiment, just a few years back. No mention of the hundreds of other "study" victims in other states was made. And no one talked about the women! The women who bore syphilitic children who grew up to be afflicted adults! Women like Aunt Hattie, who died broke, in a nursing home after being diagnosed with "dementia." Women like my Aunt Naomi who died in a mental hospital after a table (supposedly) fell on her head. How was I supposed to explain all of this to my father?

Serene cemetery final setting
for bodies donated to science

By CYNTHIA HOWELL
Democrat Benton Bureau

HASKELL – On Arkansas Highway 229 between the Benton Services Center and the Haskell city limits is a grassy field, surrounded by young pines and honeysuckle vines, from which one can see rolling hills and cattle grazing in the distance.

The serene setting is also a state-owned and operated cemetery where bodies that have been moved from now-destroyed Little Rock cemeteries are buried, along with unclaimed bodies and those donated for scientific research to the University of Arkansas for Medical Sciences.

Leroy Smith, registrar for the Benton Services Center, said during a recent interview that the cemetery was established in 1968 and between 30 and 70 bodies are buried there yearly. The bodies are transported to the cemetery once or twice a year.

Graves at the two-acre cemetery are marked with a number imprinted on a flat metal marker.

The corresponding names are listed in records kept by Smith at the center.

Many of the bodies were transferred to the cemetery when construction of the interstate highway system through Little Rock during the early 1970s forced a cemetery to be moved. Some of the bodies at that Little Rock cemetery had been moved years earlier from the site of the State Hospital, also in Little Rock, before its construction.

Smith said the cemetery is not a paupers' field. The bodies buried at the cemetery must come from the UA medical school – except when an occasional patient at the center specifically requests to be buried at the site.

The bodies from the medical school have been used for educational purposes. The school uses bodies that are donated or unclaimed for its research.

According to Arkansas law, the state must bear the responsibility of burying unclaimed bodies, Smith said.

Smith said it would be a shame if people discontinued donating the bodies for medical research simply because the bodies are buried at the state cemetery.

The bodies are treated reverently before, during and after burial and short, formal burial services are conducted by Glen Womack, the center's chaplain, Smith said. The services are attended by Smith. "There cannot be a burial without my being there to record names and numbers," he said.

Harley Tollefson, the center's administrator, and Jimmy Henshaw, the greenhouse and maintenance supervisor for the center, also attend services.

Henshaw, Smith said, has been involved in improving the cemetery by instigating a Little Rock unit of Navy seabees to work in the cemetery, primarily constructing stone entranceways.

Very few bodies at the cemetery are former patients of the services center, Smith said, because of the center's efforts to locate relatives. Less than one unclaimed body is sent to the medical school each year by the center.

The state is charged for the burial by the services center. The bill includes charges for the man hours spent, the digging of graves and the transportation of bodies.

Smith said that, although individuals may place flat tombstones with names and dates on the

Arkansas Democrat/Frank Fellone

Fred Petrocelli points out small grave marker.

Article: Serene Cemetery final setting for bodies donated to science
Arkansas Democrat Gazette. By Cynthia Howell.

Dennis and I arrived at my parent's house the next morning. I clutched the articles from Little Rock State Hospital in my hand as I walked up the steps to the front door. I smelled hot fried apple pies cooked fresh off the big cast iron skillet. Every year Madea would pick apples from the tree in front of the house, peel them, core them and make hot apple pies for her children and grandchildren. You were really in luck to actually show up as she was cooking them, because there was nothing like Madea's just-cooked fried apple pie. And today was my lucky day! Not only was I lucky enough to arrive while the pies were cooking, Madea had just put on a pot of fresh coffee that smelled wonderful mingling with the aroma of the pies. And not just any coffee. She still used the percolator that she had bought in 1951, the year I was born. I loved her coffee! I felt a little sorry for the new generation who thought that dripping hot water through some coffee grounds and into a carafe ended up to be coffee. Coffee was made to be cooked in a percolator, and served only when it was fully "perked." I decided that the news from Little Rock Hospital could wait a few more minutes. I poured Dennis and I a cup of coffee, and placed each of us a hot pie on a plate. We talked a little about our trip to Senegal, and caught up on what all the other relatives were doing. Madea was the "clearing house" for family information. Everyone would share their news with her, and she would update everyone else. We caught up on the family news. Aunt Ollie and Aunt Essie were fine. Daddy's sister, Shug was sick. Stella, her husband Bobby, and their kids Elaine and Bobby, Jr. were fine. Elaine had just broken up with Lester, her boyfriend. Bobby Jr. had a new set of drums and was driving Stella and Bobby nuts! My older brother Tommie wanted to have Thanksgiving at his house this year, and celebrate Amanda's birthday, which was just before Thanksgiving.

Then they caught us up on my older brother, Calvin. His Karate studio was picking up business and he had just bought the space next door to expand it. His son, Donnie was trying to get Madea and Daddy to take him fishing.

Next, I caught them up on my family. Dennis and I had taken our three daughters fishing the other day. We caught a few channel cats, pitched a tent and roasted hot dogs at the lake. We took the youngest, Zuton to the park to feed the ducks and laughed as she tried to catch them. Finally, I picked up the papers that I had placed on the coffee table when we arrived.

"I flew up to Little Rock last week." I announced.

"You did? What for?" Daddy asked. He wasn't surprised. I was always flying somewhere, while trying to further the family's genealogy.

"I went up to try to get Grandpa Charley's death certificate."

Madea walked into the room at that point. "You know that Arkansas loses all those certificates. They had your Daddy's when he went into the service, but when he tried to get his passport, they couldn't find it. We had to fill out another one."

"Well, this time I got lucky. I found Grandpa Charley's and Grandpa Huey's too!"

Daddy put down his coffee cup and looked at me as if I had two heads. "You found my Daddy's death certificate? I knew he must be dead, but I never thought that we would find out for sure."

I took a swig of coffee to kill a little time. The task before me was an unpleasant one. I could finally tell my father about his father's death. However, the circumstances surrounding that death were going to be hard to hear.

"Daddy," I began, "Remember when I told you that I would find out what happened to Grandpa Charley? That was the most important promise that I had made in my life. I took it very seriously because I could not imagine having a parent disappear and never come back. I knew that if something like that happened to you or Madea, I couldn't rest until I found out what happened. And I promised you that I would tell you everything that I found out, remember?"

"Yeah, I remember," Daddy looked at me a little curiously. No doubt he heard the quiver in my voice as I tried to fight down the pounding in my chest. I took a deep breath, and continued. "When I went to Arkansas, I finally found out what happened. You were about eight years old when he died."

"Eight years old?! He died about the same year that I saw him for the last time?"

"Yeah. I think he died just days after you saw him!" Hands trembling, I carefully put my coffee cup down told them what I had found out.

"In the 20's and 30's there were experiments on a lot of Black people. In one city, there were over 400 men who they knew had a disease, but they didn't tell them that they had it. They decided to use the men so that they could study the effects of the disease. Even the government knew about it. In fact, the government helped by providing money and making sure that the men wouldn't get the treatment that they needed. They used the men as guinea pigs for the experiments. They decided that the best way to get more information about the disease was to wait until the men died, and then study their bodies." I paused and looked at my father. I clearly had his full attention.

"In one area" I continued, "they called it 'The Tuskegee Syphilis Experiment.' But actually the study included lots of other places, including Arkansas, and even some prisons like Leavenworth Kansas." I paused and took a deep breath. I avoided my father's eyes. "Grandpa Charley died from the disease. But instead of returning his body to the family, they kept it and experimented on him. Then they buried him in a pauper's grave. Years later, they dug up his body, and sent it in for more research. They finally buried him at a cemetery in Haskell, Arkansas."

The look in my father's eyes will haunt me for the rest of my days. He looked like someone had punched him in the gut. But he wanted to hear all of it.

"They did all that to my father! And they couldn't at least give us his body back?" he demanded.

"They had already marked his body as "Unknown" and given it to science." I answered as gently as I could. "I'm sure that they didn't want people to figure out what they were doing."

I answered all of his questions, and then repeated what I had found until he was satisfied that he had heard it right. Exhausted from the news, he glanced at my mother. "Red, can you bring me some more coffee? Where's the remote?" He picked up a pillow and lay down on the couch. I knew that it was Daddy's way of ending the conversation. He needed to digest this revolting bit of information. He would save more comments for another day.

However, Madea wasn't quite through. "Those people should be ashamed!" she asserted. "They always treated Black people like dogs. I remember you had a 13-year-old-cousin, Uly. They said he whistled at a white woman. They beat that boy so bad..." her voice trailed off as she remembered the incident. "Then Uly disappeared until he was a grown man. They say that those white people held him in slavery. Things weren't like they are here in Denver. That's why we didn't want to raise you in the south. We didn't want to you to grow up hating people just because some of them don't do right. We all God's people! All the same people! But some people jest got the devil in 'em!" She went into the kitchen and got Daddy's coffee. We changed the subject and watched a game on TV for a while. Then Dennis and I left.

I went back home and tried to get the pain in my father's eyes out of my head. I had fulfilled a promise, but at what cost? Still, I knew that my father needed to hear the truth. He was no stranger to the horrors of racism. I reasoned that the imagination was often more brutal than the truth. But I had to admit that the truth about Grandpa Charley might have been worse than even the most horrific nightmare.

Driven to find out more about my ancestors, I turned my

thoughts to Grandpa Huey's parents. If Blacks could be treated so callously even as late as the 1970's, what was slavery like? And how had it impacted the family legacy? I pulled out the 1870 census that I had printed from the computer. Now that I had Grandpa Huey's death certificate, I knew that he was born in Mississippi in about 1848 and that his father's name was the same as his son's name, "Harmon Lewis." Grandpa Charley was named after his grandfather! Now my task was to find the census with "Harmon Lewis from Mississippi" and to find out what truths surrounded my great-great-grandfather.

Over the next ten years, I uncovered a lot of information through my research. I learned that the first Harmon Lewis was born a slave in Mississippi. He later "married" Nancy, another slave on the plantation. Harmon was sold away from Nancy when grandpa Huey was just a baby. After being sold to the Lewis family in Mississippi he "married" Syntha and they had thirteen children, some of them born in slavery. I discovered that Syntha had been sold at least five times to various slaveholders. When she was ten years old, her "owner" died without a will. She and the other slaves on the plantation were separated to settle various debts owed to a multitude of people. Because the slaves were a commodity, very few of their families were kept together. Syntha was used to settle a $450 debt. Then, when she was just twelve years old, she was sold as a "fourteen-year-old wench" and bore her first child. The children that she had before she "married" Harmon had been sold away from her. Some of the children that Syntha and Harmon had in slavery were willed to Lemuel Lewis' children after Lemuel died. Lemuel had several children who then frequently loaned and/or sold the slaves to one another. Although Harmon and Syntha did manage to find, and re-unite with most of their children after emancipation, one of Syntha's twins, (Emily), died less than seven miles away, without ever knowing her mother. Both Syntha and Emily died by fire. Syntha's parents also lived in Mississippi.

Syntha was reunited with her own mother after emancipation.

I found that (Mississippi) Harmon's father was Choctaw/Cherokee Indian named Tom, who was married to an African woman named Jane. Tom was captured and enslaved when he and a band of other Cherokee's raided the plantation where Jane lived. Their children were identified as "mulatto" on some documents and "colored" or "negro" on others. Many of the descendants of these children still live in the same area of Mississippi today.

I also found information about my mother's ancestors. Her Grandfather Frank was born into slavery to an African woman named Mariah, and nicknamed "Kitty." Kitty had at least six owners and least twelve children in slavery. The children were all sold away from her except my Grandfather, Frank. Frank and Kitty were sold together as a "lot" when Frank was about 10 years old. She was sold for $1200, and he for $900. Grandpa Frank had indeed been married seven times during his 80-something years. Grandpa Frank is buried in Louisiana, near his mother Kitty.

My Grandma Sarah's father Green Harris was indeed full blood Creek Indian as my father had always told us. Green's mother, Lizzie was very light skinned. Briefly, she went on to "pass" for white, and married a wealthy white man. It is very possible that her husband's family found out about her heritage, because his father disowned him and cut him out of his will. Green moved to Louisiana, and was identified as "colored" on the 1870 census, because the census taker decided that the family was "colored."

I uncovered many historical facts about my family during my search. I knew the names and the places. Old newspapers revealed events in their lives. Nevertheless, there was still something that I needed to do. I needed to go back and "walk the walk" that my ancestors had. I had taken the first step when Dennis and I went to Senegal. Now I needed to start in the first place that I could really identify. That place was present day Columbia, Mississippi, which is the county seat for Marion County.

19

"Roots Discovered"

ennis and I arrived in Mississippi about the middle of May. I had communicated by email to a woman named Christine, who had been generous enough to answer my internet "query," and tell me that she lived on the property on which my ancestors had formerly been enslaved. Christine was a genealogist too and as such recognized how important it was for me to see this land. I didn't know what to expect. Initially, Dennis and I thought we would try to find the graves where Harmon and Syntha were buried. After hunting through many graveyards, we finally realized that because Syntha had been killed in a fire that leveled her home, there might not be a grave. We decided to move on to the next task. We headed to the address that we had from Christine's email.

As we neared Christine's property, I noticed that Dennis seemed to be analyzing his surroundings.

"What are you looking for?" I asked.

"Didn't you notice that people that look like us disappeared a while back?"

"Oh, yeah." I conceded, "I don't see any more Black folks."

Dennis drove the car starting stopping and turning when I called out instructions to do so. Suddenly he stopped the car in the middle of the road.

"What are you doing?" I asked. "We need to keep going straight."

"Didn't you notice?" He had a worried look on his face.

"Notice what?" I replied.

"We started disappearing about seven miles back." He stated. "Black people started disappearing!" he reiterated as he glanced at me.

I took in our surroundings. I had grown up in Colorado and some of the horror stories that I had heard from those who knew more about the south than I did started swirling around in my head.

I remembered warnings such as "Don't let the sun go down on your black ass in Mississippi!" or "Don't get caught in cotton town!" I knew that in the past, some of these warnings were even codified in law in what was called "Sundown Towns" where it was actually against the law to be there after dark. Although there were no such laws today, I was fully aware that there were certain areas where you couldn't be too careful.

Dennis slowly started the car moving down the road again. After many stops and turns, we found ourselves at a stop sign, not really clear as to what direction to proceed through the intersection. Suddenly Dennis mumbled, "Uh Oh! We got company."

An older white male on an all-terrain vehicle pulled up beside the car on the driver's side. Dennis rolled down the window and the man asked, "Whatcha doing around here?" to which Dennis replied, "Oh, I'm looking for 'Lee Lane.'"

There was a young child riding on the back of the vehicle with the older man. An interesting thing about life is the innocence at hand of a child before adults ruin that dimension. Before Dennis could say anything further, the child, approximately eight years, old stated, "That street is just up the road!"

If looks could kill, the child would have died at that moment, a victim of the hate-filled look given to him by the old man.

"Oh Yes!" Dennis quickly replied. "Now I remember what direction to go in. Just a little confusion for a moment."

The old man, with a look of amazement on his face, asked, "You been around here before?"

"Sure we have! Several times before but we came from a different direction and just got turned around wrong this time. Thanks a lot."

We started driving away from them and Dennis, glancing in the rear-view mirror said to me, "We got company!" The old man was following us from a distance. We reached the street we were looking for, made a right turn and Dennis pointed to a sign that said, "Dead End- No Thru Street." As we got to the end of the roadway Dennis said, "Going to turn the car around facing the intersection so that nothing is behind me." As he turned the car around, he motioned for me to look back at the main intersection. The old man on the vehicle was present and pointing a finger at us. A crowd of about 15 people was standing at the intersection with him. Dennis stated. "I might have to run somebody over with this big Cadillac. Hell if I'm getting trapped back here!

There were several houses on all sides of us as we wondered which one was the right one for us. Suddenly a woman appeared from one of the houses, walked up to the car and asked, "Can I help you folks?"

We explained that we had come to the area to see Miss Graves.

"You know her?" the lady asked.

"Yes we do." I replied. "We came all the way from Colorado to visit her."

The lady said nothing else and began walking toward the crowd. Dennis turned nervously to me and asked, "Don't you have the phone number the lady we're coming to see? Give her a call." A quick call gave us the information we needed, — all we had to do was turn to our left and her property was staring us in the face. Meanwhile, the crowd at the intersection vanished after the neighbor talked to them. We assumed she told them that we "were okay."

We found the home that we were looking for on the property. I knocked on the door. A young-looking woman, with a pleasant face opened the door. "Hi, you must be Johari." she offered.

"I am. And this is my husband Dennis." After we had exchanged introductions and a few pleasantries, Christine began to tell us about the land. The white Lewis' had owned over 1000 acres. The work was done mostly by slaves. The slaves had built the "big house" on the property, but it had been torn down some time ago. I thanked her for the information. "Would you like to see the graves in the back?" she asked.

"What a question!" I thought. I had come a long way, hoping for this moment. I smiled to myself. "Sure," I said to Christine. She offered to accompany us if we needed her to. We declined. I wanted to explore the graves on my own. Following her directions, we headed behind the trailer and past a pond in the back. I looked around, imagining my enslaved ancestors working and sweating in the hot sun. I looked at the huge oak trees, wondering if any of them had been whipped on those trees, and then I quickly pushed the thought away. But apparently not quickly enough, because out of the corner of my eye it appeared that three or four enslaved women were washing clothes in the pond, and crying. But like the slaves in the water at Goree Island, the tears were made of blood.

Dennis and I continued up the hill, trying to follow Christine's directions. "Go to the first road and take a right up the hill. Go a little ways until you see a broken fence. Just on the other side of the fence, you will see the graves. But they are easy to miss because they are mostly covered with brush." she had said.

Dennis and I came to a small clearing. Neither of us could decide if it was a road, or if it was a path. We kept going. Soon we came to another road, this one wider than the last. We took a right turn and kept going up a hill. We went about ¼ of a mile, and then decided that the smaller path must have been the road that Christine was talking about. We tried to backtrack but apparently took another wrong turn because neither of us saw a fence. We had almost decided to go back to Christine's and ask her to take us to the graves when Dennis pointed to a clearing among the trees.

"There it is!" he said.

"Where? I looked where he was pointing, but I didn't see anything that looked remotely like a cemetery.

"Right there!" he pointed again. Then he headed towards the clearing. I followed, not because I thought he saw anything, but I just didn't want to lose him in the woods. Then I saw it! There was a broken fence covered with leaves. Then on a small hill at the top of the clearing, was a tall monument. The stone was about four feet tall, the type of stone commonly used in the 1800's. My heart pounded as Dennis picked up a stick and cleared away the brush from around the fence. He took my hand, and together we climbed up the hill. When we got to the top, we saw two monuments, but the writing was so old that we could barely make out the letters. We cleared more mud and brush from the stones, and the words became clear. "Lemuel Lewis, Born 1804. Benjamin Lewis, born 1842. Margaret Summeral, wife of Ben Lewis, born 1846. These were the graves of the people who had enslaved my ancestors! Then we noticed that on the other side, beneath more trees were some slabs of stone in the ground. Most of them had sunk far into the ground. Dennis and I pushed away the leaves and tried to read the writing on the stones. But it was impossible! The stones were broken, and any trace of writing had long faded. There was a stark contrast, even now, between the two graveyards. I wondered if it was my ancestors under the slabs of rock. The sun was beginning to set. However, the Mississippi heat was still hot. Dennis and I took pictures of the stones, and headed back towards Christine's house. We told her we had found the graves. With the kind of hospitality that is typical in the south, she graciously offered us a tall glass of iced tea, and asked if we would like to stay for supper. We declined, and climbed back into our car.

The next morning we headed north, through Mississippi, taking note of how the Mississippi river flowed. It would have been a way of paddleboat travel during the slave trade. We made our way through Louisiana, and stopped in Minden, Madea's birthplace. We scoured the city for gravesites, attempting to find Grandma Kitty and Grandpa Frank.

We found gravesites for a few relatives with familiar sounding names, but Grandma Kitty and Grandpa Frank remained elusive. Needing a break from the hot sun, we stopped at the Webster Parish Library to browse their collection of old newspapers. I was browsing through the year 1917 when I came across headline entitled *"White Man Held for Reeves Murder; Negroes and White Youth Say Henry Waller, Planned the Crimes."* It was a horrific article about four children who were hacked to death with an ax on Christmas Eve. They had first rounded up "all of the negroes" in the community and later found that Henry Waller, a white man had planned the murders and executed the family. Although I knew that the white children were certainly not the ancestors that I was searching for, I continued to read to see what had happened to the family. As I turned the page to the next article, the headlines jumped out at me. There was a photograph of two Black men on the front page. The caption above the photo said "Two Negroes to Hang for Reeves Murder!"

FROM ALERS

Two Negroes in Reeves Case Will Hang March 1 **21**

Action To

BATON ROUGE, La., Dec. 8.—Governor Pleasant Saturday signed the death warrants of Mark Peters and Chester Tyson, both negroes, of Webster parish, who were convicted of implication in the murder of the Reeves family.

The board of pardons last week recommended that the sentence of these two men be commuted to life imprisonment, but the governor did not accept the recommendation of the board and sentenced the two men to be hanged in Baton Rouge Friday, March 1.

Four men are now in the penitentiary as implicated in the Reeves murder. Walters, a white man, was given a life sentence.

al deal-
peration
adminis-
the ad-
be di-
tion and
-operate.
and gen-
a tele-
of coal
city." It

you re-
ral fuel

Man Who Knocks Red Cross To Mother is Convicted

The Shreveport Times
January 31, 1917

Shocked, I continued to read to see how the Black men ended up hanging for the white man's murder. As my eyes moved over the page, two names jumped out at me: "The death warrants of **Mark Peters** and **Chester Tyson,** both negroes from Webster Parish, were signed by Governor Pleasant on Saturday. They were convicted of implication in the murder of the Reeves family."

My mind raced back to something that my mother had said. *"One of your cousins was picked up the night before his wedding for a murder that he didn't commit. They knew that the white man did it but he was sentenced to hang for it."* I was familiar with these names! Chester Tyson and Mark Peters were both my great-un-

255

cles! A chill went down my spine as I continued to read.

"….Long said that Henry Waller used an ax that belonged to the late *John Tyson, husband of Mariah Tyson!*"

So, the stories that I heard were true! Uncle Chester and Uncle Mark were sentenced to hang for the murders. But I also learned that their sentences were commuted so that they could live and testify against Henry Waller – the actual ax-wielding killer.

NEGROES NOT TO HANG UNTIL WHITES TRIED

(Associated Press.)

BATON ROUGE. LA., Aug. 10.—Governor Pleasant yesterday ordered a stay of execution until Friday, December 13, of Chester Tyson and Mark Peters, negroes, convicted of participation in the Reeves family murders at Minden, December 25, 1916. The negroes were to have been executed here at noon Friday.

The governor announced he would continue to reprieve the negroes until Henry Waller and John Long, both white, had been tried on different courts of the Reeves murder charge under which they were convicted and sentenced to long penitentiary terms.

The Montgomery Advertiser
August 10, 1918

"Johari?! Johari!" Dennis was coming over to the microfilm reader and waving his arms to get my attention. "We better get going before it gets too late."

"What did you find? You look all wild-eyed!" he noted as packed up my belongings.

"I found out about the murders. You know poor Chester spent

years in that prison for a murder he didn't do? Oh yeah, I found some information about Henry Waller using grandma Kitty's ax, and did I tell you that they rounded everybody up…..and…"

"Henry who?" Dennis asked, as he hurried towards the door.

"Waller. He used grandma's ax and blamed Chester."

"Ax?" Dennis asked, hurriedly getting into the car. "Can you grab that map for me? Let's see if we can find any more graves. Did you find anything at the library?"

Ninety minutes later, we pulled up to St. Paul Church. A graveyard peaked out from behind the church. Dennis and I got of the car and went to the edge of the graveyard. The left side of the graveyard looked starkly different from the right. The left side had large stones, and a manicured lawn. The right side of the graveyard was unkempt and many of the graves were marked only with the temporary markers from the funeral home. We headed to the left side, and reached the largest stone on that side. "Queen Esther Jack."

"Who is Esther Jack?" Dennis asked.

"I have no idea. Whoever she is, her family had lots of money. Maybe we are in the wrong graveyard." I offered.

We covered the left side of the graveyard, not recognizing any graves. I saw a stone marked "Courtney" and vaguely remembered that someone in the family was married to a Courtney. However, neither of us saw any Lewis graves.

Then we headed to the right side. There was a grave that was marked by a doll, dressed neatly in early 1900 attire. The words were hand carved in the stone. "Luella Woods," the stone said. Then underneath the name was carved "Cousin Little Sister." I flashed back to something Madea had said when she spoke about her family. She had mentioned playing with a "Cousin Little Sister." But realizing that we were in the south, and there might be 10 "Cousin Little Sisters," we kept looking. I came across a grave marked "Nettie Powell." I asked Dennis to take a picture of it, because I remembered that Madea had said that Nettie Powell was her teacher. Near Nettie's grave was several other Powell's. We snapped pictures of Edgar Powell, and Lewis Powell." We walked some more. Then I saw it. A wagon wheel covered with flowers! A wagon wheel! Daddy had described the place in St. Paul cemetery where Grandpa Huey was buried. This must be the wagon wheel that sat above Grandpa Huey's grave! I hollered out to Dennis and he ran over to see what I was so excited about. "It's Grandpa Huey! Hurry! Take a picture." He snapped a picture as I looked at the grave next to it. "Sarah L. Rankins!" Grandma Sarah's grave! "Dennis! Hurry! Here's Grandma Sarah." We made our way through the entire right side of the graveyard. Arthina Lewis. Ionnie Lewis. Henry Lewis. One after another, I came across the Lewis relatives. We took pictures of them all. Adrenaline still pumping from excitement, we headed to West cemetery where Madea said Grandma Gertrude was buried. There we uncovered more ancestors on Madea's side of the family." We were on the way back to the hotel when I saw the sign, "Grove, Louisiana."

"Wow!" I said to Dennis. "We are in the town where those murders happened.

"Murders!? What murders?" He was clearly confused about why I was suddenly talking about murders.

"The murders that I found out about at the library. Grandpa Frank's brother Chester was supposed to hang for them, remember?"

"Oh yeah!" Dennis remembered. "Maybe we shoul…"

"Stop!" I yelled. "Did you see that sign? Let's turn around and go back!"

"What sign?" Dennis said, turning around.

We turned around and headed back towards the sign. "Newsome Cemetery." It was a name that I remembered from reading Grandma Kitty's death certificate. Grandma Kitty was buried here!" As we entered the cemetery, I saw a broken headstone right by the gate. It said "Mealie Banks, 1804 to May 28, 1919. Age 115."

MELIA BANKS
1804-1919

I was stunned! Born in 1804? She would have experienced a lifetime of slavery, *and* had lived to see freedom!

"Oh my God!" I yelled. "This is Grandma Kitty's mother! Her name was listed on Grandma's Kitty's death certificate"

I knelt down near the side of her grave, and brushed the leaves away from the stone. I was overcome with emotion as I pondered the life that she might have led. Dennis snapped a few pictures and we continued to make our way through the cemetery.

GRAVE OF HUEY LEWIS
St Paul Cemetery, Taylor, Arkansas
The "Wagon Wheel"

GRAVE OF LUELLA WOODS
St Paul Cemetery, Taylor, Arkansas

Finally, the day grew dark. We had filled about ten rolls of film, and uncovered more than five generations!

Seeing Mississippi and the graves in Arkansas and Louisiana was bittersweet. On one hand, there was a much greater appreciation for all that my ancestors had gone through. As we visited each grave, or town, I could only imagine what we, as a people had done to survive. Christine had said that the (white) Lewis's owned 1000 acres. As I looked at the land, I imagined what backbreaking work it had been to plant and harvest 1000 acres of cotton and tobacco under deplorable conditions and the threat of the whip. Dennis and I were drained as we headed back to the hotel. We still managed to talk long into the night. Although we were supposed to head back to Denver the following day I felt I needed to make one more stop. I knew I had a cousin named John Richards in Pine Bluff, Arkansas. He occasionally called my mother to see how the family was doing. I remembered my father talking about growing up with John and John's brother Cooley, in Taylor. John would be about 87 years old now. I welcomed the chance to reconnect with him, and Pine Bluff was just a slight detour off of our return route. As we pulled up to the house there were several people milling about in the yard. Curious, one of the women came up to the car.

"Hi, my name is Celeste. Are you all lost?"

"No, we're looking for John Richards. He's my cousin. I'm Tommie Lewis' daughter."

"Oh! Hi Cuz!" Celeste laughed. "Come on in!" John's in the house.

As we made our way into the house, John squealed in delight. "I remember when you were real little." He laughed. "And you still got that out-west proper accent"

John made us feel right at home. We told him about the family history mission that we were on, and asked him if he knew anything about Grandpa Huey or the rest of the ancestors.

"I grew up with Grandpa Huey." he stated. "He was a little man but he worked real hard. He was my mother Litha's Daddy. I guess

261

they told you how he died?" John didn't wait for an answer. He loved to talk and he went right on telling us about "the old days."

"I used to box, and they called me 'Big John'. And nobody would mess with 'Big John'. Me and your Daddy use to play basketball and I would whup his ass. He thought he played better than me, but he didn't. We all lived in Taylor for a lot of years cuz all the old folks was in Taylor. Grandpa Huey and his brother Old Man Lewis Powell didn't live too close together, but we was all family!"

"His brother who?" I had never heard this bit of news before.

"His brother, Lewis Powell. The Powells were teachers in Taylor. You heard of the Powells?"

"Well yes, I've heard of them but I didn't know that we were related to them.

"Oh yeah!" John retorted. You know about slavery don't you? In slavery white folks sold people and stuff. Like, say I was white and I owned you. I could sell you or your kids anytime I wanted."

"Yeah, I know a bit about slavery but I guess there's a lot about the family that I don't know." I conceded.

"Well, you see, that's what happened to the Lewis' and the Powell's. They got separated in slavery. Grandpa's brothers are the Powell's and some of the Jack's too. All of em got separated.

"The Jacks?!" Dennis piped up. "You mean the Jack's with the nice graves and all the oil?"

"Yep!" John stated. "They said that Grandpa Huey had oil on his land too, but they never pumped it!

John went on to tell me other tidbits about the family and the old days. He was a fascinating source for my genealogy. Too soon, it was time to go. We left with a promise to return soon.

We headed out to the highway looking for the sign that said "I-70 West," so that we could head back to Denver. We made a wrong turn and ended up on highway 229. We passed a sign that said "Haskell City Limits." Right behind the "Haskell" sign, was one that said "Arkansas Medical Center Cemetery."

"Turn right!" I shouted at Dennis.

"Huh?" Dennis asked as he swung the car onto the dirt road. "Do I need to make a u-turn?"

"No go straight!" I said excitedly. "Just one more stop, I promise. I think we just found Grandpa Charley's grave"

We opened the gate and peered out at the grassy field. At first it was hard to tell that it was a cemetery, because most of the markers on the graves lay flat and were hard to see from a distance. But after a closer look I noticed that the circular markers all seemed to bear a grave number. I looked at each of them until I came to number 58.

"Here!" I yelled to Dennis. "He's buried over here!"

Dennis came dashing over with his camera and knelt near the grave. He pushed the marker slightly so that he could get a better picture of it. He frowned, gently wiggled the marker, and twisted it. Then he pulled it straight up out of the ground. He looked curiously at his discovery.

"What is it?" I asked.

"Juice can." He flatly stated. "It's nothing but an old juice can!"

I studied the can that he held in one hand. It was an old can that had been filled with cement, and the number "58" crudely written in the center. Most of the other graves bore the same type of marking.

"Unbelievable!" I said, disgustedly! "A man spends his life trying to care for his family and do the right thing, and at the end, he's reduced to a rusty old juice can, that doesn't even bear his name!

At long last I had found Grandpa Charley's grave. Beneath the soil lay evidence of a very tragic episode in America. Grandpa Charley's grave and the graves of others surrounding it proved that even after emancipation; even after the "civil rights" and "equal rights" movements; and even as late as 1972 — which was more than 100 years after "freedom," black men were still as expendable as lab rats.

On the way out of the cemetery we noticed that there were a few new markers on some of the old graves. I wondered if others had uncovered similar tragedies about their loved ones, and had finally marked their graves with a dignified headstone.

We left the cemetery and finally headed west on I-70. The following day, we were back in Denver, Colorado.

I continued to pursue the family history at every opportunity. A few years later, my daughter Olisa and I were driving back from Tuskegee, Alabama. We had been checking out colleges and I had been looking for family links. As we passed a sign that said, "Welcome to Minden," I turned to Olisa and pointed to the sign. "That's where your Grandma was born. Right here in Minden, Louisiana. And you have a lot of family in Taylor Arkansas. Our family cemetery is right behind the church!

"Oh, Mom!" she squealed. "We should stop!"

I smiled, because I had been thinking the same thing. "Yes, we should," I agreed, turning off Highway 20 to Highway 371 towards Taylor. I wanted Olisa to see where her relatives were buried. And I wasn't surprised that she wanted to go there. Olisa had developed a passion for learning about her history. I had no doubt that one day she would be almost as obsessive about it as I was.

It was early afternoon when we pulled into St. Paul cemetery. We got out of the car and headed towards the graves. We went from one grave to another as I pointed out where everyone was buried. By the time we got to Grandpa Huey's grave by the wagon wheel, tears were streaming down Olisa's cheeks. She fell to her knees and began to pray. I knew how overwhelming this moment was for her. It wasn't that long ago, that I saw the wagon wheel for the first time and had the same reaction. Grandpa Huey's grave held a lot of distinction, not only because of the way that he died, but also because he was the last known enslaved family member.

We were finished looking at the graves, and slowly making our way to the front of the cemetery when I noticed a woman going in and out of the church. She got in her car, and then apparently remembered something in the church, because she got out of the car and went back into the church.

"Wouldn't it be something if she was one of our relatives?" I asked Olisa.

"Yeah," she agreed. "But what are the chances of that?"

Now, we had reached the back of the church and the woman was coming back out again. She was a nice-looking older woman with a kind face. She looked up and saw us.

"How you?" she asked.

"Fine!" Olisa and I answered in unison.

"You know some people out there?" She pointed to the grave-yard.

"Yes, Ma'am," I said. "My Grandpa Huey Lewis, and my Grandmother, Sarah Lewis Rankin, are buried there. Do you know of them?"

"I sho' do!" she said with apparent delight. "My name is Minnie Walker. My husband is John Walker. My husband is your daddy's cousin. My husband is your Aunt Della's son!"

"He is?" I was excited now. I had the good fortune to run into a relative in Taylor! And one that liked to talk. She told us that my Aunt Della was Grandma Sara's sister. We must have stood in that church parking lot for an hour! During that time Miss Minnie, (as I called her), delighted us with stories of the past, mostly about people who were buried in the cemetery in front of us. Then all too soon, she announced that it was time for her to go.

"Miss Minnie?" I asked. "Do you know if a Charley Lewis, III lives around here?"

"Junior?" she asked. "Sure! Charley Junior just lives around this road and down the next. I see Junior all the time. He's your Daddy's brother's son. He's your first cousin. He probably back there. You should stop and see him!"

Olisa and I thanked her and headed down the road, in the direction she had pointed. We arrived at a trailer that looked just like the one that she described. There was a man in front of it, working on a tractor, trying to get it going. Olisa and I got out of the car, and the man walked up to us with a curious look on his face.

"Don't reckon I've seen ya'll before. Did you lose your way?"

"I think we just found it!" I smiled. "You wouldn't be Charley

Junior would you? My name is Mary. I'm Tommie Lewis' daughter."

"Little Mary?" Junior squealed. "You's Little Mary? Well I ain't seen you since you was about three years old. Come give yo' cousin a hug!" We all laughed and hugged each other. Then Junior called out to a boy that was standing by the trailer. "That's my grandson," he said. Then he shouted to the boy.

"Hey boy! We got kinfolk right here come to see us. Run and get yo' Mama boy! Run!"

His grandson took off running and disappeared behind the trailer. He returned a few moments later with a smiling woman wearing an apron. It was Junior's wife. We hugged her, and then we sat in the chairs that they offered us. We sat in those chairs for the better part of an hour, as Charlie delighted us with one story after another about the old relatives who had grown up in Taylor. It felt good to have a connection with a "long lost" cousin. Finally, we said goodbye to Charley and his wife, and his sons, who had joined us. We left with a promise to come back often. In my mind, I was already planning my next trip! I knew that I would be back soon.

20

"Generation X"

It was a cool crisp Friday in September of 1985. I had taken a "floating holiday" from work, and got myself a sandwich and a cup of coffee. I picked up the paper and sat down on the couch in front of the TV. I looked forward to catching up on the news and leisurely reading the newspaper. I clicked the "on" button on the remote and took a sip of the coffee. The reporter caught my attention as I heard him say, " ...at George Washington High School." I looked up from the paper. Lisa and Niecy attended George Washington High! I wondered what was going on at the school. As I looked at the TV, I saw many of the students walking out of the school with picket signs and chanting something. I smiled to myself. "Well that's a familiar sight," I thought, flashing back to the 1960's! Then the reporter said, "We go now to Lisa Green, one of the students who is responsible for leading this walk-out today. "Lisa Green?" I thought. "My daughter or another Lisa?" Then I saw her. Yep! It was *my* Lisa.

"Miss Green, I understand that you have given the principal a list of demands that are to be met before you and the other students will agree to return to the classroom. Can you tell us what those demands are, and how they led to this walk-out today?" The reporter stuck the microphone under Lisa's nose so that she could speak. She grabbed the microphone from him and began to list the demands.

"First of all, I would like to say that we have tried to resolve these issues many times in the past, and the principal has refused to meet with us. We had no choice but to walkout to get her to listen. We walked out because there is no African American History taught at this school. And the history that they do teach is 'revisionist' history that is grossly inaccurate!"

"Uh, oh," I thought! Now this *really* sounds familiar. It sounded like the protests of the 1960's. Lisa continued her tirade.

"And it is not just the history books that we have a problem with. *All* of the books that they give us are outdated. We are using books that are 20 years old that are passed down after students at the white schools get through with them. Some of the books are as old as dirt!"

"She's right." I thought. It had been that way for years. Poor materials and old books. Even some of the teachers admitted to looking at G.W. as a starting point to get experience and move up to a "real" school with better salaries and better materials.

"Thank you Miss Green." The reporter turned to another student to get another perspective.

Lisa turned and joined a group of students who were standing behind her. She raised her right fist in the air and began to chant.

"NO-NO-WE-WONT-GO...NO-NO-WE-WONT-GO" The other students joined in until there was a loud chorus chanting "NO-NO-WE-WON'T-GO." Then one of the other students climbed on top of a platform. The student turned around and started to lead the students with another chant.

"WHAT DO WE WANT!?" she shouted.

"Justice!" the other students answered.

"WHEN DO WE WANT IT!?"

"NOW!!" they shouted back. I walked up closer to the TV to get a better look at the student on the platform. It was Niecy, my other daughter! That figured. Niecy was in the thick of it too! But I can't say that I was surprised. Niecy loved a good protest!

The camera "cut" back to the reporter who was summing up his take on the situation at G.W. "The students here feel that because their school is predominantly Black, they are receiving poor materials in their school. They also believe that the teachers at the school receive far less pay than in schools in white areas, and that this results in the better teachers refusing to accept positions at G.W. They are demanding a raise of at least 6% to bring the salary for the faculty on par with other schools. School officials are asking the parents of these students to come down to the school and encourage them to return to the classroom. Over 60% of the students have walked out. Classes may be cancelled for the day if they do not return soon." Some of the parents were already beginning to arrive. I sat my coffee down, and grabbed my purse and keys. The newspaper and coffee would have to wait until later. I had to get down to the school, and get my daughters back in class!

When I got to the school, I waded through students and reporters in an attempt to find my daughters. I found them. A crowd of protesting students surrounded them. Lisa was on the top of a car with her fist in the air leading a chant, and shouting:

"We want 6%! We want 6%! We want 6%!"

When Lisa saw me, she happily climbed off the car and ran over to me. She didn't expect me to be angry because she knew that I had had my share of protests in the past. One of the reporters ran over me and stuck a microphone under my nose.

"Are you a parent of a student here at G.W.?" he asked.

"Yes. I'm Lisa's mother."

"Are you here to send you daughter back to class?"

"That depends. If this is the only way to call attention to the problems and find out just how poor the materials at this school really are, then I'm all for it! And the students are correct about how disparate the salaries are for the teachers who teach here in comparison to other high schools. Why do you suppose they are paid less?" I asked the reporter.

"I'm sure you have a theory," he answered.

"Yes, I do." I stated. "It's because this is a Black school. We are not willing to invest in the basic needs of a Black school, but I am quite sure that tomorrow morning your paper will be full of stories about how the test scores in Black schools are so much lower."

Satisfied that I had the reporter handled, Lisa went back to her chanting. After I talked to the reporter, I headed inside to speak to the principal. By now, the administrative officials were huddled together promising to "look into the situation." Several of the parents joined them and we talked for about 45 minutes. Finally, the administration promised to try to correct some of the problems. While the students protested outside, we came to a preliminary solution. However, the school day was almost over, so school was dismissed for the rest of the day. A few hours later, I went home to listen to the news.

The salary for the teachers increased a little bit after several meetings, (not quite the 6% that the students wanted) but there didn't seem to be much change in the books and materials for the students. In fact, a few years later, there was a similar scenario.

It was a Tuesday, but I had the day off because I was going to work the weekend shift. The phone rang at about 10:45 that morning. It was the parent of another G.W. student. Her daughter was a classmate of Zuton, my youngest daughter.

"Are you watching the news?" she asked.

"No. Why?" I answered.

"Because your daughter and my daughter and a whole lot of other kids just did a 'walk-out' from school!"

"Here we go again," I thought. I turned on the news and sure enough, Zuton was in the thick of it. I grabbed a jacket and my keys and jumped in the car.

When I arrived at the school, some of the teachers were herding the parents into the lunchroom, which was not yet open for lunch. Some of the parents were outside of the school pleading with the students to go back to class. I got out of my car and walked towards the front door of the school. I saw Zuton break away from the picket line and run towards me. Then I spotted my friend Juju's daughter who was still on the platform. She just smiled and started chanting louder. When Zuton reached me, she was still holding her sign, and she was out of breath.

"Mom! We tried to talk to the Principal! She won't listen," Zuton complained as she reached me. I knew the story all too well, because I had complained about it myself over the years. Many of the books were every bit as bad as they had been years ago. Some of them had half of the pages torn out. In some of the classes two or three students had to share one book! I had suggested to Zuton that she and a few of the students write down their grievances and ask the principal to meet with them to see what could be done. Apparently, my suggestion had somehow gone awry.

"Well, what did she say?" I asked.

"Nothing!" Zuton said. "She refused to talk to us!" I wondered if Zuton and I had the same definition of "ask." I doubted that the principal would outright dismiss a plea for a better education, if they had asked her properly.

"Okay." I said. "Let me go inside and see what's going on!" I headed to the door of the school, along with Zuton and a few of the other parents. We joined the others in the lunchroom. I noticed some of my friends there, who also had students who attended "George." Some of them had been on picket lines with me in the 60's when we were in school, so this was nothing new to them. Many of us were more amused than angry with our kids, because we had had our fair share of protests, walkouts, and sit-ins. We greeted each other by raising a fist in the air, which was known as "the "power sign," in the 60's. Then we quickly turned our attention to the situation at hand. We were parents now, and we had to approach the situation a little differently than we might have in the past!

A teacher was at the microphone in the front of the lunch-room.

"We will not tolerate students leaving class!" he exclaimed. "Every student who is not back in 20 minutes will be suspended from school!" A groan and a loud buzz were heard from the parents and students as everyone began to make their position known.

Seku, one of my friends and a "warrior" from the 60's civil rights movement, stepped up to a microphone that had been set up in the middle of the room for the parents.

"I talked to my daughter about the situation at this school. I told her to meet with the principal, and try to work the situation out," he said. "What happened in the meeting with the principal?"

"Ms. Johnston has not met with the students," the teacher said. "Mrs. Johnston and this school have zero tolerance for belligerent students. This school requires the students to follow the rules. They can't just make demands and leave school when they don't get their way!"

"Ok," I said. "Let us speak with Ms. Johnston, so that we can see why it came to this walkout. There was more conversation and then the teacher finally went and got Ms. Johnston. When Ms. Johnston came in, one of the parents asked her if she had met with the students about better books and materials at the school.

"I don't have time to stop and address every little thing that the students want to talk about," she stated emphatically! "And I'm taking time out of my busy day, to come down here and talk to you people. All I need from you is to get the students back to class." She turned her back and started to head back out of the lunch-room door.

"You People?!" I thought. In the 60's that was looked upon as a racist phrase that was used to put Blacks in their place. Nevertheless, I decided to give her the benefit of the doubt that she did not intend it to be racist.

"Ms. Johnston? Hey! Ms. Johnston!" I tried to get her attention before she left the room. I was going to ask her about setting aside some time to listen to the students. She turned to look at me.

"Look!" she said. "I don't have time for this! I have work to do! And if this lunchroom isn't cleared out, and the students aren't back in class by 12:30, I'm going to expel every one of them!" With that, she turned and left the lunchroom.

Then I became angry. "No wonder the students felt like they had to walk out," I stated to the crowd! "What is more important than kids who want a better education? She should be glad that these kids are interested in their education!"

"I think we should get the students in the whole school to walk out!" Seku shouted. "Hell! I'm not sending my daughter back to class until they meet with us!"

Now the parents were angry and talking about the "lack of respect" that Ms. Johnston had shown us.

"Mom," Zuton asked. "Do you want us to go back to class?"

"What do you think is the right thing to do, Zuton?" I asked. But I already knew the answer. I knew Zuton well enough to know that she wouldn't "go down" without a fight. At least, not when it came to her education.

"I think we should stay gone until they listen to us!" she stated emphatically.

"Then let's do it!" I agreed. "Let's walk!"

"Yeah, let's walk!" Seku's wife, Juju shouted. The parents were now in agreement with the kids. A line started to form in the lunchroom and we all marched to the door. Zuton started to chant.

"HEY-HEY-WE-WONT-STAY...HEY-HEY-WE-WONT-STAY." By the time we got to the door, we were chanting in unison.

"HEY-HEY-WE-WONT-STAY!" We chanted all the way out of the school. The students who were still outside saw us saw us marching, and heard us chanting and began to clap. They cheered and formed a line behind us. We formed a line that was about two blocks long, chanting, "HEY-HEY-WE-WONT-STAY." Seku led the protest line to Mt. Gilead, a Black church that was about two blocks from the school. There, the parents and students formed work groups, and developed a strategy to get the school admin-istration to negotiate a plan for better books and materials in the school. For the next two days, the students and parents met every morning in front of the school. First, we would form a line in front of the entrance. When the school bell rang, we would hold our signs high, and march to the church. We formulated our plans in writing. The Pastor of the church would take the list to the school, along with an offer to meet with our group. By now, the press was involved. Mrs. Johnston's refusal to meet with us was getting a lot of coverage. Then the press got a few copies of the books that the students at George were using, and copies of books that one of the white schools were using. They reported that the books being used at G.W. were so outdated that history books had no current history. But the science books really gave them something to talk about. Some of the experiments in the science books used tech-nology that had been surpassed 15 years before. They began to speculate that the books might bear a correlation to G.W.'s poor test scores in math and science. We were elated that the press was calling attention to the problems. Their coverage was starting to make Ms. Johnston sound like an uncaring principal. By the third day, Ms. Johnston agreed to meet with our group. We heard that she was now under fire from the school board. By the end of that day, plans were put in motion to get better books and a new cur-riculum put in place by the following quarter. By the next January, the students were proudly using new books, and the curriculum included a Black History class!

However, there were other problems at the school. There was also a big disparity in the suspension rate. Black students had a much higher suspension rate than white students. Then one day, Zuton called me from school after being threatened with suspen-sion. Dennis and I went down to the school to talk to Mr. Osmond, who was the assistant principal at that time. He told me that Zuton was being suspended from school for wearing red. He explained that the school had a "zero tolerance" policy against gang attire and the students knew "wearing colors" was cause for automatic suspension. He went on to inform us that Zuton was threatening to call the *Rocky Mountain News* if he didn't also suspend the white students who had on red attire that day.

"Zuton?" I asked, "What is this about?"

"Jessica and I have on the exact same thing. We are dressed exactly alike. But because I'm Black, they decided that I'm a gang member just because I have on red. They suspend Black students for all kinds of stuff. But not the white students."

Just then, Jessica arrived. Close behind her was a Black male student, looking dejected. They handed Mr. Osmond their notes. Mr. Osmond read the first note and then looked at Jessica. "Fighting again?" Mr. Osmond asked. Jessica shrugged her shoulders and sat in a chair by the door. I looked at the clothes that Jessica was wearing. Sure enough, her clothes were *exactly* like Zuton's, all the way down to the shoelaces! Suddenly I got it! Jessica and Zuton were trying to prove a point. They decided that they would prove that the suspension rate was discriminatory by showing that Black students were suspended for things that white students were not. They were particularly upset when one of their Black friends who was an "A" student wore a red t-shirt and was sent home, while a white student, who was in fact a member of a street gang and wearing the gang attire, was left alone. Zuton and Jessica had been friends for a long time. They put their heads together and got matching outfits. Then they made sure that they were seen by school officials, knowing that Zuton would probably be suspended, while Jessica would not. After Zuton was pulled from a class that they have together, Jessica took steps to make sure she would be sent to the office too. She wanted to make sure that the principal saw them in their identical attire. Neither of them wore the baggy pants or the signature "gang" jacket. They simply wore red outfits. After Zuton was sent to the office, she threatened to sue, and I got the call to come to school.

Mr. Osmond was writing something on his pad. He gave the piece of paper to the Black student who had walked in with Jessica. "Rod," he said. "Take this to the attendance office. I am through with you! You are suspended for three days! He wrote something on another note and handed it to Jessica. "Jessica," he said. "This is the third time you have been down here this week. I will let it go one last time, but next time I am going to suspend you! Now get back to class!"

Dennis and I looked at each other. "Is this the way things are normally done? Dennis asked. "Look at the way Jessica is dressed! Why is our daughter being suspended while Jessica goes back to class?"

"We treat all the students alike here." Mr. Osmond said. "Zuton is aware of the dress code and chose to violate it."

"First of all," Zuton said, "the dress code simply says that 'gang attire' is not allowed. But who gets to decided what gang attire is? Why is my attire 'gang' and Jessica's isn't? We are dressed exactly alike!"

Mr. Osmond looked at Jessica who had not left the room yet. Looking confused, he looked back at Zuton.

"Well apparently no one noticed how Jessica was dressed!" Mr. Osmond halfheartedly explained.

"And *that's* the problem!" I yelled. "It is automatically assumed that Blacks who wear red are gang members. And furthermore, why doesn't your 'zero tolerance' policy apply equally to both black and white students? You suspend my daughter and I'll sue. Hell! I just might sue anyway!"

An argument ensued. For the next thirty minutes, Dennis, Zuton, Jessica, Mr. Osmond and I tried to get our respective points across. Dennis was becoming hoarse from the "discussion." Finally, Mr. Osmond said. "Ok. Zuton can go back to class. But please adhere to the dress code in the future!"

Dennis pulled the door open. Three students who were apparently listening at the door almost fell through it! We gave Zuton a hug and told her that we would talk to her after school. Then we headed for home.

"The more things change, the more they stay the same," I remarked.

However, things did begin to change. Most of the students became more accepting of poor books and high suspension rates. By the time Zuton graduated from G.W., protests seemed to be a thing of the past. A few students would still "push the envelope" and fight for their rights. However, few of the other students would join them. Most of the students now had bigger problems to think about than being suspended from school, or even getting a good education. Today's students had to focus on how to stay alive with the growing gang problem!

21

"Crips, Bloods and the Hip Hop Generation"

It was nearing the end of the 1980's. The stereo was blaring in the basement. Niecy and her friends were in the basement listening to something that they called "music." Hip Hop. I think they called it. You couldn't dance to the stuff! They even had electronics that did voice-overs. All of the notes sounded the same. In fact, all of the songs sounded the same. There was little singing and lots of shouting.

"NIE—CY," I shouted towards the basement. "TURN THAT THING DOWN!" Niecy came bounding up the stairs.

"Did you call me Ma?"

"Yeah, but I'm surprised that you heard me over that stuff you guys call music."

"It is music, Mother!" (she always called me "mother" when

279

she was impatient with me about something). "You're just old," she teased.

"I'm glad I had the chance to listen to music when music was music." I retorted. "These new 'artists', if that's what they call themselves, don't even know what harmony or melody is! They just put on baggy pants down to here and backwards hats and strut across the stage yelling vulgarities to no one in particular. I'm surprised they don't trip on those pants! And their back-up singers put on skirts up to here that leave nothing to the imagination and wiggle to whatever that mess is that's supposed to be music. You should put on some Temptation's or Gladys Knight, or some Aretha! Now that's music!"

"Oh, Mother!" she was impatient with me again. "I don't believe that you're dissing Tupac that way. Tupac is deep! Have you ever listened to Tupac?"

"Tu Who?" I asked.

"Tu Pac!" she said emphatically. "Tupac Shakur."

"Ok." I said. "Go turn your guy 'Toothpick' down a little. He's giving me a headache!"

"Yes, Mother!" she sarcastically relented. Then she turned around and hopped back down the stairs singing something like, "Oooh, tell me where the booty went — oops there it is!" She turned "TuWhat" down to a dull roar. I smiled to myself, thinking back to the flack I got from my Mom and Dad when my friends and I did some of our old dances. Some of the "moves" made them speechless when they saw them. One evening a couple of my friends were showing them one of the latest dances.

"What kind of dance is that when you're way over here, and he's way over there?" Madea asked.

"They call it the Monkey," I replied, dancing to the beat with my back humped over, left foot co-coordinated with right arm, and then vice-versa.

"I'll bet they do!" she retorted. Now I realized just how stupid the dances of the '60's must have looked to her. The monkey, the jerk, and the dog must have seemed strange, not to mention obscene. She would rather hear Mahalia Jackson or Billie Holiday. But the Monkey or the Jerk? Her generation could have never imagined anything so bizarre! So I understood what Niecy thought of my music, and my generation.

But even though hip-hop seemed to require no musical talent, I had to admit that this new generation was savvy when it came to electronics. They knew how to get wired! Six-inch cellular phones! Ten-inch computers! They could carry their whole life in their pocket. And who would have ever thought that you could put a letter in a machine, and in minutes, it would print out on another machine in another city! I thought that fax machines were ingenious! And it seemed like it was just yesterday when I became positively giddy, because I saw a microwave oven bake a potato in 8 minutes! I thought that was the ultimate! No more waiting an hour for a baked potato. New technology was great! However, this new "computer age" was also a scary thing for some of us "older people." Would the "waves" from the microwave someday kill us? Would cell phones lead to brain tumors? Moreover, we wondered if the Hip Hop Generation would lose all social skills with the rise of the computer era. There was already less need for social interaction. You could get anything you wanted "on-line." Business phones were increasingly answered by machines instead of people. Would this generation wake up one day and discover that they forgot how to do what we used to call "shoot the breeze?" Would they even know how to sit on a porch and just talk?

I was still deep in thought when Niecy came bounding back up the stairs. "Mom!" she yelled. "Hurry and turn the TV to channel 7!" I rushed over to the television set and turned to channel 7. The news was on. They were talking about a murder that had taken place the night before. I recognized the home that flashed on the screen. It was in the Park Hill neighborhood, and was sealed off by police tape. A policeman was leading a Black teenager in handcuffs to a squad car. The cameras zeroed in on the teens face as he got close to the car. He looked very familiar!

"Niecy!" I demanded. "Isn't that the guy who was over here

yesterday?"

"Yeah." she said. "You remember James. He lived next door to Grandma, remember? I told him he was going to go out like that. They're going to lock him up for good this time!" I looked at the TV and then back at Niecy. A multitude of emotions washed over me in that instant. Curiosity. Anger. Resignation. It saddened me that it had become somewhat "normal," to turn on the evening news and see one of Lisa's or Niecy's or even Zuton's friends led away in hand cuffs. Most of them were kids who had grown up in the neighborhood. I remembered many of them as sweet little kids. Now they were headed for a lifetime in prison. Teenagers were killing teenagers for reasons as dumb as wearing red! It never made sense to me, why someone would do that. They called it a drug war! Crips against Bloods. Red against blue. Drive-by shootings, and retaliations. The Park Hill neighborhood that I loved had been turned into a war zone! The park that we had hung out at after school had been overtaken by teen-aged thugs. The park was becoming a favorite place to be "jumped in" to the gangs. Being "jumped in" was an initiation in which a potential gang member allowed the entire gang to beat him senseless. If he (or she) survived it, they became a part of the gang.

Growing up as someone who wanted to unify the Black community, this new generation was hard to take. I never thought I would see the day when the kids in our community disrespected each other with such zeal!

Nevertheless, I didn't realize just how bad the gang problem had become until tragedy hit my own family. It was a cool evening in January when I walked up to my door, having just come from the grocery store. Dennis yanked the door open before I got to it.

"Bobby Jr. has been shot!" he yelled as I hurried up the walk. I couldn't believe that I heard him right. Bobby Jr. was my nephew. He was my sister's son. He had called Dennis earlier that day, and asked him to come over to listen to him play a new set of drums that he had just gotten.

"What?" It really wasn't a question. It was more of a plea for him to tell me that I had heard him wrong. But the look in his eyes erased any hope that I had misunderstood. The look was a mixture of fear, dread, and frustration. I hurried inside and dropped the bags on the floor. Dennis grabbed his keys and headed for the car with me close behind. We jumped in the car and drove to Bobby Jr.'s house, which was about 2 miles away. On the way over, Dennis said that my Dad had called him and told him that Jr. had been shot, and that they were headed to his apartment. Thoughts were racing through my mind as Dennis spoke. There had been numerous shootings in the neighborhood that year, as a result of the gang problem. Many had resulted in death. They called it "The Long, Hot, Summer." And they called Holly Street, the street that Bobby Jr. lived on "death row." As we pulled up to the house, the scene before us seemed surreal. There were dozens of police cars surrounding the apartment where Bobby Jr. lived. An ambulance was parked outside. I noticed two policemen trying to hold my sister back as she tried to force her way into Jr.'s apartment. Madea and Daddy were running towards me and Dennis, to tell us what had happened. Tearfully, Daddy told me what they knew; Bobby Jr.'s friend Derrick, who lived down the street from my parents, had called his mother and told her that he and Bobby had been shot. He told her that he didn't think that they were going to "make it." Although he was in intense pain, he had a very important message for her.

"Mom," he'd said. "If we don't make it, just remember the name 'Baby George.'" Derrick's mother had run to my parent's house and told them what he had said. Then the three of them ran the two blocks to Bobby Jr's house, but the police officer wouldn't let them in.

"Baby George?" Dennis shouted. "Baby George is that thug that wanted to go out with Lisa, but we weren't havin' it. He's one of the most vicious gangsters around here!"

Just then, I heard an awful wail, and I looked towards Bobby's apartment. As long as I live, I will never forget that sound. It was a sound of pure anguish and pain. It was a cross between a scream and a cry. I looked up to see where the scream was coming from. It was my sister, Stella. The policeman was trying to pull her away from the house and get her to sit in the squad car. She was screaming and crying, "No. No. No. Let me see my son! I want to see my son!"

"Stella!" I cried. "Stella!" I tried to run over to the car, but a police officer stopped me. "Let me go!" I screamed. "My sister needs me!"

"Are you a relative of the people who live at 3627 Holly Street?" he demanded.

"Yes!" I shouted, still trying to get out of his grip. "My nephew lives there. Now let me go!"

"Ma'am, I'll let you go but you are going to have to calm down!"

"Don't tell me what I have to do!" I shouted. Dennis had reached us by that time.

"Let go of my wife." he said. "I'll take care of my wife. Just tell us what happened. Is my nephew okay?"

I pulled away from the policeman, and collapsed into Dennis' arms, sobbing uncontrollably. He held me until I calmed down a little bit. Then the policeman spoke.

"There was a shooting at 3627 Holly. We know that three individuals were shot. At this time, we don't know how seriously, they were hurt. Two of them were taken to the hospital. The ambulance there is for the third."

The policeman then turned to Dennis to get more information.

"Does your nephew live alone sir?" he asked Dennis.

"Yes. He lives alone." Dennis answered.

"Does he have any children?"

I became angry! "Look," I said. "We don't have time for chit chat! You can ask us questions later. I'm the one who needs answers now. "I just want to know if my nephew is okay!"

I saw a squad car going by. Stella was in the car. The policeman answered the question before I could ask it. "They are taking her to the hospital to see about her son." he said. "Would you like me to take you to the hospital? They are going to Colorado General."

"No. We have our car." Dennis answered.

We looked around for Madea and Daddy, and saw them standing next to our car. We got to the car and told them that we were going to meet Stella at the hospital.

"Did you talk to Stella?" I asked my Dad.

"I talked to her for a minute before they took her to the hospital. I'm really worried about your sister. This is really hard on her."

"I know." I said angrily. "They wouldn't let me get to her."

When we arrived at the hospital, we went to the emergency room. My sister and parents were there, along with Derrick's mother.

"Have you heard anything yet?" I asked no one in particular.

Derrick's mother answered me. "They said that Jr. was hit twice with a 9mm automatic Uzi. Derrick was hit in the throat, but it might have been a different kind of gun. The neighbors said they heard shots, and saw two men run from the house. There was also a young woman in the house who was shot. Her name was Sheila. They took her to Denver General. She didn't make it! My God, she has two little kids, that don't have a mother no more!"

It seemed like everything was moving in slow motion. Dennis must have led me to a chair, because the next thing that I remembered was getting up from the chair when a doctor walked into the waiting room. He headed for my sister, who was standing up at the time. I walked over to them so that I could hear what the doctor had to say. "Mrs. Frazier, We did the best that we could but I'm sor..." Stella interrupted his sentence with that awful anguished scream.

"Don't tell me that!" she screamed. "I don't want you to tell me that!"

"Mrs. Frazier, I'm am very sorry." he said, "The damage from the wounds was just too extensive."

I don't remember much about the next few hours. I remember hearing that Derrick might not survive either. In addition, if he did, he might have injuries that severely hampered his quality of life. I remember meeting Sheila's dad. He wondered how he was going to tell her two young children that their mother wasn't coming back.

They say that when something is too awful for us to handle that our mind blocks it out. I guess that is true because the next thing I remember is that someone from the Grief Counseling department came into the waiting room where we were. The clock on the wall indicated that it was early morning, but seemed to me that we had only been there a short time.

The counselor walked over to Stella. She was sitting on the couch, head in hands, overcome by what we had learned.

"Mrs. Frazier?" the woman asked. "We have people who can help in times of crisis. Would you like to talk to someone?"

Stella lifted herself up off the couch and looked at the woman, square in the eyes, with the most heartbreaking expression that I have ever seen. "My son is dead." she said flatly. "What is there to talk about?"

The next day when Dennis and I arrived at my parent's house, we waded through the reporters in the yard and went inside. Madea, Daddy, Stella, her daughter Elaine, and other family members were there. Stella looked up at me.

"Why would anyone want to kill my son?" she asked. "I knew that she didn't expect an answer because there wasn't one. I just shook my head, and tried to keep the tears from rolling down my face. Stella put her head back down on the couch and stared into space. I looked down at the newspaper that was on the table. The headlines stared back into my face.

"Two killed in gang-related violence!" it said in big bold letters. I became angry! Bobby Jr. was not a member of any gang! The press always made any crime in the neighborhood gang-related, whether it was or not. Bobby was the nephew that came over to visit Dennis and me a few times a week and teased me about my "nasty coffee that was always too weak. He was the kid who always surprised me with his knowledge about cars and science. When he was little, I teased him and told him that people who said that

Blacks didn't have scientific minds had never met him, because he had a brilliant scientific brain!

"I know Auntie," he would reply. "I am good!"

I thought of him as the kid who liked to play the drums and loved our back yard barbecues. He and Dennis would talk for hours about music, cars, and almost everything else under the sun. Now the newspapers had decided to report that Bobby Jr. was "gang" and then embellish the story to appear gang related because gang stories were what sold papers these days.

The next week was a blur. Dennis told me later that I went to the hospital to identify the body, and that I met with the funeral director to make sure they did a good job in making sure that Bobby Jr. looked his best. He told me that I went over to Bobby's apartment and cleaned up the house. He told me that I had carefully packed up Bobby's things and had given them to my sister. It would be an entire year before I remembered big chunks of the past week.

For the next few weeks, the media dissected the story from every angle imaginable. They kept doing "remotes" in front of Bobby Jr's house, always mentioning that Holly Street was called "death row" by many in the neighborhood. Then they would show pictures of youths who had been killed in the neighborhood around Holly Street. They talked about how crime had plagued the Black community, preventing people from enjoying any parks in the neighborhood. Moreover, they made it sound as though every Black youth was in a gang. They interviewed every neighbor and selectively reported tidbits that disrespected the neighborhood, and disregarded the truth.

However, just a few days later, the police did indeed find "Baby George." A few days after that, they located his accomplice, Wendell "Doc" Jones. The new cell phone technology helped to find them. Baby George's cell phone signal led the police right to his door. They arrested him without incident, and denied him bail. Soon my family was sitting in a courtroom with Judge Hufnagel sitting on the bench. Baby George was led into the courtroom.

The district attorney who was prosecuting the case, leaned over to me and said, "We got a good judge. They call her 'Hang 'em High Hufnagel!" he smiled. Now the judge was reading the charges:

"One count of kidnapping. One count of attempted murder. Two counts of felony murder. One count of drug possession with intent to distribute."

"How do you plead?" Four times, she asked the question.

"Not guilty," he repeated four times, one for each charge. They led him back to jail where he stayed until it was time for the trial, over a year later.

The trial was gut-wrenching. Little by little, the story came out. Baby George and Wendell Jones had gone to Bobby Jr.'s house, looking for another person who was a drug dealer, who had crossed them on a deal. They were at the wrong house. Not finding who they were looking for, they became angry and decided to kill anyone, and everyone who was in the house. They shot Bobby Jr., Derrick, and Sheila. They thought that all three were dead. They didn't want to leave anyone who could identify them. Derrick lay still until they left the house so that they would believe that he was dead. As they fled the house, the person who they were looking for was coming out of the house next door. They grabbed him and forced him into their car, planning to take him somewhere and "shake him down," for stealing their money.

For two weeks, we sat in the courtroom and listened to testimony, trying to make some sense of what had happened. Despite Baby George's and Wendell's threats to kill him, the man that they kidnapped turned state's witness, and testified against them. Derrick was also under police protection because Baby George had a "hit" out on him to keep him from testifying. Baby George's attorney's strategy was to discredit the other drug dealer, by revealing his former drug convictions. Nevertheless, the man was very compelling and convincing about Baby's George's and Wendell's part in killing Bobby Jr. and Sheila. In addition, Derrick was unwavering in his eyewitness testimony. Finally, the trial ended and both sides made their closing arguments.

The jury deliberated for two days before they reached a verdict. Finally, the district attorney called us at home. "We have a verdict. Please meet us in the courtroom at one o'clock. We filed into the courtroom at 12:30 pm and sat on the hard benches to wait for the judge and jury to arrive. The jury was led in. I looked at each of them, trying to get some indication from their faces as to what they had decided. However, the jury was expressionless, and did not meet our eyes. Then the judge walked in and everyone in the courtroom stood up, in accordance with courtroom etiquette.

"Please be seated." the judge said.

"Does the jury have a verdict?"

The jury foreman spoke, "We do, your honor."

The bailiff took the papers from the foreman and handed them to the Judge. The Judge looked at the papers and put them down on the desk in front of her. She looked at the jury and asked the questions;

"To the charge of possession of drugs with the intent to distribute, how do you find?"

"Guilty your honor."

"To the charge of kidnapping, how do you find?"

"Guilty, your honor."

"To the charge of attempted murder, how do you find?"

"Guilty your honor."

"As to charge number one of felony murder, how do you find?"

"Guilty your honor."

"As to charge number two of felony murder, how do you find?"

"Guilty, your honor."

The courtroom started to erupt in a loud buzz, and the Judge banged her gavel on the podium.

"Quiet!" she ordered. Then she continued, "I will now poll the jury!" A lump welled up in my throat. We had gotten a guilty verdict on all counts. However, I had forgotten that the judge still had to ask each juror individually, if they agreed with the verdict. It was just a little too soon to celebrate!

"Is this your verdict?" she asked juror number one.

"Yes, your honor." juror number one answered.

"Is this your verdict?" she asked juror number two.

"Yes, your honor." She asked the question twelve times. Twelve times the answer was, "Yes, your honor."

The judge was finally ready to hand down the sentence. "In the state of Colorado, sentencing guidelines mandate that the sentence for felony murder is forty years. This court will abide by those guidelines." Will the defendant please stand.

Baby George stood up.

"To count number one drug possession with the intent to distribute, 10 years. To count number two, kidnapping, 14 years. To count three attempted murder 20 years. To count four felony murder 40 years, with no possibility of parole. To count five felony murder 40 years, with no possibility of parole. The time for these crimes is to be served consecutively!"

"Consecutively!" I rolled the term around in my brain. The judge had sealed his fate!

"The judge spoke again. "Mr. Shanklin, had it been possible to give you a longer sentence I certainly would have. You have shown no remorse. But I can still insure that your sentence is served in such a manner that you'll never be free again!"

Baby George had been sentenced to the maximum time on each count! And Judge Hufnagel required one sentence to be served entirely, before the next one began. This meant that Baby George would not even be eligible for parole for 104 years! If by some miracle, he lived that long, he would be 128 years old when he was released from jail!

The Judge turned her attention to the jury. "I accept your verdicts, and I thank you for your service." she said to the jury. "You are excused." With that, the she stood up. Everyone in the courtroom followed protocol and ceremoniously did the same. The Judge went through the door and into her chambers. Then the courtroom erupted. The district attorneys congratulated us on winning the case. Some members of the jury came up to the family, hugged us, and told us how sorry they were that our family had gone through that kind of pain. The courtroom was filled with emotion! Many tears of relief flowed in that courtroom that day. Even the District Attorneys had tears in their eyes.

Finally, satisfied that Bobby Jr.'s killer had gotten what he deserved, I turned to walk out of the courtroom. I did not want Baby George to ever walk in freedom or breathe fresh air again, and the judge had insured that! When I got to the last row of the courtroom, I looked down and saw a teary-eyed woman, about ten years older than me. She looked up at me. I knew her face. She had been sitting in the same courtroom as my family had for the last two weeks. She had testified in Baby George's behalf. It was his mother! The look in her eyes caused me to think about the love a mother has for her children. More often than not, that love is unconditional. I thought about what the world in general and the Black community in particular had come to. As I looked into her eyes, I realized that the 9mm Uzi that her son held that cold day in January was responsible for taking more than just two lives that day. He had also killed a part of his mother's soul. There were many who had been hurt because of what happened in just four short minutes, over two years ago! Bobby Jr.'s life was over, and because of the way he died, no one in our family would ever be the same. Each of us lost a piece of ourselves that day. Each child in the family, who was old enough to comprehend what had happened, lost a bit of their innocence about humanity. Then there was Derrick. Even though he had survived, that day would be burned in his memory as he struggled with the question of why he survived, and his best friend didn't. It would be a long time before Derrick's mother stopped worrying about someone wanting to "finish the job." Then there was Sheila. Her two little children would grow up without a mother, and know that it was senseless violence that took her life. And it would turn out that just as George's mother had sat in the back of that courtroom that day, Wendell's mother would sit in almost the same spot, three months later, and she would suffer the same kind of loss as the Judge again sentenced another mother's son to spend the rest of his natural life in prison.

For the rest of the 1980's and into 1990's, the "gang problem" took its toll on the community. It wasn't just the Black community that was plagued by the gang problem. Hispanic gangs also fought for "territory." And as quiet as it was kept, there was even a huge gang problem with Asian Gangs, who many said were even more vicious than the others. However, people identified the Black community most closely with the gang problem. Generation X lost at least 15 years trying to solve the problem of the Crips and the Bloods. Thousands of young Black men were jailed during "the drug war." Many will be in jail for at least twenty years! Some will never walk in freedom again!

The
Millennials

The Tenth Generation

"Generation Y"

Why go to a movie when you have a theatre at home?

22

"Hope for the Future"

A few months after that, Niecy had little time to *think* about the gangs much less spend time with them.

It was a crisp, cool day in 1991. It was that day when I made the transition from Mother to Grandmother. It was one of the most wonderful days of my life! Niecy called me that morning, while I was at work.

"Mom, I'm in labor!" she said excitedly.

"Yeah, okay." I said in a bored tone.

"Mo-ther!" Niecy said in a tone that indicated that she would not be dismissed. "For real this time! I really am in labor, Ma."

"Ok." I said, "Time your contractions and call me back."

For the past two weeks, Niecy had called almost daily, claiming to be in labor. Not that she was trying to "snow" me, but she really thought that she was in labor. However, a few hours later she would call back and announce. "Sorry Ma, false alarm!" So naturally, when she called on that day, I thought that she was mistaken. After all, it was a whole week before her due date! When the phone rang two hours later, I picked it up with a laugh. "False alarm?" I asked.

"No Mom," she said excitedly. "I told you! I'm in labor for real this time! I just called the doctor and he said to come on in when they get five minutes apart!"

My own excitement started to build. "I'll pick you up!" I said. "And by the way, don't eat anything or you'll be sick" I remembered back to when I had Lisa. I ate breakfast in the morning. Then I had a 24-hour labor, and I was sick as a dog.

About two hours later, I picked Niecy up and headed to the hospital. She was calm and the contractions were still light. "Did you eat anything?" I asked.

"Yeah I did. Actually I knew it might be a long time and I might be hungry."

"You'll be sorry you did that!" I glanced over at her.

"Oh, Mother," she groaned. "You worry too much! We were about five minutes from the hospital when I noticed that Niecy had gotten very quiet. I looked over at her. "Are you okay?" Niecy's face was a weird shade of green. Her hands were over her mouth.

"I think I'm going to throw up!" she announced. I pulled the car over to the curb, so that she could get out of the car and get some air. Too late. Two minutes later, I looked at what had been a clean car this morning. She had thrown up all over the car.

"Sorry Mom," she said dejectedly.

"It's okay," I answered. There would be time later to say, "I told you so." I would wait until I could really rub it in!

The baby arrived about nine o'clock that night. I thought that Niecy had an easy delivery, but I don't think she agreed! Nevertheless, it didn't matter. She had a beautiful daughter, and I had a beautiful granddaughter! Raisha Janae. Niecy named her Janae as a twist on Jane, my middle name. Raisha signaled the beginning of the next generation in my immediate family.

Raisha kept her busy day and night. It was fun to watch Niecy with Raisha. When Niecy was growing up, I imposed the "Mother's curse" on her and I told her that I hoped she had a daughter just like her. Now my wish was coming true right before my eyes. Payback was sweet. Raisha, precocious as she was, brought the kind of joy into my life that only a grandmother knows! By the time Raisha was two years old, she was dancing around, booty in the air, singing, *"Can you tell me where the booty's at? Whoops! There it is!"* Yep! Double payback! One of Raisha's favorite shows was "Cops." The police cars on the show were okay but what she liked most was the theme song. When it came on, she sang and danced to the beat, *"Bad boy! Bad boy! What you gonna do? What you gonna do when they tell on-a you?"*

She kept us laughing all of the time, but she had her tender moments too. Her favorite kid's show was "Barney," the big Purple dinosaur. She would always sing along with Barney at the end of the show, *"I love you. You love me. We're as happy as can be...."* She would end the song by going up to the TV and hugging the screen, which was as close as she could get to hugging Barney. I thought that it was the cutest thing!

Nevertheless, Raisha started to grow up quickly! Of course, she wasn't as old as she thought. She was about three years old when she decided that she should be thinking about a job. Dennis and I were at Niecy's house on a hot July afternoon.

"Raisha," can you go get Nana my juice? It's in the bottom part of the refrigerator. Raisha looked at me as if I had two heads!

"I can't get you no juice out of that refrigerator! I can't touch that refrigerator cuz I don't even have a job!" she announced. I think I laughed for an hour. Yep! It would be interesting to watch the grandkids grow up. You never knew what they were going to do.

Over the next twenty years, I would make thirteen trips to the hospital, and witness the birth of my other grandchildren. Kiante in 1994, and Brianne in 1996. Then Zuton married David and started her family. Zumante was born in 1999, followed by Ashantay in 2001 and D.J. in 2003. Then in December 2005, I flew to Atlanta and arrived in time to witness the birth of my seventh grand-child, Monye. Again, a beautiful baby girl. At that time, Zuton was pregnant with a boy. She delivered Elijah Green in March 2006. We now had four granddaughters, and four grandsons! Then in August 2006, Modupe Yekpewa, my 9th grandchild, made her entrance in Atlanta, Georgia! Dennis and I hoped we would have at least ten grandkids, especially after we asked Raisha if she was going to take care of us when we got old. Raisha was about 6 years old at the time.

"I thought that was what old folk's homes were for?" she re-plied with a serious look on her little face. Dennis and I looked at each other. "See I told you we need at least ten grandkids," he laughed. "Maybe one of them will take care of us!" In July 2007, Maxwell Antonio fulfilled our wish. He was our tenth grandchild! And joyfully we had even more than ten. In July, 2008, Aina Kes-an, made her entrance as number eleven. Then in May 2011 Ojo claimed position number twelve followed in July 2011 by NiaMani who completed our "baker's dozen."

It seemed like a New York minute between the time that Rai-sha was born and when she entered middle school. Her school, MLK, was named after Martin Luther King, Jr. Bussing had failed. Most schools had become resegregated and Raisha's school was almost all Black. I thought back to my alma mater, Manual High school. I went to Manual before bussing was implemented. I loved Manual. Manual had spirit! It was the end of the sixties, and at that time, Black folks still called each other "My sister" or "My broth-er." Although this terminology is still used today, in the 60's it was shorthand for our common struggle. At Manual, we all looked out for each other, and took it personally if our basketball team lost to a white team. But when I walked into MLK, I suddenly realized that I was in another world! I had heard awful things about MLK. Things like daily fights and weapons carried by students. Things like young girls being raped in the bathroom. Things like after school parties where some of the boys would sneak drugs into girls drinks, and then rape them, sometimes gang rape them. And just last week, at Montbello High, which was MLK's sister high school, a 16 year old kid was stabbed and killed by a 17 year old kid.

One day I was feeling particularly frustrated with the school system. I walked into the school, and went directly to the office to get Raisha's schedule and find her.

The office assistant was obviously bored when she looked up at me. "Are you here to pick up a child?"

"No, I'm not." I answered her. "Actually, I'm here to sit in on a class and see what in the world is going on at this school. I repeated some of the things I had heard about weapons and rapes. She listened to me, seemingly bored by the whole thing. Then she spoke the saddest words that I had heard in years, "Well, you know how kids at this age are."

I was in shock! After all, I had told her, she didn't even care! She thought this kind of behavior was normal! She had become desensitized to the violence. What had the world come to? I talked to her for a while longer that day. She was surprised that a parent or grandparent had come to the school just to see how things were going. And I had found that they were not going well!

It was with a heavy heart that I went home that day. I wanted to take my granddaughter out of that school, and grab the younger ones before they got to middle school. Private school was best, I reasoned. However, private school was also expensive. More and more parents were putting their children into private schools, but few in the Black community could afford it even with the "voucher program" that the Bush Administration wanted to implement. In my mind, I asked the question that I'm sure many thought about. "Why can't we just fix the public schools, and do right by *all* of the kids?"

I was concerned about the future for my grandchildren. If the schools were this bad now, how bad would they be in another 5 or 10 years? New laws mandated higher testing scores which caused teachers to "teach to the test" instead of focusing on learning. Low performing schools were in danger of being converted to charter schools. In theory, these measures were supposed to improve the schools. In reality it lead to allegations of corruption by some of the teachers who cheated on the tests to avoid school closures and job loss. Students seemed to learn less than they did before the "improvement measures" were instituted. Basic civil rights were once again under attack. This resulted in low self-esteem for students who often gave up and dropped out. Fixing the school system that had been broken for years seemed like an insurmountable task. I began to wonder if it would ever be fixed.

Health care in the community suffered as well. Too often, families had to choose between buying medication, paying the rent or purchasing groceries. Usually, food and shelter won out and people went without their much needed health care. Emergency room visits increased while regular doctor visits became a luxury for the affluent. I recalled going to the pharmacy to fill one of my medications. It was for 10 doses of medication for chronic pain. The cost was $325! The prescription went unfilled while I took triple doses of an over-the-counter medication that helped very little.

In addition to the other problems, the gang problem was still getting worse! Jump-ins, killings, and drive-by shootings were common place. Many of the parks that had been previously used by families with children were taken over by gang members.

Sadly, a few years later, I found out just how cruel the world could be.

Zumante, Zuton's firstborn son, and my fourthborn grandchild was severely asthmatic. Asthma was a common condition, especially in children. However, in Zumante, the condition was chronic, and required aggressive measures to keep it under control. Zumante's asthma was bad enough and his needs great enough that he was diagnosed as a disabled child. Eventually, a combination of technology gone bad, a poor health care system, and human beings who had been desensitized by years of "caring for" the less fortunate, led to tragic results.

On the evening of Thursday, July 16, 2009, my phone rang. Zuton's voice, filled with panic, was on the other end. "Mom, I need you!" she shouted into the phone.

"What's wrong?" my heart was in my throat.

"Zumante is having an asthma attack. We are going to take him to the hospital."

Zuton always called me when Zumante or one of the other children was sick. If it required a hospital visit, I would usually meet her there, to be any help I could, and to cheer the children up by my visit. But this time seemed different. Zuton seemed extremely upset. Then she asked me to hold on. The next few moments were a blur. I remember hearing someone scream. Then I heard Zuton plead "Wake up son! Wake up Son!" I panicked!

"Zuton!" I screamed. "Zuton!" I couldn't breathe. I was oblivious to the others who were in my living room and staring at me, wondering what was wrong. Olisa was sitting on the couch and talking to her friend Talinga. The children had stopped playing and had come into the living room to see why I was upset. Niecy, who was visiting at the time, was standing next to me, and staring at me. I pushed the phone at her, and slumped to the floor, my heart in my throat. I couldn't speak through my panic and I hoped that Niecy could be my voice. As she spoke on the phone, my eyes were fixated on hers. I looked for a sign – any sign that everything was ok. But the sign never came.

The ten-minute drive to the hospital felt like an eternity. When Dennis pulled into the parking lot, I bolted from the car, ignoring his warning to be careful of traffic. When I got to the sign-in desk, I threw my license at the security guard and screamed, "My grandson was just brought in by ambulance – I need to be let in." After a brief exchange of words with the security guard I finally joined Zuton and Niecy, who were standing outside Zumante's room in the ER. There was a group of doctors standing over him. I turned to Zuton to ask her what was happening, but her full attention was on the activity taking place in Zumante's room. It was Niecy who answered my question.

"Zumante was down for a while." Niecy chose her words very carefully. He is breathing now. The look on her face spoke far more than the words she had obviously chosen so carefully.

"Oh my God! Oh my God!" I cried. "Will he be ok?" The fear in her eyes reflected my own panic.

Zumante, who was breathing, but still unconscious, was taken to the ICU. He stayed in ICU for four days, sustained by a myriad of equipment and surrounded by family and friends. On Monday, July 20th, we were informed that the machines were the only thing keeping him alive and that he was not expected to survive without them. He was buried the following week, in the children's section of St. Simeons Cemetery.

I never thought that I could, or would want to survive Zumante's death. I cursed God. I looked for a message in this horrible tragedy. I tried to accept it. In the end, the only thing that I could do was to do my best to keep my sanity and my faith. But it wasn't easy. Children were not supposed to die! I would gladly accept Zumante's place. I hated the fact that his siblings now had a reason know about the uncertainty of life and the arbitrary nature of death! Ashantay, who was eight years old at the time, questioned her own mortality.

"I have asthma, too." she asserted as we visited Zumante's grave. "How do you know that I won't die?"

"Because God won't take two of my grandchildren from me." I answered, hoping that it was true.

"Yes, but you don't know that, do you?" she challenged.

I couldn't argue that point with her nor could I promise her that "time heals all wounds" or that "everything will be ok." In my heart, I knew that nothing would ever be the same again, and that our wounds would always bleed. I would search for ways to try to empower her and my other grandchildren even in the face of tragedy or adversity. I wanted them to have the coping skills to handle all of the heartbreaks of life. I wasn't sure of how to do that in the face of my own insecurities.

I do my best to make sure that they have strong examples. Many of those examples come from passing on the stories about their ancestors. Instead of hiding some of the ugly truths, I have chosen to tell those stories, emphasizing the faith that carried them to the other side. I will make sure that they know that from our earliest ancestor in this country, we have always had a struggle that was different from any other race. I wanted my grandchildren to know that there was unstoppable strength within each generation. It is very important to me that not only do they know the names of those who came before them, but that they also know of the adversities that they overcame. As horrible as it was, and is, to face Zumante's death, I know that Syntha and Jane and countless others had children taken by force and somehow made it through. I know that there will be a day when my grandchildren will ask questions about their family history. It's important to make sure that they have access to those answers. I want them to know that no matter what the problem, they can reach deep within themselves to find the strength to prevail.

23

"We've Come This Far By Faith"

"**L**adies and Gentlemen, the next President of the United States – Barack Hussein Obama!"

I watched CNN News in amazement as Barack Obama was proclaimed the next President of the United States. I could not believe my eyes. A Black man? A Black man was President? I never thought that I would see it in my lifetime. When I did allow my imagination to even entertain the thought, I always imagined that it would be a Republican like Colin Powell, who both Blacks and Whites respected. I fully expected it to be someone who did not look Black, and would not appear to be an advocate for civil rights.

On second thought, as I mulled over the last eighteen months or so, between the time Obama announced his candidacy and the moment when he was elected President, things fit perfectly. Over the past two years, he had become "acceptable." And after the wild economic and social ride of the Bush administration, it appeared to me that in retrospect, the election of Obama should not have been that much of a surprise after all.

I thought about the day that Obama announced his candidacy.

He was completely unknown in many parts of the country. The snippet of his speech that ran repeatedly on the news, was one where Obama declared, "There is not a Black America and a White America and a Latino America and an Asian America; There's the United States of America!" That phrase was his introduction.

Many took his speech to mean that he would not be biased in favor of Blacks. They labeled him "inclusive." Some Blacks took it to mean that he would not look after their interests. During the next few months he would be vetted in order to impress upon America just what kind of President he would be.

Barack Obama tried very hard to prevent race from becoming an issue in the election. However, because he could possibly be the first African American president, his every move would prove to be prefaced by that fact. Much of the discussion about what one could or could not say about race was absurd. For example, the media regularly reported Obama's standing in the polls with Black and White voters. But one evening when Obama mentioned that he was polling well in the Black communities, he was accused of making race an issue in the election.

I began to notice a disconnect between the old Civil Rights guard who had fought during the 50's and 60's, and the younger, college crowd, who didn't remember what it was like to ride in the back of the bus, or wonder if a job was denied you because of the color of your skin. It was a fascinating time that I never thought that I would see in my lifetime. I was surprised and amused by all of the White folks walking around with tee-shirts that prominently and proudly featured a "brother." I decided to talk to a few people and see what they thought about the election. My mother was 84 years-old during the election cycle. I was having coffee with her one morning when I decided to broach the subject.

"What do you think about Barack Obama running for President?" I began.

"Oh I hope he doesn't win! If he does, they're gonna kill him!" she asserted. I was somewhat surprised by that until I thought about the things that she had seen Black men go through in her lifetime. When she was a teenager in the 1930's Black men had little say in their own lives, much less the lives of others. Lynching was in full swing. Jim Crow was the order of the day. Anytime a Black man attempted to assert any degree of power, he was in real danger of being branded an "uppity nigger," and threatened with bodily injury or death. In my mother's mind, she was afraid that white people with power would have him assassinated!

I asked my sister what she thought of the election. She liked Obama. She thought he would be a good President. She didn't mention race at all. But I'm sure she thought about it. My theory about an Obama Presidency was not unlike many of my friends. I thought it would be great to finally have a Black President, (especially one who we felt would be a hundred times better than the last president) but I didn't think that it would improve the condition of African Americans. I was more excited to have an African American First Lady raising children in the White House. And I was almost giddy at the fact that Michelle Obama's mother, who was an older Black Woman and had firsthand knowledge of racism and Jim Crow, would move into the White House. And I wanted Michelle to be President!

But I felt that any Black president would have to be extra careful avoid appearing to have too much focus on Black community. As a matter of fact, I made friendly wagers with several of my friends that during the course of the election, Barack Obama would have to remove any hint of his African American culture to make himself "palatable" to "mainstream America."

I saw this pan out in a big way several months later when it was revealed that Obama was a member of a Black Church that was pastored by Reverend Jeremiah Wright, a long-time advocate of Civil Rights. He spent two decades under Wright's leadership, never seeming to have a problem with his well-known politics. The Black Church has a unique history in the United States and Reverend Wright was not unusual in comparison to most of them.

But over the course of a few weeks Obama totally and completely redefined his relationship with Reverend Wright, a man he respected enough to title his book "The Audacity of Hope" which was the title of one of Wright's many sermons.

Obama first distanced himself from Wright before his 2008 candidacy began. He knew that Wright's politics would prove to be problematic. He was ready for the fallout, and as expected, he condemned some of the statements from Reverend Wright's past Sermons. But it was not enough to quell the negative press that surrounded him. Obama was still was forced to spend much of the following few weeks defending his position and trying to convince naysayers that he was Christian and not Muslim.

Soon, Pastor Wright made public comments defending his sermon that had asserted that the September 11 terrorist attacks were the result of a corrupt American foreign policy. Obama, under fire for even knowing the man was forced to renounce ties with his Pastor. Obama finally held a speech entitled "A More Perfect Union" where he talked about the issues of race and caused many in the Black community (including Rev Jesse Jackson) to conclude that Obama had pacified the white community by "talking down" to Black people. Finally, Obama totally denounced Reverend Wright, pulled his membership from the (Trinity) church, and, angrily disavowed Wright calling him "disrespectful and insulting."

It appeared that finally, he had done enough to convince America that he was worthy of the white vote. He had also done enough to convince many others that he had neither the desire nor the means to improve the problems within the Black community. Many in the Black community felt betrayed. In the 60's, there was a one-word phrase that was used to describe Blacks who pretended to have a cultural sensitivity, but who turned their back on the community —"sell-out!" Many felt that the term now applied to Obama. But at the same time we knew that America's volatile history between the races would continue to limit the power on an Obama Presidency. We knew that he would not be allowed to focus too much on the Black community without being accused of nepotistic behavior.

Actually, I didn't want to be right. I wanted to see what a post-racial America looked like. But it was not to be. What was apparent was that America was racially confused. There seemed to be numerous opinions about whether racism was still a factor. For many people, the fact that there was a Black President seemed to prove that we were a "post racial" society. For others, the nightly news, the criminal justice system, and disparity in schools and healthcare proved otherwise.

Ironically, the Obama Presidency exposed the racism in many areas, as people took to the streets with racist signs, and posted blatantly racist soliloquies as they hid behind anonymous blogs. Moreover, each person seemed to be convinced that their opinion was the accurate one.

"American isn't racist!" insisted some. "How can you say it is racist? We just elected a Black President!"

"And how can YOU say THAT when he had to erase any hint of his black culture? People still regularly call him a "nigger" and refer to Michelle as an "ape" others pointed out.

But the next years would prove telling. Obama narrowly won a second term, beating out Hillary Clinton in the primary, and then inching past Mitt Romney in the general election. Obama's second term proved even more contentious than his first. His biggest battle was with Congress. In fact, a CNN special narrated by Fareed Zakaria ((Dec 7, 2016), reported that 15 of the most powerful Republican senators plotted Obama's demise by holding a not-so-secret meeting and vowing not to pass any democratic-party led legislation on Obama's watch. Many openly admitted it. It was very obvious though, because manyof the bills that Republicans had previously supported were now agressively opposed. And for the first time in recent history, the Senate refused to hold confirmation hearings to replace a vacancy for a Supreme Court Justice (after the death of Antonin Scalia). The Supreme Court went eight months with only eight justices while refusing a hearing on Merrick Garland, Obama's Supreme Court nominee. Merrick Garland was a known centrist who many Republicans had supported before. But now, the goal was to hold out so that the next President could select the nominee.

By the end of Obama's presidency, brutal police killings of Black men dominated the nightly news. The *Black Lives Matter* movement was in full swing due to the increasing racist attacks. I realized that not long ago, I had assumed that Black youth were becoming complacent, and out of touch with racism. Now, with a sense of pride in today's youth. I began to witness a newly unleashed Civil Rights Movement, the likes of which I had not seen since the 1960's. I recognized the passion, and the drive as something similar to my own teen-aged years. And I knew that this movement could make a difference.

I thought back to a conversation that I had with some friends about ten years ago when six Black Students (ages 14 to 17 years old) at *Jena High School* in Louisiana sat under an old oak tree in the schoolyard. Many of the white students became angry because they believed that only white students should be allowed to sit there (they called it "The White Tree"). The next day three nooses were found hanging from the tree. A fight broke out, and a white student was beaten and suffered a concussion in the melee. The Black students were charged with attempted murder. One of them (Mychal Bell) was charged as an adult and faced up to 100 years in prison. People were outraged that the Black students were overcharged while none of the white students faced any disciplinary action. The case touched of riots and protest across the country.

"I'll bet that this is the start of another Civil Rights Movement." I remarked to Ladana.

"Well if it isn't, it should be." she replied.

The *Jena Six* movement was relatively short lasting. However, over the next ten years a culmination of various forms of racial incidents arose on Obama's watch. Numerous Black men were killed at the hands of police officers. The names are now familiar: Trayvon Martin. Michael Brown. Eric Garner, Tamir Rice. Freddie Gray. Philando Castile. Unnamed black man. The Black community was enraged because not only were the killings often un-justified, there seemed to be no consequences for the officers that killed them. Whatever the offense or perceived offense it was that lead to their killing, I was reasonably certain that had they lived, their sentence would not have been the death sentence that the police had meted out.

Whereas the Obama Administration began with hope for racial reconciliation, by the end of his presidency, the nation was bruised, battle-worn from racial strife, and facing increasing divisions.

Obama started his run for the office by proclaiming that "There is not a Black America and White America and Latino America and Asian America, there's the United States of America. But he ended his term with allegations of racism and racist actions, the likes of which that this country has not witnessed in over fifty years. Police actions were reminiscent of the lynching days, with zero consequences for killing of Black people, whether they were men, women, or children.

Conversely, following Obama, the incoming President, (Donald Trump) began his run, by speaking about Mexican immigrants, by proclaiming, "When Mexico sends its people, they're not sending their best...They're bringing drugs. They're bringing crime. They're rapists. And some, I assume are good people."

Thus, although the Obama administration began with many people thinking that racism was over, it ended with many thinking that racism is worse than it's ever been. However, along the way there was also an increasing awareness of the divisions. We saw black youth and white youth standing side by side and fighting racism in the *Black Lives Matter* movement, and other civil rights venues.

On the other hand, many people believe that Donald Trump is causing further racial divide with derogatory comments about Mexicans, Muslims, African American and others. America is now perceived by many Americans and even those abroad to be totally divided along racial lines. As horrible as the divisions seem to be at this moment, there is another opportunity for widening our understanding of each other. My hope is that by the end of the Trump term, we will have started the healing process that comes after every period of racial and civil unrest.

Thus, we begin the next phase. America has always danced around the "race question" without confronting it head-on. We take two steps forward and one step back. Nevertheless, I choose to keep the Faith. But there is one thing that I know for sure. We still have a long way to go to become a "post-racial" society!

Hope and
Faith

The Eleventh Generation

"The Generation of the Future"

T.T. AND BESSIE LEWIS
Nassau, Bahamas

24

"Long Memory"

It has taken me more than twenty years to compile our family history. I still discover information regularly. It was enlightening to learn that we were not always enslaved. The first generation in our family was free. "Violet, a free-born negro" as she was called at the time, exhibited courage and strength to fight a system that she knew was unjust, although her chances of prevailing were very slim. Violet never lost faith that she would one day see freedom for Bett and her other children.

Bett, and her brother Thomas and her sister Nancy, the second generation, fought all of their lives to try to stay free. In the end, they were enslaved, but during that enslavement, they were ingenious in finding ways to keep their families intact, and pass down cultural traditions that would arise again in the future.

The third generation would see atrocities brought to our native

Africa, as Kitty was kidnapped, branded, and brought to the colonies in chains. And it brought violence and death around Tom, a Cherokee/Choctaw native who was captured and enslaved. Our Creek ancestors, the Harris', also suffered horribly as they endured a bloody removal from their native land.

Harmon, and Syntha, the 4th generation, endured the humiliation of enslavement. Their children were torn from their arms as their family was separated at least six times! Syntha was used as a "breeder" while Harmon was helpless to stop it.

And even though the fifth generation, Huey and Arthina, and Frank were emancipated from slavery during their lifetimes, they still bore the marks of slavery complete with scars from "the lash" which the sixth generation, Gertrude, Charley, and Sarah could see. The Sixth generation claimed freedom, but as Charley quickly found out, they still were not free. Parents watched as their sons and daughters were lynched and tried to pray their way through the madness. They still could not vote without fearing for their lives. And they were looked upon as animals that could be used for experimentation.

Nevertheless, they had great hopes for the seventh generation, Tommie, Bessie, Hattie, and their 16 brothers and sisters. However, the seventh generation would suffer residual effects from the harms and restrictions placed on their parents. They also had their own battle — The battle of Jim Crow and the color line. However, much like generation number four who lived both slave, and free, their generation began their journey in the back of the bus and by the end of their journey, they could sit front and center!

The eighth generation, including me and Dennis, Stella, Calvin and Tommie, relentlessly fought for those civil rights, even in the face of vicious police dogs and fire-hoses. We claimed victory for those rights and felt that the country was well on the way to equality. We were proud to hand the ninth generation a piece of dignity.

Nevertheless, the ninth generation — Lisa, Niecy, Zuton, Bobby Jr., Elaine, Donnie, Denard, T.J., and Gigi, still had deal with a different kind of "bondage." Racism still existed, but usually took a different, more subtle form. School bussing was supposed to level the playing field. By 1989, it was obvious that bussing had failed. Black schools still lacked basic materials that would afford them a good education. Affordable health care lagged behind in the community because many people held jobs that did not offer health insurance. And gang warfare took an ugly turn. It was almost as if Black youths showed themselves the same kind of disrespect that the enslaver had shown to their ancestors. In the end, they would be subjected prison sentences that rivaled slavery. Nevertheless, many of them still attained that which their ancestors could only dream about! They were part of the technological age that would bring the world to their fingertips. Medical advances soared, and diseases that killed in the past were now treatable! In addition, they broke the barriers once again, by becoming Doctors, Lawyers, and Congressmen in larger numbers.

The Tenth Generation ushered in the first Black President. But we must make sure that they are aware of what it took to reach that historic moment. And they must realize that "power can be fluid, and can dry up over time. The tenth generation, including Raisha, Kiante, Brianne, Zumante, Ashantay, D.J., Elijah, Monye, Modupe, Maxwell, Aina, Ojo, NiaMani and all of their cousins need to know how each generation fought for dignity, and the right to raise their children in a better world.

I made a vow to teach them about the past and instill in them a sense of self-worth. They must also recognize other kinds of subtle bondage, that still exists, such as the criminal punishment system, and institutionalized racism that can be found in many places. It should not be lost on them that even as late as 2004, states like Florida and Ohio, still had plenty of cases where Blacks were tricked, intimidated, or subjected to other methods designed to keep them from the ballot box. They have a tough job because today's racism can be confused with "classism" without the overt actions of the past. They must remember that pride and self-esteem are necessary for success and self-preservation.

We must keep the faith and keep hope alive so that future generations will have a good sense of self-worth! As Jesse Jackson says, "I AM SOMEBODY"

Finally, we must insure that our children do not forget the struggles of the past, because as we have seen, those who forget their history are doomed to repeat it!

Afterword

For ten generations — over 250 years, the Lewis and Green families have endured various types of bondage in the United States of America. Nevertheless, there has been a common bond in our family from the 1740's when "Violet, a Free Born Negro" was enslaved, to 2011 when NiaMani, the last grandchild as of this writing made her entrance into this world. That common bond reveals that during the struggle, we never lost hope. Each generation had the same vow — to make the world better for the next generation. In that vow, was optimism for freedom, hope for peace, and faith in the future!

Johari

Photograph Credits and Comments

African Village. Senegal, West Africa. Dennis Green, Photograph1996

"Am I Not a Man and a Brother?" Courtesy Library of Congress.

LC-USZC4-5321. Broadside Collection portfolio. 118, no 32A. Cir. 1837.

Door of No Return. Senegal, West Africa. Dennis Green in Photo.

Johari Ade', Photographer. 1996

Door of Slave Mansion. Senegal, West Africa. Dennis Green, Photographer

Goree Island. Senegal, West Africa. Photo was taken from the Ferry. Dennis Green, Photographer.

"Last Slave House in the Family." Florence, South Carolina. Personal Collection of the Author.

"Uncle Jimmy" Photo is of Jimmy Rankin. Taylor, Arkansas. Personal

Collection of the Author.

"Taylor, Arkansas," Pop 657. Dennis Green, Photographer. 2002.

"Green and Hattie Harris." Cir. Est. 1915. Photographer Unknown.

Personal Collection of the author.

"Huey Lewis". Cir Est. 1938. Photographer Unknown. Personal Collection of the author.

"Harmon Charley Lewis" Cir. Est. 1920. Photographer Unknown.

Personal Collection of the author.

"Tommie and Bessie Lewis' 35th Wedding Anniversary" 1974.Mary Green, Photographer

"The Lewis Family" Parents' 35th Wedding Anniversary. 1974 Personal Collection of the Author.

"Dan McGee" Cir. Est. 1938. Minden, Louisiana. Personal Collection of the Author.

"Favorite Aunts." Naomi Booker. Est 1934. Hattie Mason Est 1977.

Arlie Glover, Est. 1998. Essie McGhee 2005. Personal Collection of author.

"The Green Family, 2003." Courtesy Wal-Mart Photo Studios. Denver. CO.

"The Older Grandkids" Personal Collection of the Author.

"The Younger Grandkids" Personal Collection of the Author.

"Olympic Gold Medallists - Black Power Salute". http://www.britannica.com/eb/art-86748/African-Americans-at-the-1968-Opics-show-their-support

"Olisa. Graduation at Florida A & M." Courtesy Bob Knight Photography. Tallahassee, FL.

"Newspaper Article – Serene Cemetery Final Setting" Arkansas Democrat Gazette. Early 1980's. Article by Cynthia Howell.

"Grave of Huey Lewis" Personal Collection of the Author. Photography by Dennis Green. 2002.

"Grave of Luella Lewis." Personal Collection of the Author. Photography by Dennis Green. 2002.

"Home Movie Theatre." Personal Collection of the Author. Photography by Dennis Green.

"Silhouette of Tommie & Bessie Lewis." Nassau Bahamas. 1996. Personal Collection of the Author. Photography by Dennis Green.

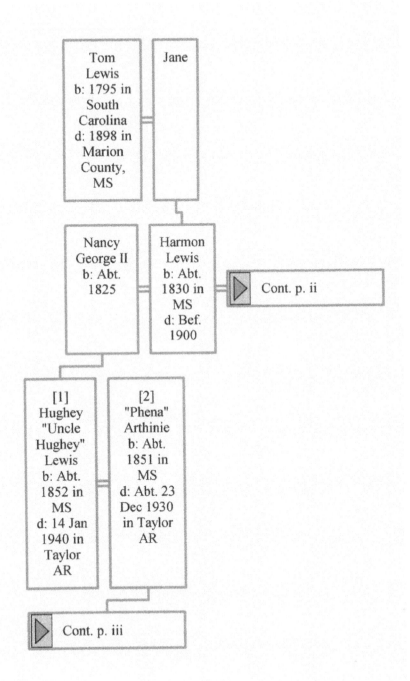

Tom Lewis
b: 1795 in South Carolina
d: 1898 in Marion County, MS

Jane

Nancy George II
b: Abt. 1825

Harmon Lewis
b: Abt. 1830 in MS
d: Bef. 1900

Cont. p. ii

[1]
Hughey "Uncle Hughey" Lewis
b: Abt. 1852 in MS
d: 14 Jan 1940 in Taylor AR

[2]
"Phena" Arthinie
b: Abt. 1851 in MS
d: Abt. 23 Dec 1930 in Taylor AR

Cont. p. iii

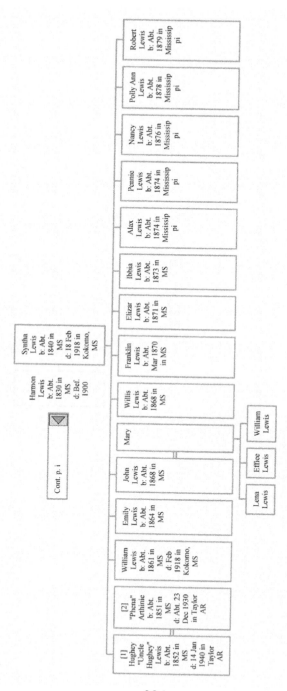

Cont. p. i

Harmon Lewis
b: Abt. 1830 in MS
d: Bef. 1900

Syntha Lewis
b: Abt. 1840 in MS
d: 18 Feb 1918 in Kokomo, MS

[1] Hughey "Uncle Hughey" Lewis
b: Abt. 1852 in MS
d: 14 Jan 1940 in Taylor AR

[2] "Phena" Arthinie
b: Abt. 1851 in MS
d: Abt 23 Dec 1930 in Taylor AR

William Lewis
b: Abt. 1861 in MS
d: Feb 1918 in Kokomo, MS

Emily Lewis
b: Abt. 1864 in MS

John Lewis
b: Abt. 1868 in MS

Mary

Willis Lewis
b: Abt. 1868 in MS

Franklin Lewis
b: Abt. Mar 1870 in MS

Elizar Lewis
b: Abt. 1871 in MS

Ibbia Lewis
b: Abt. 1873 in MS

Alax Lewis
b: Abt. 1874 in Mississippi

Pennie Lewis
b: Abt. 1874 in Mississippi

Nancy Lewis
b: Abt. 1876 in Mississippi

Polly Ann Lewis
b: Abt. 1878 in Mississippi

Robert Lewis
b: Abt. 1879 in Mississippi

Lena Lewis

Effiee Lewis

William Lewis

324

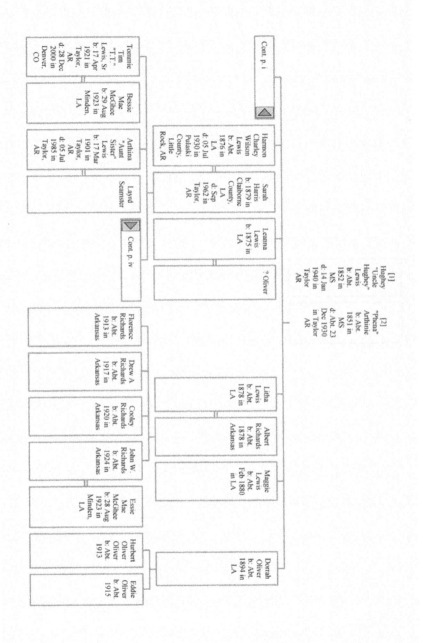

Cont. p. i

[1]
Hughey
"Uncle
Hughey"
Lewis
b: Abt.
1852 in
MS
d: 14 Jan
1940 in
Taylor,
AR

[2]
"Phena"
Arthine
Lewis
b: Abt.
1851 in
MS
d: Abt. 23
Dec 1930
in Taylor,
AR

Harmon
Charley
Wilson
Lewis
b: Abt.
1876 in
LA
d: 05 Jul
1930 in
Pulaski
County,
Little
Rock, AR

Sarah
Harris
b: 1879 in
Claiborne
County,
LA
d: Sep
1962 in
Taylor,
AR

Leanna
Lewis
b: 1875 in
LA

? Oliver

Tommie
Tim
"T.T."
Lewis, Sr
b: 17 Apr
1921 in
Taylor,
AR
d: 28 Dec
2000 in
Denver,
CO

Bessie
Mae
McGhee
b: 29 Aug
1923 in
Minden,
LA

Arthina
"Aunt
Sister"
Lewis
b: 17 Mar
1901 in
Taylor,
AR
d: 05 Jul
1985 in
Taylor,
AR

Layrd
Seamster

Cont. p. iv

Litha
Lewis
b: Abt.
1878 in
LA

Albert
Richards
b: Abt.
1878 in
Arkansas

Maggie
Lewis
b: Abt.
Feb 1880
in LA

Florence
Richards
b: Abt.
1913 in
Arkansas

Drew A
Richards
b: Abt.
1917 in
Arkansas

Cooley
Richards
b: Abt.
1920 in
Arkansas

John W.
Richards
b: Abt.
1924 in
Arkansas

Essie
Mae
McGhee
b: 28 Aug
1923 in
Minden,
LA

Dorrah
Oliver
b: Abt.
1894 in
LA

Hurbert
Oliver
Oliver
b: Abt.
1913

Eddie
Oliver
b: Abt.
1915

325

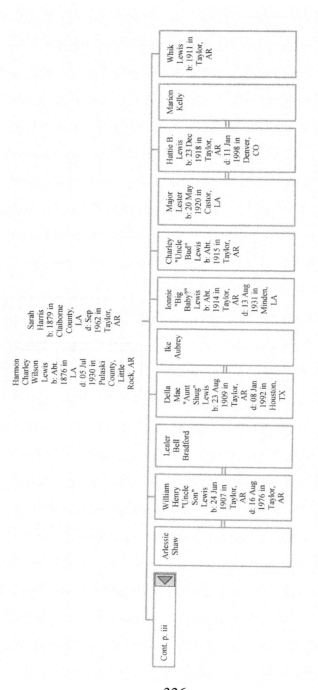

Harmon Charley Wilson Lewis
b: Abt. 1876 in LA
d: 05 Jul 1930 in Pulaski County, Little Rock, AR

Sarah Harris
b: 1879 in Claiborne County, LA
d: Sep 1962 in Taylor, AR

Cont. p. iii

Arlessie Shaw

William Henry "Uncle Son" Lewis
b: 24 Jun 1907 in Taylor, AR
d: 16 Aug 1976 in Taylor, AR

Lealer Bell Bradford

Della Mae "Aunt Shug" Lewis
b: 23 Aug 1909 in Taylor, AR
d: 08 Jan 1992 in Houston, TX

Ike Aubrey

Ionnie "Big Baby?" Lewis
b: Abt. 1914 in Taylor, AR
d: 13 Aug 1931 in Minden, LA

Charley "Uncle Bud" Lewis
b: Abt. 1915 in Taylor, AR

Major Lester
b: 20 May 1920 in Castor, LA

Hattie B. Lewis
b: 23 Dec 1918 in Taylor, AR
d: 11 Jan 1998 in Denver, CO

Marion Kelly

Whik Lewis
b: 1911 in Taylor, AR

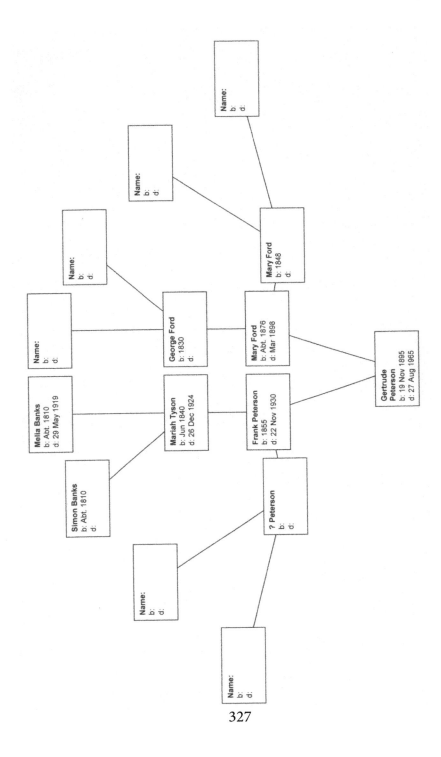

CPSIA information can be obtained
at www.ICGtesting.com
Printed in the USA
LVHW090447231221
706981LV00001B/11